BOHEMIAN GHOSTS
A Memoir

DEWEY PAUL MOFFITT

ISBN: 099048470X
ISBN-13: 978-0-9904847-0-7

Editor: Kayte VanScoy
Treehouse Editorial • Austin, Texas
Cover artwork: David Sockrider
www.tourpaintings.com
Author photograph: Tim Sutherland
www.timsutherlandphotography.com
Layout and design: Decibel Arts Press
FIRST EDITION

Published by Decibel Arts Press • Denver, Colorado
decibelartspress@gmail.com

*"I can hear the wheels turning way off in the distance
or maybe just maybe, that's only the wind
or the bohemian ghosts, or the vagabond spirits
are all that remain of my oldest friends..."
-Jay Randall, "The Road to Saint Paul"*

*This book is dedicated to the loving memories of those
friends who made our world a better place, our lives a
more joyful experience, and their infinite light a shining
beacon of inspiration. Here are a few of them:
Paul "Fimster" Crabtree; Bob Pinkerton;
Mark "Shaggy" Hughes; Brandon Breed;
Virgil Lester "Buddy" Smith, the IIIrd; Billy Bennett;
Bryant Brandenburg; Norma Scheurkogel;
Amy Fisher; Tony Rock 'n Roll; Terry Dalton;
Nick Williams; Chris Haney; Becky Killpack;
Spiros Holevas; Richard Bratko; Kenny Greenbaum;
Charles "Chaz" Scales; Corey Dwyer; Brad Huff;
Michael Hinton; Jamaica;
and Brooklyn Bobby Sheehan.*

*For all of my family and friends far and wide,
past, present, and future.*

CONTENTS

EPILOGUE

Preface
And
Acknowledgements

I feel it is our purpose within this human condition to spread our experiences outward, to share our journey with others, intellectually and creatively. Whether it be through our own music, writing, painting, laboring, simply smiling at a stranger, or listening intently to another's experience. We all possess this power whether we are tuned in to it or not. We are not always aware of these intentions that are set forth, but we possess an amazing ability to examine and express them.

This memoir is about a transformative process, a personal journey that was, in part about my experiences within the bohemian Grateful Dead community and what I took away from it; where it has taken me on this human expedition; the cycle of inspiration, initiation, and sacrifice that gave birth to many of my artistic endeavors. It's about rites of passage, lost loves, bad decisions, fortunate breaks, self discovery, family, friendships, brotherhood, deceit, betrayal, death and rebirth. To me, inspiration is the process of giving breath to the soul. It is my belief that life's very creation comes out of the act of being motivated within, to create something, anything, external. But ultimately these very internal motivations were not born within us, but passed on to us, absorbed from the souls we interact with. Create something, anything, and you will inspire another to repeat the cycle. From inspiration comes the act of initiation into a society and culture where we then adapt to those situations and the people around us. Ultimately, the ego is reinforced and nurtured usually to an absurd point sometimes resulting in our own self-destruction. From there, the art of sacrifice and humility becomes another important tool in our journey.

The tales told herein are set within my unique human experience with the unfolding understanding of how it all connects to the greater spiritual cosmos we all belong to. Our lives transpire so mysteriously at times that we cannot see the bigger picture of how our soul spirits affect one another. This is my piece of it, as best as I can recollect and reconstruct the major and sometimes minor events that have, so far, shaped who I am today, in this present moment. Some readers may sense a bit of obvious dropping of names throughout my tales which is very true and a potential criticism that I must proudly accept and acknowledge. It would be difficult to share my stories without doing so. There is also quite a lot of uninhibited use of illegal substances which provided much spiritual aid to my research. Well, it goes with the teritory. I would urge my readers to consider supporting decriminalization efforts and also the work of Families Against Mandatory Minimums–an organization and cause that I fully support.

I owe special acknowledgements to the following individuals who have greatly inspired, supported and encouraged the finality of this writing and publishing experience: Dani Jordan, Kayte VanScoy, Moe Taylor, Luke Schmaltz, and Scott Jackson. A very special appreciation to those individuals I have written about, whether your name appears altered or as-is, whether I have done justice to our experience or it became slightly askew, whether the bulk of our escapades ended up on the cutting room floor, I thank you all for this experience and allowing me to continue this journey with the most positive intent.

PART I
Inspiration

CHAPTER 1

Today's Tom Sawyer

The gypsy put her hands on my face. Her eyes cut deeply into my being and beyond.

"Oh honey... you have a long journey ahead of you. Such a fulfilling life. All of your desires will be met. But you will have to work hard for them. It won't be easy. You're going to fall in love a lot. That won't be easy either. There will be serious relationship problems. But you're a shining star. I've never seen a chart like this before."

She continued staring and even seemed slightly tearful.

I looked over at Butterfly, such a cute hippie girl out traveling on the road. She dragged me into this place because she wanted a tarot reading. We had stopped for a day off to relax and browse a few shops in New Brunswick, New Jersey. And there we were in some hippie new age shop. I didn't want a fortune. But after Butterfly got her reading the woman just focused in on me. She got my birthday and cross-referenced a bunch of books.

"Butterfly! Help! Get this crazy voodoo bitch away from me!" Well I didn't say that, but that's what I was thinking as I peered over at the little angel for help.

"Well, that was something huh?" She commented as we left the shop.

"Yeah. I'm not sure I buy all that mumbo jumbo stuff though."

"But she peered right into your soul. It was electrifying!"

"It feels like she put a curse on me."

Butterfly came into the Middle Earth presence after the infamous K. Fimster lured her back to our hotel following a Grateful Dead show in Raleigh. That was the summer of 1990. Mind you, his intentions were pure. As for the Middle Earth thing, a detailed explanation shall be revealed in due time, but for now, just know that it was a tight-knit group of great friends that traveled together on Dead tour. He was merely looking after her. She had taken too much acid. It was her first show. She lost her friends. She found us and decided to stay on tour and abandon her job in Atlanta. With some minor persuading from Middle Earth, we gave her a perfectly safe haven and her new hippie name.

There are too many episodes like that one to accurately recall them for the purposes of this chronicle.

I spent the first ten years of my life, more than half of my juvenile days, in a small American factory town in northeastern Ohio. This was sacred land that adorned a junction of three muddy rivers named after either a black bear or the act of a black bear dancing across the rivers. Before the white man's invasions, several Native American Indian tribes had called Coshocton home and, for some, the capital of their nations. Some were murdered for it and other tribes driven from it by the white's tenacious expansions. After the dust settled and the native blood dried up, many of my father's ancestors emigrated there from Ireland and Germany. The British and Swiss DNA from my mother's side of my family had already spent several centuries in the new world.

For generations my roots thrived alongside the town's industrial prosperity. The ancient spirits that danced among the region's hills seem to have had the last laugh, however, as the town today is not quite what it used to be. I loved growing up in that small American town. I knew there was great local history that I couldn't quite understand, but I could feel it. As proud as I am of having lived out the 1970s all-American childhood experience, it seemed obvious, even to a kid, that the town's opulent years were becoming a thing of memory. Coshocton had left its glory days long ago and now struggles to keeps its people and streets breathing. The air, water, and ground are polluted in one way or another and the reminiscent smells of the Buckeye and Sycamore trees have long faded and been replaced by the exhaust of an old container factory that manufactures cardboard boxes. When I have rarely returned to my town, I could barely recognize her from the memories of my youth. She is now a long lost love that I often try to forget, but am always secretly fond of from a distance.

Music was a big part of my childhood. My father listened to the outlaw country groups, mostly Johnny Cash and Willie Nelson. He bought me a guitar when I was nine, and I took some lessons at Main Street's Glass Music store. I was hooked. My older brothers were listing to the Rolling Stones and KISS. My sisters listened to Todd Rundgren and Three Dog Night. My father took me to most of my first concerts, which were held at the County Fairgrounds, and at our downtown bandshell on the courthouse square.

My parents divorced when I was seven, which I'm certain was for the best considering my father's addictive infidelity and the amount of domestic violence I witnessed back then. In fact, my earliest childhood memory is of my first birthday that ended in my mother being physically beaten against a wall by my father. He never beat me but I recall my siblings getting roughed up quite a bit. Those are some ugly memories that troubled me for many years and left me with a lot of hatred for him. He did do something great for me as a child, though, and that was to encourage me to discover music.

The greatest thing my mother did for me occurred a few years after the divorce. She took it upon herself to leave our little Ohio village behind. She chose the warmer climate near the swamps of southern Florida. We initially set up camp in a small suburban community right in the heart of the Palm Beaches, Greenacres City. But that only lasted a few months because she had quickly become disconnected from the boyfriend with whom we had been squatting with. When I was eleven, we shifted a little further south to the county border. We moved into a small condominium with my mother's good friend, Carol Ashman and her two daughters, who had also recently escaped from the same little Ohio town.

The Spanish Oaks condominium development, where we lived

with the Ashmans, in Central Boca Raton was at the slanted intersection of Northwest 13th Street and Glades Road. To the north, Florida Atlantic University; a couple miles to the east, the great Atlantic Ocean. It was a vast and different world from the small town Ohio life, the only life I had known. It took me no time at all to make new friends and adjust to the fast times of the 1980s South Florida lifestyle.

Tom Sawyer (yes, that really is his name), an older high school kid, was waiting for me at the abandoned security booth at the Spanish Oaks entrance. He gave me a tiny strip of paper with five hits of LSD– "Around the Worlds" or "Globes" they were called. I was thirteen. I lied and said that I had done acid many times before. He had hesitated in handing over the doses. I think he was on to my fib, but I somehow convinced him that it was no big deal. But it was a big deal, a very big deal. Spanish Oaks soon transformed into a bizarre, majestic wonderland full of wild, laughing palm trees, dancing alligators, and the ghosts of ancient Spanish explorers. And right then and there, from that point forward, life started to get really weird. My heart and mind were opened up and they would never be the same again.

Despite dabbling in the many different social and antisocial groups at Boca Middle School and Boca High, my rebellious and curious spirit looked forward to escaping those awkward confines. My best friends were Rob Pena and Andre Puccio. We had many drug-fueled teenage adventures and shared a passion for classic acid rock music, like a lot of teenage boys in the eighties. Rob turned me on to Led Zeppelin. I turned him on to Pink Floyd. I turned Andre on to Black Sabbath and he in turn introduced me to the world of the Grateful Dead. We changed one another's lives with that music. Hollywood's smoky Sportatorium, West Palm's dilapidated Municipal Auditorium, and Sunrise's sophisticated Musical Theatre were all our playgrounds. It being the eighties and us being rebellious stoner teens, it was mostly hard rock concerts that we attended–Ronnie James Dio, RUSH, Def Leppard, Judas Priest, Iron Maiden, KISS, all the greats.

One time in ninth grade, I even skipped school and took a series of city buses up to the Municipal Auditorium for a KISS concert. My mother had let me go to many concerts in the past but only with groups of friends.

On this occasion, she had not given me permission. I had told her that I would be staying over at either Rob's or Andre's house that night which was a brave bold-faced lie. I took it upon myself (fourteen at the time) to map out the bus routes it would take to get to the auditorium, which was a half hour away by car. It took a few hours on the bus, but my solo adventure landed me at the venue well before noon. I had a lot of tenacity and fire at that age, and if I wanted to see a concert, well there was really nothing that was going to stop me.

In the parking lot, I met the guitarist from the opening act, Chris Holmes of WASP. We smoked a joint together outside their tour bus. *Dude, what were you thinking smoking a joint with a fourteen-year old?* At, like, eleven in the morning too! For me, this was glorious. I then got to hang out with the musicians inside and watch the crew set up all the staging and rigging of the lights and sound. I remember thinking how cool it would be to have a job like that some day.

A couple of years earlier I watched a lot of wrestling at that auditorium. I saw "The American Dream" Dusty Rhodes, Ric Flair, Andre the Giant, Hulk Hogan, the Iron Sheik, and other legends battle it out. I even got to meet some of them and get their autographs. But the wrestling scene quickly faded for me.

On that day, it was all about the music. Chris had furnished me with a backstage pass, so after the show I got to hang out and converse with KISS. I mostly talked to drummer Eric Carr and his sister Lisa. What the hell we talked about I can only imagine today. By the way, WASP singer Blackie Lawless was a total dick. The other guys were pretty cool to me though. I wonder if they ever thought, "Where are this kid's parents?" But it was a cool experience to be behind the scenes like that at a young age, and I'm sure it fueled my propensity to be a part of the action in the years to come. There was one big problem that night; I had never worked out a solid way home. I think I had lined up a ride with my friend Greg Goss at some point; but by hanging out after the show I had missed the ride. I clearly didn't think it through and sometime after midnight I had to do the unthinkable...

call my mother.

"Um, Mom... yeah, you see I'm not really at Rob's. I'm sort of, well... you know that concert you told me I couldn't go to?"

Shit, she was so pissed off at me. But an hour later she showed up at the auditorium. I think I freaked her out more than anything. She couldn't have her baby boy left in the big city with a bunch of rock stars. I might've just gone on tour right then and there. But that would have to wait a few years. The circus wasn't quite ready for me yet.

My favorite concert venue was the legendary Hollywood Sportatorium, which has been recognized as one of the worst concert venues of its day. They had horrible acoustics, a leaky roof, and a few riots. But the parking lot scene was always a massive party. The scene inside the hall was unruly, rebellious, loud, hot, muggy and downright cool, with foggy layers of pot smoke permeating the air. I once got rained on, drenched in fact (remember this was an inside venue) during an entire AC/DC show, and loved every minute of it. I used to sneak in tape recorders and bootleg the shows. My cunning creative genius came up with a good system after a gate security guard once found a tape recorder on me heading into a RUSH concert. He patted me down and discovered the recorder tucked in the front edge of my pants. I was asked to check it in and pick it back up after the show. I immediately noticed a flaw in their system after he stopped the pat down once discovering the recorder. From then on, I snuck in two recorders, one in an obvious spot that they would always catch and confiscate, and another tucked in my boot. It never failed.

My teenage wasteland was not limited to the grimy concert halls, but also included the occasional keg parties with the surfer crowd at 40th Street Beach, and with the stoners at the local bowling alley, Don Carter's. Now that place was our refuge. Playing video games, smoking cigarettes and joints, droppin' the occasional hit of acid and flirting with girls. I don't think we ever actually bowled one game during those years. This scene was of course adjacent to the newly built Town Center Mall, where we would often lounge out in the food court or thumb through the vinyl records at Spec's Music. Oh and I can't forget to mention the "Horseshoe," an infamous dirt road located near the bowling alley that hosted all sorts of notorious raging keg parties.

That place was turned into a strip mall not too long after our teenage soirees.

Before my career started, I used to loiter for hours at Tapeville USA and Island Water Sports Surf Shop, in the plaza across from Spanish Oaks. The old pink "Boca Mall" on the east side of town was an occasional hang out too. I got my first job there at the music store Great American Sound. Eventually, I would also work at Q Records and at Peache's Records & Tapes.

My life shifted dramatically one Friday night–May 30th, 1986. My mother dropped my friend Andre and I off at Don Carter's. We had just walked in the main doors, and while Andre went off to get quarters for the video games, my eyes stumbled on the fateful stare of the most beautiful sight I had ever seen.

"Who...?!?" was the first cognitive splatter that came across my mind. Electrical sparks flew in our briefly locked glance. The second thought was, "Uh-oh." I had never recalled such a spontaneous emotional change before. My stomach swirled uncomfortably. She was buying a pack of Marlboro Lights from the cigarette machine with another girl. They walked by and gave a flirtatious smile. I tried to play it cool and stood there in somewhat of a daze until Andre pulled me away and into the arcade room.

I kept looking for her. Normally I held the high score on Grand Prix Auto Racing, but that evening I couldn't keep my concentration. It was obvious that my head was not into the game, so Andre and I walked around to look for the girls. A few minutes later we were having a conversation with them. Andre took an immediate liking to the other girl. They were sisters. We convinced them to go outside and get high with us.

Elle and I spent nearly every day for the following eight weeks or so either together or talking for hours on the phone. She was my first love. Her hypnotic eyes and honest smile mesmerized me. Her smooth, black hair and tall, slender figure teased my adolescent urges. She was the first woman I've ever known to make me feel so alive. She became my new best friend in a very short period of time.

I recall that first awkward and nervous kiss with her. We had been walking across the mall parking lot towards the bowling alley, holding hands. My brain had been obsessed with when to make my move when I suddenly decided to just go for it. I stopped walking, she turned to me, and I went for it. We stood there in that parking lot kissing for what seemed like forever, and everything after that was suddenly calm and comfortable.

Unfortunately, it was a summer teenage romance that would turn sad. I had already had plans in the works to move away, back to Ohio at the end of the summer, and at the height of our courtship. It was an arrangement my parents and I had agreed on a few months earlier, before Elle and I had even met. The initial decision was made based on my lack of good grades in school. I had agreed to go live with my father.

One of the saddest, and yet most beautiful days of my life was when we had to say our goodbyes. We were hanging out in the park a few blocks from her house, stalling the goodbye as long as possible. It was getting close to dinnertime, and her sister walked over to bring her back home. Storm clouds were moving in, and suddenly a monsoon came screaming out of the skies. It was one of those hot, sticky, steamy rains. We were trying to wait it out in a picnic shelter, but her sister had finally urged her to brave the storm before it got worse. We kissed passionately, felt sad, and then they walked off beyond the rain-drenched palm trees.

I was consumed with emotion as I stared off into the wall of water, watching my love disappear in the haze, not knowing when or if I ever would see her again. I felt sick, frightened, confused, without a mature understanding of our magnetism. A few minutes passed, when suddenly an amazing thing happened. She reappeared out of the fog, walking towards me for one more last soaking wet kiss. It was an unbelievable, passionate, romantic moment that I will never forget.

I moved away the next day, I never knew how to properly describe the way I felt for Elle. She was my first love and that was a new feeling for me. She had suddenly become a mystery. I was crushed when she got a new boyfriend, just weeks later, but we still wrote letters back and forth, and I longed for her deeply.

I spent tenth grade back in Coshocton, but things were amiss. I felt a world away from my dreams and desires. I stuck to my commitment to stay there and improve my grades, although I lived with regret that entire school year. Things were not as fun back at Dad's. There were no smoky concerts, no keg parties, no beach. Life was a drag. What the fuck had I been thinking?

Finally, the end of the school year came, and I returned to the Florida lifestyle. I was hoping to spark things up with Elle again, but she was still dating another guy, which left me confused and slightly bitter. At some point I ended up dating her best friend Jill very briefly. That created so much jealousy between them that they actually got into a physical brawl over me one day. Yes! Girl-fight! And I got her back, but that only lasted for one day. The next day she had felt too guilty about leaving her boyfriend, so she wrote me a heartfelt letter describing why we couldn't be together. Things between us never really got back on the right track after that. I chalk it up to inexperience and adolescent insecurity. I had no clue in the world how to be in a real relationship and somehow I managed to fumble the whole thing up pretty bad. The energy and chemistry was there, but we were young, shy and most likely scared of our emotions and the possibilities.

Elle got away, and I would soon set off to wander about the country in search of truth and a meaning to my existence. I tried to return to her again, but my revelations were always poorly timed, and I escaped again and again, running towards an unknown and unclear destiny. That is the power and uncertainty of that confusing emotion Love, and the questionable decisions we make to fill the void without it, and not to be alone.

I had accepted that Elle and I were not going to work out, which was made a little easier by the fact that I had suddenly become popular with some of my female classmates. Oh, those high school memories I wish not to recall. I blew so many opportunities back then. Most of my close friends were females, and I think that was one of the reasons for my popularity. I was asked by two different beautiful girls to go to the prom, and yet I refused to go. I was such a shy person and an anti-establishment thinker and thought of the prom as too pretentious. Although one of the main reasons was actually because I was a poor kid, living in a wealthy community. One girl actually offered to pay my way, but being so stubborn, I passed that one up, too.

Regardless, my path was heading in another direction. I am certainly fortunate that I have shared my heart with so many amazing spirits. My heart's spiritual journey may have been sparked with Elle but little did I know back then the long and strange trip those crazy, charismatic women would lead me on.

Andre had turned me on to the phenomenon of "Dead tapes"—bootlegs of Grateful Dead shows on cassette tape—first, though, and I quite liked everything I had heard. An actual show was a completely different matter, however. An experience I had been anticipating for years, because my brother Shawn, nine years older than I, had gone on many Grateful Dead tours by the late 1980s.

For my first show, Shawn and I headed off to the center of Dade County and the inner city Miami Arena. My brother split off in his own direction as soon as we hit the parking lot. I ventured forth solo, through the madness of the scene. Somewhere along the line, I stuck out my tongue and accepted a dose of LSD from a stranger. The arena transformed into a giant floating bubble and I was like another bubble just bobbing around inside of it. The first set sounded warped and distant. The band on stage looked like a tattered puppet show taking place in the background. None of it was familiar to me. It was like suddenly I had never even heard this music before. The first sign of recognition was the first set closer, Chuck Berry's "Promised Land". Oh boy, did that bring me around a little as my bones started to wiggle and shake to the rhythm and vibrations of the bubbles. Tidewater four-ten-o-nine!

The second set opened with a smokin' "China Cat > Rider" that I should've been ecstatic over, but the acid was clearly winning and the music was only coming through in waves, literally. The mantric verses of "Saint of Circumstance" brought me in for another landing. I didn't know what I was going for, but I was going to go for it, for sure. By the time "Goin' Down The Road Feelin' Bad" hit, I was a true believer! Man oh man, I was a dancing fool like I had never known to the full stream Grateful Dead boogie. The "Dear Mr. Fantasy > Hey Jude" finished me off and nothing was left of my brain but a puddle of exhausted enlightenment and a new found sense of freedom.

After the show, we descended on my car only to discover that I had lost the keys. We called a locksmith from a pay phone and waited, tripping, laughing, and staring for what could've been hours...

When the locksmith finally arrived, I suddenly found my keys, which were right there in my front pocket the whole time. I guess I just needed the acid to wear off a little. Instead of driving home that night, we set course to continue the adventure by heading across the state to the bayside retreat of St. Petersburg for the next round of Dead shows.

CHAPTER 2

Driven By The Wind

B y the fall of 1990, I had been completely transformed by the magic and music of the Grateful Dead scene for several years with several tours under my belt and dozens of new friends from the road. I had even created my own newspaper/zine, *Inspiration*. That fall, using my self-appointed status as an underground newspaper proprietor, I secured a press pass for a debate between Timothy Leary and G. Gordon Liddy. The event was held at the Florida Atlantic University, which was directly across the street from Spanish Oaks, where, if you recall, many of my teenage psychedelic expeditions had taken place. I was fortunate enough to get a photo, conversation, and interview with the legendary Leary, who insisted I call him Tim, and I subsequently published it all in the third issue of *Inspiration*.

The revelation to publish my own newspaper hit me a couple of years earlier at one of the east coast Dead shows, like a lightning bolt, during "Terrapin." Inspiration moved me brightly. It also might be blamed on the intensity of the Snoopy-and-Woodstock–decorated cartoon blotter I ingested that night.

My concept was similar to the Rhode Island-based hippie rag, *New World Rising*, that my friend Grateful Fred had been publishing. I filled *Inspiration* with artwork and poetry from like-minded travelers alongside information on environmental activism, Rainbow Family gatherings, and Grateful Dead tours. At the time, many of these grassroots movements existed as sort of a continuation of the former Yippie movement. Papers like *New World Rising* and *Inspiration* spread information and kept people connected. My pen name and nickname at Rainbow Gatherings and in the Grateful Dead lots was Morning Dew. My brother Shawn still calls me that.

Through these vast counter culture networks and with the distribution of my zine, I met a lot of friends. Two girls from the Palm Beaches, Sunshine and Springwater, contacted me after receiving an issue of *Inspiration*. The two were inseparable friends who expressed an interest in organizing some peace rallies against what would become the first Gulf War. Along with local representatives of Greenpeace, the Sierra Club, and similar pacifist organizations, I met with the girls and we created the Palm Beach County Coalition for World Peace.

I have always had a strong aversion to violence. On summer Dead tour that year, I witnessed a frightening event where police allegedly beat a Dead fan to death in front of the box office at RFK Stadium. I had no clue how that incident started, but I witnessed a terrible ending to it. I had stumbled into the grassy knoll area in front of the box office where an overwhelming police presence had suddenly blocked off the surrounding area. Mounted cops on horseback would then not let people leave. There were a group of Deadheads shouting at the cops to, "Leave the guy alone." Several cops were on top of this guy, beating him, strangling him, and then I witnessed his body go limp. People were shouting "You killed him! You fucking pigs killed him!" To my own eyes, I certainly bore witness to this; the guy seemed to be not breathing anymore. The cops let up on him and a few in charge made a couple radio calls. A few minutes later, a nearby ambulance was let in to the area. As I watched on in horror, I noticed a medic who was kneeled over the guy shake his head back in forth in dismay. It didn't look good. The batons came out and the goon squad in blue set its sights on quickly dispersing the mob. We all split the scene as fast as we could. It had really freaked me out, but inspired me to make the most of every moment and stand up for peace and justice whenever possible.

At the final show of the 1990 Summer Tour in Chicago, I walked up to the front of the stage after the encore and stared at the "Steal Yer Face" sticker on Brent Mydland's Hammond Organ. I closed my eyes, meditating on the image, turned around and walked away not looking back to the stage at all. It was the end of the tour, and I wanted an object stuck in my mind to think about until the next tour. Three days later, when I arrived back in Boca, I got a disturbing phone call of condolence from a friend. She just informed me that Brent Mydland had died. It was devastating. My favorite moments from almost every show I attended were when Brent would let loose on his fiery organ and light up the crowd. There would be great moments again, but the music was never the same to me. Like most 'heads, I found out the same way, when I arrived home from tour. The final verse Brent sang that night was from "The Weight":

"I gotta go," he sang, "but my friend can stick around..."

Back in the Palm Beaches, my new friends Sunshine and Springwater absolutely electrified me. Their deeply driven spirits were out to make a real difference in the world. Their compassion, motivation, and expression spoke to me on every level. And I was immediately smitten with the soul of Springwater, a charismatic, petite blonde from Scotland with a hilarious wit. We would laugh so hard together it was truly painful. An instant bond was formed between us, and it wasn't long before our passions evolved beyond just friendship.

This was all happening during a time when I was dating a stunning redhead, Jenny. We had met earlier that year while I was working the graveyard shift at a gas station, in addition to one of my record store jobs. She lived nearby and would stop in and flirt with me on occasion. Eventually I was invited to a party where we hit it off. Jenny was from a humble family with fairly old-fashioned parents. By this time, I had let my hair grow out pretty long and been fashioning a few tie-dyes. It had been quite the personal transformation from my pre-Tom Sawyer/surfer look. There were a few weeks of romantic courtship before Jenny and I started getting physical. The first time we had sex was while on an LSD trip, and WOW, that was quite a wild experience! It joyously went on for many hours.

Jenny and I had gone through about a month of being apart while she was visiting with relatives up north. I was spending my time in the Palm Beaches organizing peace rallies with the hippie girls. When Jenny returned, I felt I had to tell her that I was feeling intense emotions for Springwater.

We took an evening stroll on the beach, and I confessed my strayed emotions. This was one of the shittiest moments of my life. I felt horrible that I was essentially breaking her heart, but I had no other choice than to be completely honest. She didn't take it very well. She was so mad at me that she insisted that I leave immediately. My own freedom tasted bitter. A couple of hours later I got a desperate and confusing phone call from her. She was rambling incoherently about swallowing a bottle of pills and was afraid that she might be overdosing. We spent the night in the emergency room.

Her selfish attempt to end her life didn't sit well with me and only increased my desire to distance myself from her and follow my heart to Springwater. From that point on, Springwater and I jumped headlong into an intensely passionate relationship. I was commuting to my job at Peache's Records & Tapes. On my nights off, we would often hang with our friends who were starting the Dead cover band Crazy Fingers. Up to that point in my life, I had been socializing in many different circles, from the goth kids to the beach bums. But I found a very likable and accepted identity among the hippie kids. Well, that, and I had fallen head over heels in love with one. I still kept my ties with the other social groups, though; they were all part of a growing LSD network that I happened to be the primary supplier for.

Springwater and I became inseparable. One Florida sunset we sat huddled together on the beach while glaring out into a turbulent sea. The wind blew warm gusts of salty air at us as ominous storm clouds moved in from behind. Half the sky was calm and innocent; the other side was tormented with thunder and lightning. The darkness soon threatened the remaining edges of our world. Caught in between the oncoming storm and the fading blue sky behind us, we held each other tight. Nothing else mattered. This may have been our greatest moment. We were so at peace with life and one another. The tortured sky did not flinch our grasp. We sat there silently smiling and weeping with each other, not saying words. The storm had moved in and covered us in complete darkness. The rains fell down but we held on tight for a time that seemed like a glimpse of forever. We made it through the storm and when it had passed, we simply walked over the dunes holding hands with the night in full darkness, leaving part of ourselves in the sand, a pureness that we would never fully attain again.

Our moments together were often intense like that. We would exhaust every ounce of our strength. Regardless of our attempts to become one with each other, nothing seemed to compare to the one-ness we had that night, during a storm, just holding each other, on the beach, with no fears, and when nothing and no one else mattered.

We were a part of a loving family of bohemian freaks who referred to each other as husbands and wives, which was mostly Sunshine's idea. Not exactly a cult, but instead very Rainbow Family–oriented. There was an impromptu silly, yet sweet, acid-laced ritual by the pier one night joining Springwater and I in union. We were infatuated with each other and devoted for what I had hoped would be a lifetime.

I remember telling one of the guys in the Peace Coalition, Bill Chalk, that I was happier than I'd ever been in my life. I told him I had everything figured out: I knew the keys to happiness and how to hold on to them. Well, Bill was a wise fellow and he loved the fact that I had found such happiness, but he could see right through my arrogance.

"Be careful there Dew... because it's been my experience that every time you think you've got life figured out, something big will happen to pull the rug out from under you. This will happen over and over and over again if you don't realize that you actually don't know shit. Learn to be happy in the moment and you'll be able to take life's hits a lot easier. Trust me, there is great wisdom in humility."

I would soon learn that Bill actually knew a thing or two more than I about such matters. I was reminded of the Grateful Dead anthem, "Uncle John's Band," in which Robert Hunter writes about life looking like Easy Street and then danger knocking at your door...

CHAPTER 3

Follow Your Bliss!

W hile I was hanging with my new family in the bohemian underworld of the Palm Beaches, Jenny was stirring up trouble for me at home.

As it turned out, she had befriended my mother and older sister—continuing to hang out with them while I was off on new adventures. My family had not met my new love yet, nor were they willing to even give her a chance. Nasty words were exchanged about me at home, and things soon reached a boiling point.

Taking a break from Springwater one night, I was relaxing at home. Jenny had been out shopping with my sister. When they got back to the house, Jenny wanted to hang out. We were just chilling and talking together when, after a while, I started to feel strange, like the onset of an acid trip. It was then that she confessed to dosing my lemonade. I guess she just figured I wouldn't mind. Well of course I just smiled and went with the flow. And in a moment of extreme weakness and poor judgment, this led to her sexing me. And so much for me thinking that I had everything all figured out. Regardless... I knew that I had really fucked up.

The next morning, I felt like the worst person in the entire world. I had cheated. I got extremely angry with Jenny and told her to stay away from my house and to never speak to me again. I had never wanted to repeat the mistakes of my father and become a cheater or dishonest person. There was only one thing I knew to do and that was to be honest and confess to Springwater right away. Maybe she would understand.

I called her and said that we needed to talk. She was apparently already upset about something. She told me about this apocalyptic nightmare she just had. She was being chased around in a land of giants that she could not escape from. Looking for me everywhere to help her but I was nowhere to be found. Doors were being knocked down and houses were smashed, families and lives devastated, towns destroyed!

I realized that I couldn't discuss my problem with her on the phone; it had to be in person. Especially after learning of her traumatic nightmare. My car was in the shop, so I took a long bus trip up to Lake Worth. We sat in her room and I confessed what had happened the night before between Jenny and I.

She said nothing to me. It was a horrible and devastating silence. She got up and went into the other room and asked her roommate to give me a ride home. It was one of the longest rides of my life. Styx was on the radio... the song "Come Sail Away" does not sit well with me to this very day.

I was in shock and I knew that she was too. I had now broken two hearts and really a third by shattering my own in the process. It would be a long recovery that changed my life and the further choices I would soon make sent me thousands of miles from home on a soul-searching journey of self-discovery.

At first, I was so depressed when I got home that I retreated to my room and wanted to hide from the world. But, a much bigger storm was brewing. My mother and sister had been out drinking together and when they arrived home they ganged up on me in a verbal and abusive assault like I had never experienced. They said the meanest things to me, as if I wasn't already down and defeated enough.

I called up one of my closest friends and soul mates, Beth, for help. Beth and I had worked together in the record stores a lot and had been to many club concerts together. One of my favorite concert memories with her was a wild time seeing The Ramones in Miami Beach. We had actually met them and got their autographs that day, too. Anyhow, I made an early morning escape and moved into Beth's house. She and her parents welcomed me in with open arms, but I knew that I had to come up with an actual plan for my life... and fast.

It seemed as though Springwater and the whole Palm Beach hippie family of love didn't want to have much more to do with me at the time. Who could blame them? She and Sunshine had decided to move to a college town in, of all places, Ohio. I refused to speak to Jenny or even my own family at that point. I was lost, depressed, and confused. Just days earlier I was on top of the world, but it had all come crumbling down so fast. My whole life was changing, again. Maybe if I hadn't confessed, things would have been different. But it wasn't the honest way; I didn't even second-guess my confession then. I accepted the responsibility for my actions.

It was while sitting alone in the comfort of Beth's parents' house that I saw a TV program on PBS that would inspire the most important personal transformation of my life. The program was called The Power of Myth, with Joseph Campbell and Bill Moyers. Campbell was one of the world's leading scholars on mythology and urged us all to "follow our bliss," without fear, and to not be surprised when doors of opportunity open when we do.

The program mesmerized me and tantalized my intellect. I felt spiritually alive. My depression lifted and I felt an internal calling to follow my own, true bliss. My thirst for this knowledge was pushing me to leave South Florida for good. To blindly jump into the world, without a net. The timing seemed to be appropriate. As much as I needed to escape and run from the bad things that were happening to me, I also longed for greater understanding. I longed to find my own answers on how to maintain an inner happiness, which I'd recently had little fortune holding onto. A sort of rite of passage into manhood was clearly emerging.

The next set of Dead shows were coming up in December in Phoenix and Denver. All of my internal compass arrows were pointing for me to head out to the traveling hippie Mecca, my home away from home. I needed to rise from the ashes. Although I had been doing the east coast tours for a few years, this time around there would be no nest for me to return to, no safety net to catch me. I managed to photocopy a miniature flier version of *Inspiration* to pass out at the upcoming shows. I decided to quit my job at Peaches, sell my car and personal belongings, and hit the road.

Interestingly enough, a couple of goth friends who I worked with, Brian Warner and Scott Putesky, were also going through some similar personal transformations. They quit Peaches around the same time because their band was really starting to get noticed in the Florida music scene. I used to sell them doses, and we would occasionally hang out, smoke pot, and watch Scooby Doo cartoons at Brian's grandmother's condominium. I made a couple of fliers for their band, Marilyn Manson & The Spooky Kids. Brian played me a demo recording one day that consisted of a mash-up of sorts with an interview from the notorious Charles Manson and one from Marilyn Monroe. He laid down a bunch of creepy techno keyboard tracks behind it. And this was the basis for their band name. Eventually Brian and Scott legally changed their names to that of their on-stage personas—Marilyn Manson and Daisy Berkowitz—and thus began their own world conquest of pop culture, which became well known and obviously quite successful.

Most of the year had been pretty adventurous for me, but by the next winter my emotional status was pretty tattered. I needed to venture west, do some healing, and figure some things out. Then, I thought, when the Dead played their annual East Coast Spring Tour, maybe Springwater and I could have a chance again.

Before I left, the World Peace Coalition was having a bake sale on the Florida Atlantic campus. Springwater and I met up and had a nice conversation on the lawn. Neither of us was in college then, but just sitting there on that grass and having a relationship talk about different directions we were going to go in felt so mature to me, like something out of an eighties John Cusack movie. I talked about how I needed to head out west and do a little soul searching. She talked about how she needed to go up north to do the same. We talked about the possibilities of meeting up again. I told her I would stay in contact and write to her about my adventures.

Ironically, she was moving to a place not far from Coshocton, where I had gone to live with my father, disrupting my first love with Elle. On a nice, calm, sunny Florida day, Springwater and I exchanged goodbye letters, hugged and kissed and knew that one day we would see each other again.

I read her letter after we parted. It was heartwarming and encouraging. It instilled a sense of hope in me and reassured me that everything would work out just the way it was meant to.

CHAPTER 4

The Bus Came By

I sold my little Toyota Corolla for $300 cash, along with a bunch of personal items, and raised enough money for a one-way Greyhound bus ticket to the West. Beth dropped me off at the bus station. It was a dark and gloomy day with a light rain falling. I was scared and anxious.

Several hours into the trip, we were taking a break for bus cleaning in a beachside town known for its 500 laps of NASCAR racing. I remember sitting in the front row of seats in the terminal with my personal items in the seat next to me.

The call was announced over the intercom that our bus was ready to board again. I grabbed my items and got on.

As I took my seat on the bus, panic and anxiety overcame me. My wallet was suddenly missing!

I searched all of my belongings but couldn't find it. I remembered putting it on that empty seat next to me in the terminal. We started pulling away and I shouted out for the driver to stop.

The bus stopped abruptly and the agitated driver asked what the problem was. I looked out the window and could clearly see into the terminal to the exact location I had been sitting and the seat next to it. All was empty, no wallet!

I hopped off the bus and quickly checked inside the terminal for my wallet. I asked the clerks behind the counter.

There was no sign of it anywhere.

"Thanks," I told the driver as I boarded the bus again. We pulled away, my wallet gone, and I was completely broke, heading out west on a four-day bus trip. I leaned my head against the window, overwhelmed with sadness, and silently cried.

"What a tragedy," I thought. Somehow, though, I felt as if I were being tested, because now I had no choice but to continue on my journey. No choice.

The next morning, we were taking a break somewhere near the Florida state capital when I met a cool dude named Walter. He wondered if I were heading to the Dead shows because that's where he was heading. I told him about what happened with my wallet and in an amazingly kind gesture of the kind that was common among Deadheads, an opportunity presented itself to me.

He told me that he was a parking lot T-shirt vendor and he would lend me some shirts to sell for him at the shows and I could pay him 50% a shirt for what I sold. He also fronted me some money for food to get through the next few days of bus-riding hell. He reassured my faith in humanity, but especially the kindness of the Deadhead family. That's really what it was all about, helping out strangers in need. It also secured my newly adopted "follow your bliss" creed. Indeed, doors of opportunity were beginning to open up to me in my newly found bliss. It also didn't hurt knowing that soon I would be running into my acid connections, too, and could quickly turn a profit in that world.

Clearly, the wallet incident had been merely a test. What a twist to have sold my car and possessions for traveling money only to have that money lost or stolen within hours of setting off on my journey. At first I was fearful, but I became calm knowing that at some point something good must happen. It was all happening for a reason.

Walter and I shared stories of the various shows we had attended over the years. It made the long bus ride easier, having someone I could relate to and talk with along the way. Especially once we got to Texas, where things would get a little weird and crazy.

We had a long layover near the Alamo where we switched buses. To kill time, we explored the tourist spots for a few hours. Our new bus was scheduled to depart around 11pm, but was delayed, apparently because we had no driver.

My head was filled with the history of the West, of Daniel Boone. I thought of the hardships those people endured and the sacrifices they made standing up for a better life that they truly believed in. And, of course, the sobering thought of how the Native Americans got so fucked over in all of that.

We waited inside the terminal until some time around 12:30am when the driver arrived. His nametag read "Jack."

Jack stood by the door collecting tickets as we all began to pile onto the overcrowded bus. I noticed the smell of alcohol and he slurred his speech. He was noticeably rude to several people, shouting off a few expletives occasionally. "Just get the hell on the bus, people!" he yelled at one point. Then he disappeared for a while. We sat there on a completely crowded bus for another half hour or so... before we realized... Jack had disappeared.

A woman dragging two kids behind her and a garbage bag full of toys and clothes got on. Her young children made their way to the back of the bus as she struggled behind, knocking the bag into peoples' knees.

Just then, Jack arrived and shouted for everyone to take their seats, and that we would be departing immediately. He shouted specifically at the woman in the aisle to take her seat. As she tried to rush her way down the aisle, he jerked the bus into motion and her bag of toys ripped open spilling all over the aisle, right next to me and Walter. We then both got up to help her gather some of the items.

Jack's inebriated voice came over the intercom demanding "DO NOT HELP THAT WOMAN!" He threatened to stop the bus immediately and kick all the troublemakers off. We ignored his threats as other passengers were starting to express their outrage over his behavior. We got the lady's situation quickly resolved and all seemed calm for the moment.

We were barely outside the city limits when his driving became erratic. Speeding and swerving along the highway, upsetting passengers who began talking in worried voices to one another. It was obvious that we had a very drunk bus driver for our seven-hour route to El Paso!

This was in the days before cell phones, so no one could conveniently call the outside world for help. Like riding on an airplane with bad turbulence, some people were crying, anxiously sweating, others praying, all thinking that we were about to die. You could hear people whispering with one another about what we should do.

I was one of those thinking: "This is it, I am going to die on a Greyhound bus in sweaty Texas!"

Finally, the passengers got together and elected an unlucky soul for the ill-fated mission of going up to talk some sense into Jack—my new friend and hero, Walter.

Walter stood up and approached Jack, who instantly bellowed for him to SIT DOWN! Our brave hero traded seats so he could talk to Jack.

I couldn't hear from where I was, but everyone could hear Jack's twang shouting: "... am NOT drunk and I am offended that anyone thinks so."

Jack suggested that he would sing a song for us if that would ease everyone's minds and calm us down. He then launched into a series of TV show theme songs, over the intercom. It did seem to help some.

"He actually drives better when he sings," noted a fellow rider. His negative attitude had completely turned around and by the third song. He had everyone joining in for the sing-alongs.

We stopped for a short smoke and restroom break whereupon a fellow passenger discreetly used the pay phone to alert authorities to our situation. Jack, now full of coffee, seemed to be sobering up.

A couple more hours down the road, we stopped at our next break point where police and a new driver were waiting. I cannot recall why they never just pulled the bus over. But at the stop, Jack was put in the back of a squad car and several passengers gave statements. The ordeal was over and we had a nice, sober driver and relieved passengers for the rest of the trip.

We were so elated that the situation was safer, a few passengers jumped into a sing-a-long with "Hit the Road, Jack!" A dangerous situation that led to friendship, hope, and opportunity in the midst of a tragedy narrowly averted.

CHAPTER 5

As Honest As
A Colorado Man Can Be

The legendary rock 'n' roll promoter Bill Graham was standing in the dirt parking lot at Firebird Lake, Arizona, when we met. I already admired him for his role in the music and culture that I'd made my life. This was the man who had made the legendary Fillmore Auditorium into a mecca for psychedelic bands in the 1960s. He'd managed Janis Joplin and Carlos Santana and was, when I met him, promoting all the west coast Grateful Dead Shows. I was just a raggedy hippie kid, but Graham looked me right in the eye when we spoke. We discussed the bohemian scene, its troubles and what might be in store for the future of the parking lot culture. I think he was mostly interested in why I was passing out fliers at his concert. He didn't seem to mind, though, as long they were not becoming litter. I asked to officially interview him a future issue of *Inspiration*. He was very open to it and promised to make it happen one day. I left the encounter with a positive aura, hinting that something greater was in the works.

The shows were exactly what I needed to rejuvenate my spirit. From the first night's opening sermon, "Cold Rain and Snow," to the next night's closing hymn, "Brokedown Palace," my soul was gently rocked and soothed. The second night's experience had been particularly sweet. The boys opened with "Hell In A Bucket > Bertha." "Maggie's Farm," "Black Throated Wind," "Samson & Delilah," and "Goin' Down The Road Feelin' Bad > Good Lovin'" were spectacular, bone-shaking highlights. It was a beautiful Sunday show and like most of those nomadic experiences, it was somehow everything I needed to hear at precisely the right times.

I was able to pay Walter back right away for the T-shirt loan and had leftover funds to survive on. I met some cool new friends at a campsite gathering after the shows. Some random hippie girl proposed marriage to me by the campfire one night. I can't even remember her name, but I remember that her naivety and sweetness lifted my confidence. I politely informed her that my heart belonged to another. I ended up catching a ride with her and her friends to the next set of shows in Denver. An unidentified flying object was seen in the middle of the night while we drove through the Navaho Indian Reservation. Also, a more identifiable object visited us, too, nearly killing us all. Just near the Colorado state border, a large, white owl flew out of the darkness, filling the windshield with its wingspan for a brief instant. It scared the hell out of us as we swerved off the deserted highway.

When we finally made it to the Mile High City, I caught up with some dear friends from Middle Earth, the Bama Boys. Freeman had gotten real sick, and he just sat there huddled over his grilled cheese skillet and propane stove in the snow-covered Shakedown Street. He contemplated whether or not he could go into the show. Fortunately for me he eventually forfeited his special mail order ticket, and I was further nudged forward towards my unsuspected fate.

The first I had heard of the almighty Henry Sullivan was some months, or maybe even a year or two earlier at a Rainbow Family gathering in the southeast. Drum circles thundered out and resonated tribal rhythms from all directions, deep inside a remote and enchanted muggy Southern wilderness. The full moon was being honored by a nomadic band of psychedelic gypsies. A dark dread-headed warlock named Diamond Fire spoke to me across the ceremonial flames of worship. He picked me out and peered into my soul. He said that one day I would find myself in a troubling situation at a Grateful Dead concert and that I would need to seek out a man by the name of Henry Sullivan. He informed me that someday I was going to be helped by this man.

Even for me, that was a pretty esoteric pronouncement. Yet I responded, "Sullivan... really?" How precise! "I mean are you sure its not Henry Jones, or Henry Smith, or maybe even John Henry?"

"Nope. Henry Sullivan."

"Okay, okay... putting that into the vault. I'm going to remember that, Diamond Fire."

Destiny, in the form of a man named Henry Sullivan awaited me.

Denver's McNichol's Arena howled, like a spaceship that had crashed into a dark and snowy mountain valley, lost and crying out to be discovered. The first sign of trouble was a yellow-jacketed security goon who came to escort several of us backstage over supposed duplicate tickets. He lured us with the lucrative promise of new and better seating assignments. He collected all of our stubs and I kept my eyes on Freeman's gift, which I was absolutely ninety-nine percent certain was the very top ticket in his hand. Once backstage, the usher handed the stubs over to a man in a black leather biker coat, a cross between Dennis Hopper and guitarist Tony Iommi of Black Sabbath. He ruled over the hive of yellow jackets. An official Grateful Dead tour laminate dangled on a tethered lanyard from around his neck. The lights in the arena had just gone dark as the band took to the stage. There was a loud roar from the crowd. Distantly, I could hear the opening chords to "Touch of Grey." He took out a highly technical thermal emission tool (a Bic lighter) and held the flame underneath the top stub. A dark thermal reaction revealed a browning or burning of the ticket. He declared it good. Some asshole from the group shouted abruptly that the ticket was his and quickly stepped forward to retrieve it. He gave him the mail-ordered stub and motioned for him to return back inside the arena. The guy skipped off happily as I stood there silently realizing that something was amiss. That false ticket-stub claiming shyster just ran off with my fucking ticket! Then, just as quickly, the remaining stubs were all tested and declared fake. My stomach dropped. I had been duped. Mister Leather Coat motioned for his hive of yellow goons to herd us out the back door and into the parking lot as he turned in the opposite direction and confidently walked away.

Frustration and anger overwhelmed me and I suddenly flashed

on Diamond Fire's prophecy. I pushed my way back through the yellow jackets and stood my ground. "I demand to speak to Henry Sullivan!" The yellow jackets grabbed me as Leather Coat stopped and turned around.

"Let him through," he said. I walked slowly toward him with a gulp. "I'm Henry Sullivan," he said. The yellow jackets closed in, gripping me by the arms. I explained about the asshole stealing my stub, about being told that we would be reassigned seats, Bama Boy Freeman, the mail order system, and the fact that the whole thing was going down wrong.

"It was all wrong man!" I was near tears. The yellow jackets tightened their grips on me and demanded that I turn around and go with them immediately. Henry waved them off and told them to give us a minute. He pulled me to the side and asked me how I knew his name. I informed him that someone from inside the "family" said to ask for him if I ever got into trouble and that he would help. He paused, scratched his chin and stared intently at me. His rough tone softened up and he spoke sincerely.

"Look, you've already made a scene here and although I do believe you've been wronged, I can't fix it right now, but one day I will. I promise I will," he said kindly. "Now go back out into the parking lot and find another ticket. You'll get back in. Then find me at the next run of shows, and I'll take care of you."

What choice did I have? He apologized and walked away. The yellow jackets swarmed on me and proceeded to roughly drag me towards the exit. I shouted a few choice words at them in protest. Henry turned back around and instructed them to "Ease up," and they did. The background chorus faded as I calmly walked out the back door of Denver's McNichol's Arena to the faded sounds of the choir's opening number reminding me that I would indeed get by and I would undoubtedly survive.

In the parking lot, my adrenaline was pumping but I was determined to get back into the show. I went straight to a known scalper. When I tried the Bic lighter test on his tickets, none of them passed. "Asshole!" I thought. I told him that he had fake tickets. He argued with me. He asked if I was going to buy one or not. I asked for a discount, but he wouldn't go below twenty bucks. I caved in and rolled the dice on a known counterfeit. In a sweet ironic twist I got back into the arena, but this time I didn't make the mistake of going to my assigned seat.

That night I was treated to an awesome "Dark Star > Terrapin" that set off an awe-inspiring three-night run. I also managed to get into the next two nights to witness the grand finale of a "Dark Star" reprise out a fantastically stellar "Space" jam. I felt transformed, like a three-night cosmic carnival ride had just dumped me off at the snow-covered altar of freedom and bliss. Ahhh, sweet religion. Soul rejuvenated, direction unknown.

CHAPTER 6

Rocky Mountain High

Dave Shroeder, also known as "Sticker Dave," was a Middle Earth friend who had been living in the Rocky Mountain ski resort community of Summit County. The Bama Boys had headed up to Dave's place after the shows, and I ended up with some crazy girl in Boulder. I eventually lost the girl and ended up sitting alone at Penny Lane, a well-known coffee shop on Pearl Street. I befriended a kind man named Tom who owned the Beat Book Shop, and he offered me a room at his house for a few days. Eventually after bumming around Boulder, directionless, I was rescued by the Bama Boys.

Sticker Dave lived in the Swan Meadow trailer park nestled behind Lake Dillon, a sweet and welcoming winter refuge. The cold road had grown weary on me and I really appreciated the warmth of Dave's home. The last time I had seen him, he was visiting me in Florida the previous summer. He stayed with my family for a couple of weeks, and we managed to do quite a bit of partying. When my whole world fell apart that winter, I called him up and he offered a room in his home, if I could make it out to Colorado. It had been in the back of my mind for sure, but my bigger plan was to head out to the west coast for the annual New Years Eve run of Dead shows. Dave said he could certainly use another roommate and I was welcome to find a job and stay for the winter. From the warmth of the Florida sunshine to the brisk Colorado mountains? Sure, why not? And onward the Bama crew rolled further west, without me.

I immediately started looking for work. There was a HELP WANT-ED sign in the window of a Dairy Queen in the town of Silverthorne. I went in and asked the man for an application. He said that he wouldn't give me one because he had no intention of hiring me. I was confused. The man said that I couldn't work there with long hair and he knew that I probably wasn't willing to cut it off. I left pissed off and sort of in shock.

I sat down on a wooden bench out front and began to feel down-right pitiful when a door opened up from the restaurant next door. A man in a chef's coat approached me, lighting up a cigarette. He could see that I was upset, and asked me what was the matter. After I told him, Byron, the kitchen manager of the Sunshine Cafe offered me a job right there on the spot.

The serenity of those mountains gave me the healing and inner quiet that I had been seeking. Somehow, in this new place, I felt at home and settled in for some winter soul searching. I wrote to Spring-water that I hoped we would reconcile someday. I explained the best I could that I loved her deeply and wanted to see her again, as soon as possible. Then I phoned her, and she was receptive and nurturing. There was hope.

Meanwhile, I hitchhiked to work almost every day. I could see why Byron hired me on the spot: the Sunshine Cafe crew were my kind of people. There was the infamous Tyrone Sloan, Dave Plyman, Dave Owie, Bob Moon, Warren Rosencranz, Amy, Maurine, and Rachel just to name a few. Richard "RJ" Johnson was one of the restaurant's investors and he became a lifelong friend. Then there was the unforgettable Robin Page. Robin and I knew right away that we were kindred spirits. She called me her younger brother and took me under her wing. She vouched for me at all the local bars, though I was not of drinking age, and dragged me around to some of the greatest parties in the county.

The Sunshine Crew was already well known for partying their ass-es off. By that winter I was the youngest of the group at only nineteen but everyone was very kind and friendly to me. I really liked those people and could write a book just about them and the wild adventures we went on, but for now, just one must-tell story...

Oh how I loved the sweet southern sounds of the Allman Brothers Band. I had met their road manager, Kirk, at a Dead show in Chicago a couple of years earlier. I think I was wearing an Allman's "Eat A Peach" shirt when Kirk approached me and we hit it off, talking for about an hour or so. What a great guy and a kind soul. I bumped into him again in Miami, just a couple of months before I left South Florida for good. I was at Springwater's one Sunday morning and her roommate, Roberto, and I were looking through the newspaper. There, buried in the classifieds, was a small two-line advertisement that read:

ALLMAN BROS. CONCERT TODAY
TAMIAMI PARK–MIAMI 1PM

That's it. No other ads or announcements for the show existed that we knew of. It didn't make much sense, really, but we were up for an adventure, so we went down to Miami to see what was going on.

It was a crystal clear blue sky day in the park. There was a small mobile stage nestled in-between palm trees just beyond the end zone of a football field. Now there were about 2,000 people there, Frisbees, dogs, hippies, peace, love, with plenty of room for everyone to dance. Hardly any security whatsoever–this was like some crazy impromptu show. It also happened that at the time I possessed a great batch of LSD. We were so excited that the universe had aligned things in our favor that we dropped the acid and got lost in the music. I enjoyed a wonderful hallucination of palm trees dancing with musical notes that were floating up from the guitars during the solos. I bumped into their band manager Kirk who informed me that the band were about to go into Criteria Studios to record a new album and they were testing out some new material at the show. He introduced me to a few of the band members but everything was too fuzzy to make any sense of the encounter. I had that reassuring feeling that I would bump into them again down the road, though.

And now, back to the cool Colorado mountains, where a blizzard is falling upon the tiny ski village of Vail while an avalanche of psychedelics swirled around the intimate little Dobson Ice Arena for yet another great Allman Brothers Band show. The Sunshine crew was on hand, all of us smashed on mushrooms. I said hello to Kirk, but again, my psychedelics were kicking in too strong to hang out in the backstage environment.

Now the real kicker happened the next night, when the Allmans were scheduled to play down in Boulder. We already had tickets that night to see the very popular German heavy metal band, The Scorpions, in Denver. Robin Page and I tried our best to convince the gang that seeing the Allman Brothers for a second night in a row would be a much better experience. God knows we tried! But, we were out-voted and ended up at the Scorpions.

Hmmm... leftover mushrooms... seemed like a good idea at the time! Robin and I decided to indulge and shroom again. But that night was very, very different than the night before. A colossal arena, spandex, metal heads, leather and spikes everywhere. The lights went down, explosions roared, "WE LOVE YOU DENNNVEERRRRR!!!" The Scorpions screamed into their classic rocker "Big City Nights." I mean, really, it's a catchy tune. In fact, I really dig it. But, we had already wrapped our little hippie heads around some psychedelic organic fungus, and, well, how can I explain it? It was sort of like a day-glow, candy-colored amusement park in magic mushroom land getting ripped apart at the seams by a thousand steel locomotives at full speed. WHAT THE FUCK IS GOING ON HERE?!? PUT DOWN THAT SLEDGEHAMMER! Enter the yellow jackets, mega security force paranoia, and Robin and I were both on the aisle just totally losing our shit! Sensory overload, WE GOTTA GET THE FUCK OUTTA HERE... NOW!

Robin and I abandoned the rest of the crew and high-tailed it out the exit by the end of the first song, laughing hysterically along the way. That same arena had been an inter-stellar bohemian spaceship just a few months earlier when the Dead landed there, but it had been converted into a dungeon of toxic sludge, filled with thousands of leather-clad human slaves worshiping the metal SCORPION GOD.

We tripped out in the parking lot with a bottle of Grand Marnier and waited for the show to end and the rest of the crew, who all had a rockin' good time of course, to stumble out and head home. Still, lesson learned: DO NOT TAKE MUSHROOMS AT A HEAVY METAL

CONCERT, ESPECIALLY JUST AFTER ATTENDING A TRIPPY HIP-
PIE PSYCHEDELIC SHOW. It's a rough mix, trust me!

As the winter crept on, Springwater and I wrote more letters and talked on the phone when we could afford it. We were hoping to see each
other at some point in the near future. I had made plans to return
to Florida to publish another issue of *Inspiration* before Spring Dead
tour.

I had also reached out that winter to my first love, Elle. She was
still living in South Florida and had written me a few comforting letters that winter. We were on good terms, and she confided some of her
relationship woes. Under the surface, I still had felt that our early relationship had never been resolved. I always let her know that I would
love to see her again.

Just before the beginning of spring, I put in my notice at the
Sunshine Cafe and got a Greyhound bus ticket back to the Sunshine
State. The road was calling me again and my adventures in the moun-
tains were really only just beginning. From the Sunshine State, to the
Sunshine Café, and back to the Sunshine State again... just following
where the road led me.

CHAPTER 7

When You're A Stranger

T o this day I detest those rugged, putrid, gray corduroy felt seats with the tacky rainbow stripes. I spent so much time on those buses back then that I think I developed an allergy. And there was always a sick person, a crying baby, and someone giving off deadly odors near me. Yep, it was another four-day hell ride on The Hound, but thankfully, no drunks at the wheel this time. Instead, I met a couple of girls, almost got mugged, and somehow stumbled into a happy ending. Thank God that bus didn't ride through sweaty Texas. Kansas was painful enough.

There was a long layover in the Great Arch City, and I didn't want to waste my time hanging around the bus terminal. I took a taxi over to a local mall, which had been the old Grand Central Train Station. I met a hippie girl named Gayle who worked at a shop there. I bought a Guatemalan backpack from her, and invited her to a movie. The new Oliver Stone feature, *The Doors*, was playing, and I needed to kill some time before my next train, not to mention the flirtatious spark, and that I could use the company. She politely declined though, claiming the neighborhood was too unsafe, so I headed over to the movie theater alone.

Something seemed immediately off. I sat near the concession stand, sipping on a soda, when I noticed some kids giving me mean looks. I shrugged it off until I noticed that I was the only white person in the building. No big deal, I thought, until one of the kids flashed a knife at me. Okay, obviously I'm not welcome here. Anxiety over-came me instantly. I started to shake, drenched in fear. They slowly approached and called out a bunch of racist shit in my direction. I mumbled something back, but I can't remember what. I got up quickly and headed over to the box office and told the manager that I felt un-safe and wanted a refund. They didn't seem surprised. When I walked outside, the kids were there, waiting. They headed towards me, but I jumped into a nearby taxi, and they flipped me off as we pulled away. I headed right back to the Greyhound station, which at least felt like a much safer place to be. Close call. I should have taken Gayle's advice.

At Memphis, a beautiful blonde college-aged girl boarded the bus and sat right next to me. I said hello, and she smiled, but didn't say a damn word to me. I was a little tired anyway, so I just leaned my head against the bus window and tried to ignore her. I drifted in and out of a light slumber through the ride, which was usual on The Hound... you really can't sleep on those things. Occasionally my mind would wander into what kind of conversation I could spark up with the girl. As it turned out, though, it wasn't long before no conversation was necessary and something quite surprising happened.

It was an overnight ride. Somewhere along the way, she got a blanket from the overhead storage. I awoke to find the blanket across both of our laps and her head leaning on my shoulder. She whispered something like, "Do you mind?" or, "Is this okay?" Hell, I can't re-member what she said. I really didn't care. She was really attractive. My heart was beating hard with anxiety. I nodded and she gave me a girlish giggle and her hand went right down my pants. I never got her name, and she just disappeared off the bus sometime late, in some small town outside of Nashville. And, of course, I got off sometime before then. Following one's bliss can be a frightening and sometimes very pleasant experience.

The bus pulled into that same Florida beachside town where I had lost my wallet four months earlier—Daytona Beach. I was in need of decent break. This time, though, I had learned my lesson about keeping an eye on my money. It was mid-morning, and the middle of the annu-al "Bike Week," a sort of wild motorcycle convention when we arrived. A perfect time and place for me to stray from the bus for a while and check out the beach and the bikes. It felt really good to walk around with a sense of vindication and accomplishment, considering how I felt the last time I was there.

I was browsing one of the vendor tables for a gift for Springwater when a small black hand-blown glass rose jumped out at me. I immediately thought not of Springwater, but of Elle. This confused me, but I purchased the rose.

I spent a couple of weeks piecing together the next issue of *Inspiration* on my brother Shawn's couch back in good ol' Spanish Oaks. He had taken over the condominium we used to live in years earlier with my mother. Coincidently, I found out that Springwater was visiting from Ohio, and she still had my battered heart freshly bleeding in her hands.

I wanted to get to a Rainbow Gathering and spring Dead tour eventually, so I arranged a ride with her as she was planning a return to Ohio. It would be a good time to test the waters between us. I met with her briefly a few days before we were set to leave. The encounter felt good–it was hopeful. The day before we our planned departure, however, I had arranged a date with Elle and to finally see *The Doors*.

Elle took my breath away the very moment our eyes met again. Obviously, I was still smitten. Nervous butterflies swirled in my belly in the dark of the movie theater. Afterwards, we sat in the parked car just under a secluded palm tree in the corner of the Glades Shopping Center. I remember being flooded with confused emotions. She wasn't dating anyone, and I was still in love. She was the ultimate catch. I realized I could easily date her again, but I was leaving the next day with Springwater. I gave her the glass rose, and we talked about taking a drive to the beach. She knew it meant things would happen between us, and was reluctant. I knew that it must have scared her. Hell, it scared me. I felt intimidated, even inadequate, with Elle. She knew I was planning to leave in the morning, but she didn't know I was planning to ride out with Springwater. Yet again, we didn't know when or if we would see each other again. I figured, why complicate matters further? Part of me longed to stay and pursue Elle, but I still hungered for the open road. Staying put for a girl, even my ideal woman, frightened me to no end.

As I drove away from Elle, alone in my brother's car, the dilemma weighed on me. Suddenly I became distracted by something very odd in the night sky to the north. It was a clear night with many stars and one star appeared to be moving parallel to the horizon at a very rapid pace. Then at lightning speed, it shot up at a forty-five degree angle. It continued to jolt up and down at variable speeds moving from the north to the east. I couldn't believe what I was seeing. At first I tried to reason that it was an aircraft, but knew that there was no way a plane could move like that. Perhaps it was a rogue satellite? It seemed inconceivable to me, especially since I had not recently taken any mind-altering substances. I pulled the car over and got out. I watched this little white dot dance along the horizon like a boat sailing in choppy waters. It bounced in-between stars until it suddenly stopped on the south horizon. A few seconds went by and then it zipped off into oblivion. I was astounded... I mean, what the fuck was that?

What a surreal night. I drove to the beach and sat there, thinking all night about what direction I wanted my life to go in. The previous eight months had been a whirlwind of life-changing adventure. I found myself with the choice to seek more or to hang back. I had so foolishly damaged my relationship with Springwater, but it seemed I was being given another chance. My past with Elle seemed distant. And, I had put so much effort into my newspaper and really felt compelled to get it distributed at the upcoming shows.

I meditated there in the sand and witnessed the sun rise over the sea to meet a new and hopeful dawn.

CHAPTER 8

Goin' Down That Road
Feelin' Bad

R egardless, of what I decided, it was certain that I was continuing my journey into the unknown. Despite the unearthly and
quite possibly extraterrestrial object that I had witnessed, that was
hardly the event shattering my reality. The incredible date with Elle
complicated by the coincidence of Springwater was just too much for
my heart to ignore. By the time the sun breached the horizon, I had
decided to take the ride with Springwater and explore the possibilities.
Somewhere deep in the center of my being I loved Elle more than I
could ever understand. Not only did that scare me, but it seemed that
our timing, though close this time, was still not in alignment. Perhaps
there was much more that I needed to learn.

Springwater and I escaped the south with some friends of hers
and headed up I-95 on through the Peach State and into the Carolinas.
We talked about so many things, both serious and lighthearted. We
laughed, held hands, and stopped at a couple of tourist traps along the
way. We were getting comfortable with each other again. She told me
that she had forgiven me for what happened with Jenny. We talked
about our possibilities in the future.

I began to think that maybe the Rainbow Gathering wasn't where
I wanted to get out. Maybe I should ride the whole way back to Ohio
with her? Or maybe we could both do the spring tour together? It
could have happened either of those ways, but neither of us wanted
to jump in that heavy and fast again. We needed more time. At least

she convinced me we did. She had started taking classes at Ohio University and wasn't ready to blow them off for Tour. Reason prevailed, and we stuck with the plan for me to be dropped off at the Rainbow Gathering. We acknowledged that nothing was official between us, but we talked about getting together over the summer. Maybe she would even move out to the mountains with me. There were all kinds of wonderful and exciting possibilities emerging.

She dropped me off near the edge of a Carolina forest. We kissed passionately and vowed to see each other again in a couple of months. If only things could be that easy. It was torture seeing her drive away, and more complications were about to evolve.

The Rainbow Family's Spring Equinox Gathering was being held in a remote national forest. It was typical in the bohemian sense: lots of hugs, smiles, and fun hallucinogenic drugs were passed around. The usual amounts of nudity, drum circles, and howling at the moon ensued. These gatherings were a spiritual retreat back to nature, not just for the dread-headed hippies, but also for the closet lawyer-and-doctor types, who used these gatherings as their escape from society. It was a place to let your freak flag fly without the expected paranoia that came with living in step with societal expectations.

It was at this gathering that I met yet another bohemian beauty and my next complication. She was a cute, petite, blue-eyed, blonde-headed, smiling hippie girl, Summer. We really hit it off one night by the campfire—singing, playing our acoustic guitars, making up blues songs and just basically grooving together. We gave in to the passionate bliss of our desire and got very intimate on the last night of the Gathering.

In the morning I asked if she wanted to travel with me to the Dead shows but she informed me that she was expecting her boyfriend to show up and that they would be traveling in her VW bus—but, of course I could ride with them. Hmmm... she had forgotten to mention any boyfriend before, and of course I neglected to mention my complex, sideways situations as well. As promised, her boyfriend Lee showed up that afternoon, and I was introduced to him as this cool guy that she had met and befriended.

Lee thanked me for looking after his girl. I responded with a little jealous, "Yea, so glad to finally meet you. Heard so much about you," blah, blah, blah... I politely declined their offer for a ride to the shows, instead climbing into a van with my dear friend Celeste, and we headed off to invade the nearby home of informal Middle Earth mastermind, the legendary K. Fimster.

The raid on Fimster's was a success for us, and a nightmare for his disapproving and disgruntled wife. We met up with the Bama Boys there and had his neighbors on heightened alert after turning his backyard into a miniature Woodstock. We managed to break his washing machine, further pissing off his wife, before the Middle Earth gang rode off again to officially hit Spring Tour.

It was business as usual in the parking lots. I distributed my newspaper along with some LSD that I scored at the Rainbow Gathering. Fimster's seven-year-old kid Joey got lost, but managed to find his way, ticketless, past the entry gate and into the arms of a Greensboro police officer. Bama Boy Kilgore and Jersey Jay were on the outside looking for their free miracle tickets. They were a little taken back at first when the officers asked them to step inside the gate.

"Does this kid belong to you?"

Not sure if they were in trouble and uncertain to what degree the situation was a mere hallucination, they accepted responsibility for Joey and a newly discovered way to gain free entry to a Grateful Dead show.

"Yes, Officer... we know him. We'll get him to his father... he's over there, yes." Pointing randomly into the arena and quickly scurrying away with Joey, they made it into the crowd, losing the cops in the process. The police were so overwhelmed with the surrounding chaos they had no idea what had happened. Fimster, of course, was still ticketless in the parking lot and looking everywhere for his kid, the poor bastard.

I got my miracle that night by being in the right place at the right time. I was sitting close to the backstage gate with my index finger in the air, and a member of the Grateful Dead crew who was walking by with his arms full of cases of soda stopped to talk to with me. He asked me who I was, and I nonchalantly responded "family." He laughed and handed me a silk backstage pass, saying he would walk me through. I was to return the silk pass when we got into the arena and carry some of the cases of soda for him. I couldn't believe that had worked! I arrived inside just in time to catch the beautiful coincidence of the first set closer, "Don't Ease Me In!" It was chaotic perfection at it's best.

That was the first time for me being in the Dead's backstage space without being harassed. Although, in just a few months, and a few more right-place, right-time scenarios, I would actually be living and working in that very environment. At the next show I finally ran into Henry Sullivan again, who made good on his promise to take care of me after the incident out in Denver. He miracle'd me tickets to all the remaining shows on the tour.

As for the origins of the Middle Earth gang, well it's a real twisted tale that goes back to the infamous Dead Spring Tour of 1977. The actual moniker refers to a J.R.R. Tolkien-inspired raft that was built for a northern Alabama river race back in the mid-seventies. Fimster, who had built the raft (it sank by the way) had carried the Middle Earth name to initiate fellow wanderers he came across throughout his years of touring the Dead scene. It had evolved into a rowdy bunch of party people who would meet up on tour and combine psychedelic forces to terrorize the uninitiated, not-so "on-the-bus" types. Some Middle Earth-ers were known to kidnap—er, uh—"encourage," rather, a few innocent folks along the way to quit their jobs and hit the road. Unlike the street-hustling junkie types—à la the Wrecking Crew, a.k.a. Drainbows—Fimster's Middle Earth approached the Grateful Dead world with the same conceptual notions that Ken Kesey's Merry Prankster's were famous for. Except, this bus was a sort of hijacked, metaphorical, pimped-up, ultra-high octane, acid-fueled, rocket-boosted, interdimensional, hyper improbability driven madness machine, and, well, you get the picture... The bus came by, and a whole bunch of fucks got ran the fuck over! Okay, if you didn't get all that, then lick the page number in this book corresponding to the added sum of the square root of the speed of light, and give it a half-hour to kick in.

But it wasn't all about mind-altering, drug-fueled debauchery. Most of the time, we would dig into some heavy intellectual, spiritual warrior shit. There was a movie being worked on that we were living out the screenplay to, in real time: *A Minor Motion Picture*, it was sometimes called. I sum most of it up as "some pretty damn good research!"

Fimster was sort of our guideless compass, our point of meeting up with one another. Then we'd abandon him, or wait until he passed out, and then, reverting back to our fraternal brotherhood, we would Sharpie tattoo his face and clothes with slogans like "Dose Me" and "Asshole." Our sense of humor was totally irresponsible and reckless. It wasn't uncommon to see him walking around a Dead show with a DO NOT DISTURB motel door handle sign duck taped to his head. Yeah, he was THAT guy. It was very clear that no one was actually driving that allegorical bus, and we all knew better than to let our ego-centric powers get in the way. Except, when the drugs wore off—well, that sometimes presented a problem.

On the last leg of the Spring Tour I was riding with the Bama Boys, J.B. and Kilgore. Freeman was in another car, I think. Well, we were on our way back down south. There was a night off in between shows and we decided to lay over in Gainesville, Florida. My friends from the Palm Beaches, the Dead cover band Crazy Fingers, were scheduled to play some frat party that night. When we got there we found out that the band had canceled. Or maybe we had the wrong frat house? But, regardless, a party was underway. Announcing that we were close personal friends of the band and that we possessed lots of drugs, we were granted access to all the floors of the fraternity house where we were treated like visiting royalty. It was like a scene out of *Animal House*, add some renegade band of psychedelic cowboys with handfuls of LSD tabs and whoa... you got yourself one helluva shindig!

The particular details of that night still escape me, but the next morning set in motion a series of events that I can never forget. And, sometimes, I really want to forget. I woke up with my face planted in the grass, and Kilgore standing over me, aggressively kicking me in the ribs. Waking up, I glanced over to see J.B. passed out on the ground with his arms hugging a fire hydrant. Freeman was laying about somewhere too, probably in a nearby bush.

After collecting our own carnage, we proceeded to drive away from the crime scene of Alpha Beta Psychedelia in Kilgore's trusty red Ford Escort named Calvin. I suddenly took on a case of a seriously evil bad mood. My ass was hurting in a very unpleasant way, itching and burning. Something wasn't right. I forced Kilgore to stop at the nearest restroom. Results were not good. I had a hemorrhoid! A really pissed-off, bleeding, burning, itching, FUCK YOU hemorrhoid! Oh the boys got a kick out of that one, but I wasn't having it. I BECAME that bleeding, burning, itching asshole of a hemorrhoid all day long! At one point, I actually snipped the wires to the speakers in Calvin's rear dashboard because Kilgore wouldn't turn the fucking music down. These guys were my best friends and they wanted to kill me and dump my body in a remote swamp. I couldn't blame them.

Something had to be done, so I convinced them to stop at a grocery store so I could get some preparation H. The only problem was that we were all temporarily out of cash. I doubted the store would be willing to accept LSD or grilled cheese sandwiches as payment. So, out of pure desperation and without any sort of criminal past to draw on, I tried to steal it instead. I had never before stolen anything nor had I ever even attempted any such criminal deviance. I looked both ways and the aisle was clear before I shoved the box into the front of my pants. My heart was thumping like the sound of a conga drum being slapped around loudly and rapidly by a Latin percussion player as I made my way to the front of the store. Just a few steps before the outside world, I was approached by a security guard from out of nowhere. He grabbed me by the arm and asked if I had anything to declare.

At first I was just speechless and frozen, then I realized I had been busted.

"Man, you have no fucking idea! I have some serious pain to declare here!" I tried to reason with him. How embarrassing! I got caught trying to steal a tube of Preparation H. He threatened to detain me and call the police, but somehow the embarrassment combined with my stupidity seemed to finally get through to the guy, and he kindly let me off with a stern warning. Besides, we weren't actually outside of the store yet when he grabbed me. We went off laughing our way to the arena parking lot. Well, I wasn't laughing all that much about it. The Boys, however, were rolling.

J.B. and Kilgore drove off towards the beach that night and found a field of shrooms that we ended up swinging for the upcoming

Orlando shows.

Just as things seemed like they couldn't get any worse, I ran into Summer and Lee outside the arena. Lee said, "Summer needs to speak with you about something serious," and he left us alone for a minute.

That's when the beautiful, kind Rainbow sister informed me that she thought she might be pregnant.

CHAPTER 9

Parking Lot Prophet

The hemorrhoid situation was one thing, but an unexpected pregnancy with a girl I had just met was quite another. Summer said that she would want to have the baby, regardless, and that we'd all have to find a way to deal with it. She even mentioned the possibility of leaving her boyfriend. It was quite a lot to deal with. No more than a month had gone by since my date with Elle, and then I was making plans with Springwater for the summer, and now a whole new set of possibilities were emerging with a girl I barely knew. Oh, the tangled web!

The scene at that moment in Orlando was intense. Someone Summer knew had drowned in the lake in front of the arena that day. Summer and I agreed to meet up later, at some shows down the road, where we could discuss the future. I decided to head north towards Cumberland, where I had heard about another Rainbow Gathering. It wasn't too far from the southern regions of Ohio, where Springwater was living. I contacted her to convince her to meet me there.

The Cumberland Gathering was a rain-drenched mud festival. I had a hard time being there. I was just recovering from the hemorrhoids (much thanks to a witch hazel remedy my mother passed on to me), and I was very stressed at the thought of suddenly becoming a father. I was also conflicted about Springwater and Elle.

Being stuck in Kentuckyland frustrated me. I was so close to Springwater and one day I unsuccessfully tried to hitchhike my way up to her. I reluctantly returned to the gathering, which usually serves as a peaceful refuge from the stresses of the world we called Babylon. But, some of the nastier, negative influences of the Rainbow scene had infiltrated the muddy grounds in Cumberland.

There were a lot of bad vibes around, rampant alcohol, and hard drug abuse. Although psychedelics are generally overlooked, alcohol is strictly forbidden inside the grounds. That did not stop people like Fast Eddie and his six-foot-seven or so sidekick Ira, "The Drunken Indian," from having a good time. They and a few of their cohorts were appropriately known as The Wrecking Crew. As I mentioned, they were also referred to as Drainbows, among other things. The elders were unable to control the rogue elements, and the scene had just become intolerable.

With the Cumberland blues all around and a failed attempt to reach Springwater, I made plans to skip out of the Gathering with a brother in his thirties whose name was Gypsy. The plan was to pursue the nomadic pastime of hopping freight trains. It was an ambitious plan. But, I had second thoughts after hearing his convincing stories of being beaten up by railroad men and, in some cases, friends of his going missing and presumed dead.

Instead, I, and a fellow nomad, managed to get a ride from a cool brother named Alan who was anxious to get to the Pacific as soon as he possibly could. He drove a green 1976 Nova that he had nicknamed Bertha. I was tired and went to sleep. And sleep I did; the next thing I remember, I woke up near Hot Springs, Arkansas. We had stopped for a brief side trip to apparently go crystal mining. I was up for the adventure, but as it turned out, the person we were looking for to guide us through the caverns had recently died, some guy named Crystal Mike. So back on the road we went while I went right back to sleep.

Only two and half days after we left Cumberland, I woke up in sunny Santa Cruz. Alan was desperate to get to some girl there so he could ask her to marry him. We pulled up in front of a beach house. I said my good-byes and wished him luck. He ran right inside the house to propose to her. I really was not interested in how it turned out, so I gathered my backpack and guitar and headed down to the beach.

The sweet smell of the warm Pacific gave me a sense of

accomplishment. The feeling overwhelmed me. The west coast! I finally made it to California! There I was, standing on the shore alongside an old boardwalk and a wooden roller coaster. Once again, it seemed as though all my troubles had been left behind. My journey to this place had been like a strange amusement ride itself, but it felt right for me to be there. I had a sense that there was something new waiting for me but at the time, the vision was still a little cloudy. I thought of how the early pioneers must've felt when they finally reached the shores of the Pacific, and the struggles they endured in their covered wagons. By contrast, I knew I had it pretty easy: one lucky ride in an old Nova from a fellow lovesick traveler.

I had run out of cash again and was getting quite hungry. I had heard about the mission in town where I could get a hot meal, and so off to the soup kitchen I went. The scene there was not a pretty one. I got the notion to move on just after my meal. I walked right out to the Pacific Coast Highway and put my lucky thumb back in the air. A yellow Volkswagen microbus pulled over.

As if my journey hadn't been surreal enough, fate had just landed me another set of strange episodes. Driving the bus was a man named Greg, who looked like a cross between Charlie Manson and a member of ZZ Top, with long scraggly hair and straight beard. Oddly, he was wearing a sheet for clothing and had this wandering and distant, yet glowing look behind his eyes. I asked him where he was headed and he answered me cryptically that he really wasn't sure but would take me to wherever I needed to go.

Oh, great! I thought, how do these people find me? I pondered about my options for a few seconds. The guy seemed crazy but in a harmless way. He had a good smile about him, and my instinct told me that he was a good person, so I figured why not? He seemed like he could be an interesting soul to get to know. I suggested, "North, to the great city of San Francisco!"

"I can dig it, bro," he responded with enthusiasm, and we were off to the wild bohemian mecca where the whole hippie craze began. He informed me that he had just got inspired to go for a drive, but had no obligations or commitments to be anywhere. He saw me thumbing it and knew he had to pick me up and set forth on an adventure.

So this is the real wild west, I thought, the land of bliss!

Just a few miles north, another hitchhiker appeared and I couldn't believe what I was seeing: I actually recognized the girl. It was none other than Crazy Heather. She was a Deadhead girl that I was familiar with from various shows. My first reaction was, Oh no, not Crazy Heather, please don't pull over and—too late, Greg had pulled the bus over.

She recognized me immediately, and we exchanged hugs. Just like Greg and I, Heather, too, was just out following her bliss, sort of directionless. It was pretty well known among most Deadhead circles that Crazy Heather was pretty directionless in the first place. She had no belongings with her, just wearing a sundress and a smile, ready for the Universe to deliver her next experience. She was one of those spinners at the shows that you often tried to awkwardly maneuver your way around as they twirl aimlessly in all directions obstructing your path. She had a reputation as Queen of the Wingnuts. She was tall with wild, curly, sandy hair and a very outgoing personality. She's not a person you forget.

From the moment Greg picked me up, I had noticed that strewn about his bus were several religious items. There was a Jesus hula dancer on the dash, a Bible on the floor, and Greg was wearing a cross around his neck. A few minutes after picking up Heather, Greg mentioned that he was a devout follower of Christ and wanted to be sure that we were not uncomfortable with any of it. Crazy Heather immediately shouted that she loves Jesus! That's when I realized that his appearance, although similar, was more Jesus-like than ZZ Top. I asked him if he would mind if I just went ahead and called him Jesus... like, "Jesus Greg." Of course, I assumed that would probably offend the normal person, but I also quickly assumed that Greg was not the normal type of person anyway, so perhaps he would find it endearing, which of course, he did.

It was apparent that Jesus Greg wasn't necessarily playing with a full deck. And neither was Crazy Heather for that matter—as she was clearly self-aware by her own acceptance of being referred to as Crazy Heather. Yes, I was indeed in very strange company and soon I would start to question my own sanity.

CHAPTER 10

Is There A Problem, Occifer?

We parked the bus somewhere near North Beach, dropped some acid, and went off in search of Chinatown. Although Chinatown is actually located right next to North Beach, we somehow managed to get lost and ended up tramping barefoot through the night in some wild Wizard of Oz–like adventure, through the less desirable parts of the city. There were strange and lucid encounters with locals and potentially harmful people in the Tenderloin District that seemed more threatened by us than we would have been by them under "normal" circumstances. We managed to avoid run-ins with the police until Jesus Greg stopped them in the Mission District to ask for directions. To our benefit, even the cops were scared of us.

We continued our yellow brick road romp, as fire truck sirens would sing out in symphonic harmony and echo off the concrete hills into the electric night of the legendary wonderland of colorful San Francisco. Warped hours flowed in and out of our consciousness, as we circled our way back and forth laughing through the city neighborhoods, with their grinning street lamps and dancing Rice-A-Roni trolley cars. Sometimes we found ourselves back in the places where we had started. We occasionally sought refuge and sanctuary in Golden Gate Park and its magical poppy fields. We never dared look at a map, as we could barely make out the jumbled letters of the street signs. Just as the sun greeted the new day and shed its glorious light upon the empty early morning streets, we suddenly realized that we were standing smack dab in the middle of our sacred promised land,

Chinatown!

We just shrugged our shoulders and made our way back to Golden Gate Park and napped there for most of the day. Jesus Greg read some Bible verses, while Heather danced with the wind. We befriended some punk rocker kids that we scored some opium from. They showed us some unlocked garages on Lombard Street that we could sleep in at night if we needed to.

We managed to catch some Jerry Garcia Band shows at the Warfield Theatre before our next mission was realized... VIVA LAS VEGAS! Grateful Dead style, of course. Crazy Heather was certainly on board and Jesus Greg agreed to drive once he found out that Carlos Santana was the opening act. We picked up another rider for the trip and were all set.

Las Vegas was the usual gas of wild experiences. Add lots of loud, noisy slot machines, ringing bells, circus acts, and thousands of patchouli-drenched hippies. The marquee at the old Sands Casino read:

WELCOME

GRATEFUL

DEAD HEADS!

Like we were some sort of convention or something. I'm sure the security personnel at the casinos had their hands quite full that weekend. At first we attempted to stay at Circus Circus with some friendly heads we met. The kid who had the room in his name, however, was beaten up by hotel security for swinging doses on the casino floor. We were all kicked out and asked never to return.

Meanwhile, I kept my business to the lots. I had been moving my way up the supply chain. It wasn't something I had originally sought out; it was just a means to an end for me at the time. I was more into the music and just wanted to survive on the road and experience as many shows as I could. The scene had become a home for me, a place where I could have a good time with my closest and craziest friends.

One of those close friends who showed up in Vegas was Robin Page from the Sunshine Café. She brought with her my tax refund check, which turned out to be extremely difficult to cash because

I wasn't twenty one years old yet.

We lost Heather somewhere along the line, and Jesus Greg kind of freaked out after one of the shows when he pulled his ticket stub, tripping of course, out of his pocket and it had folded in such a way that it read:

GRATFUL DEA

SATAN

instead of

GRATEFUL DEAD

SANTANA

He tripped out on that and thumbed through his *Bible*, uncertain of how to process all of it.

We camped at Lake Mead with a bunch of other freaks in what could best be described as the perfect, serene desert setting. We slept on the side of a rocky cliff overlooking the pristine, crystal blue waters. It was so majestic. I wrote letters to both Springwater and Elle. I was feeling lonesome and wanted to share my experiences with someone who could relate to my inner soul and the scene I was so immersed in. That was one tangible difference between the two girls: Springwater was a Deadhead and Elle had been more into the rocker scene. But I knew that deep down, it was of little importance. My mind was also on Summer, and whether or not a baby was due. Those thoughts really made me consider the consequences and responsibilities of just hooking up and having random encounters on tour. There was no doubt that I needed to be more careful and perhaps stop displaying my heart on my sleeve so much. Inside, I was just longing for a secure relationship, or at least that's what I thought.

I awoke in the morning to a giant hawk soaring over the cliff and flying off into the distance over the lake. I felt better having poured my heart out in the letters. But I was too stubborn to mail them, and they just remained silent in my notebook.

Just before leaving the Casino Nation, Greg and I went in search of a bank that would cash my check, but with no luck. On our way out of town, we spotted Crazy Heather hitching by the side of the road again and stopped to pick her up. We also stopped and picked up a couple more kids who were headed toward the next run of California shows.

South of Reno, we pulled into a small town. I asked Jesus Greg to pull into the bank parking lot so that I could go in and see if they would cash my check.

I walked into the bank and took a quick look around. I noticed that one of the tellers had no line, so I walked up to her part of the counter. I asked her if she could cash a government-issued tax refund check. Maybe thirty seconds or so had passed since I walked in the door, and suddenly I heard loud noises behind me. The doors of the bank had swung open and several police officers had entered very quickly with raised weapons pointed in my direction. They took a firm stance. I looked back towards a nervous bank teller and immediately thought to myself, Holy shit, the bank is being robbed! I was gripped in fear. I didn't see anyone in the drive-through window, so I looked over to see the only other customer in the bank, an elderly lady at the other teller window. Then the thought hit me... Holy shit, that old lady is robbing the fucking bank! I glanced back at the cops and my focus zoomed into a double barrel shot gun aimed right towards MY HEAD! I quickly looked back to the bank teller.

"Is everything okay?" I asked her in a sort of inner-panicky but stay-calm-and-cool-on-the-outside sort of tone.

"Oh, yes," she responded. "Just a false alarm."

Again, I nervously glanced back towards the cops and their weapons began to lower. They loosened up and began conversing with one another. The bank manager went over and spoke to them. All the while I was getting glances from them as they talked. Surprisingly, the teller began counting money to me and wished for me to have a nice day. Ah, finally I got the check cashed! On my way out the door, I was followed. The officer asked to speak to me outside.

"Is there a problem, Officer?"

Well, according to him, it seemed that I scared some folks when I walked into the bank so quickly. They just assumed a robbery was about to take place, and someone hit the alarm.

He then said, and I quote: "We don't normally get yer type 'round here. You know, with yer long hair and all." I was so shocked at what he said that I didn't have a response.

He then ran a check on my ID and began to interrogate me about where I was headed, who I was with, what was in that van, any weapons? Drugs? Etcetera. The other officers were standing by in the background eyeing the van and, well, it just so happened that Jesus Greg had a gun in the van, and I was carrying about two ten-lots worth of acid (twenty sheets, or two thousand doses). There was at least an ounce of weed and some pills strewn about as well. And who knew what the new kids had on them.

"No sir, absolutely no drugs, no weapons, nothing sir, we are a clean religious bunch, sir," I told him with my best straight-and-serious poker face. The officer glanced over and could see a cross dangling from the mirror over a Jesus hula dancer on the dash. Jesus Greg stood just outside the sliding door smiling back, looking like Charlie Manson. The other kids were sitting in the back until the officer asked them to please step outside the vehicle.

He kept interrogating where we were coming from and where we were heading. I thought it best not to mention anything about the Grateful Dead, so I convinced him that we were a religious music group heading to a concert in California and we just stopped here to cash a check from our last gig. The others nodded in silent agreemement.

He noticed the guitar cases and a couple percussion drums in the van. He asked that if he opened the cases, whether or not he would find drugs or guns. I laughed at his suggestion and he seemed to lighten up a little.

About that time, dispatch called him back with a clean run on my ID. He then informed us that he would follow us out of town and advised that we not come back anytime soon.

We drove directly out of town with a police escort. Once out of their grasp, we exhaled and said a quick Thank You prayer to the Lord. That's when the group started calling me Jesse James.

All in all, we survived the situation but it was a scary close call. It reminded me of another encounter I had a couple years earlier on Tour in Deer Creek, Indiana. At the time, I was traveling with my friend Alex, also a Middle Earther and a friend from Boca Raton. Alex and I ended up at a makeshift campground located by a Grandma's Restaurant. The field next to Grandma's had been taken over by hippies and turned into a popular camping spot for after-show shenanigans. There were nitrous tanks, loud music, and crazy freaks running amuck.

Unbeknownst to Alex and I, a Noblesville Police car had pulled in behind us. Out of the car stepped out a very large Boss Hog–looking cop who walked up behind Alex, myself, and a couple of other guys. We had been dosing pretty heavily; I was tripping especially hard. The cop wanted to ask us some questions. He introduced himself as "THE" Chief of Police. He started out very polite and said he didn't want any trouble. He wanted us to pass on the word to all the other campers that we were welcome to stay but to be sure to clean up after ourselves and not to cause any problems. That part all seemed like a routine request but then the conversation turned weird, really weird. It could have been the drugs, but I swear he put his hand firmly on my shoulder and said that he had a boy about my age out there on the road somewhere. He went on to tell me that he wanted to believe his kid was in good hands and not getting into trouble anywhere. He said he knew we all liked to take drugs and have a good time with our marijuana, balloons, and all that LSD. He was staring me square in the eyes real intently. My trip was peaking out pretty hard and I just stood there kind of frozen, wondering if I was about to get arrested or not, but the vibe was peaceful, so I didn't panic. I just thought about how weird things were going and tried to dismiss all the colors.

He said he didn't think there was anything wrong with wanting to have a good time with your friends. He went on to add that if he were to take off all his clothes and if I were to take off all my clothes right there... then we would just be two naked men standing there having a normal conversation. He explained that two men should have respect for each other as human beings and that it shouldn't matter that he happened to be wearing a badge. If we were naked, no one would know that he was a cop or that I was not.

My mind was totally melting all over the place by this time and I looked over at Alex, like, (Are you catching all this?) did he just say what I thought he said? Man this is some crazy acid! He finished by saying that he wished for us to have respect for the land, Mother Earth, and each other and more importantly that he didn't want to have to come back out here tonight. He then got back in his cruiser and split. We laughed our asses off in total disbelief at what just happened. And the party raged on, without any return visits from THE Chief of Police.

That experience was one of many great psychedelic adventures Alex and I went on. On one of the best trips, I actually had an out-of-body astral journey. Alex had scored us some LSD from one of his older friends, who apparently had a leftover stash from the Sixties, the real good shit. We were tripping in Boca at his grandmother's condo. She was away for the day, of course. The trip was rough taking off. I didn't start feeling good until I vomited rainbows in the toilet and Alex put on the Tom Petty song "Feel A Whole Lot Better" for me, which I did. I then remember sitting in a chair with a lamp to my left. At the other side of the lamp was a couch and then another chair in the corner that Alex was sitting in. I started to feel very light, like I was floating. I began to look down at my body below. Suddenly, I felt my soul bobbing at the top of the room against the ceiling and about to float through it when I looked over to my left and noticed Alex was floating too, looking right back at me, eyes wide open, bobbing along the ceiling. This went on for like half a minute or so, but who really knows? I glanced back down at my body and swoosh! I was rushed back into my flesh. I looked to my left but the lamp was blocking my view and so I leaned forward to look over at him. His distorted green face looked back at me in amazement. He pointed up to the ceiling and I nodded my head back at him to confirm: Yep that was me up there. You too? Awesome! This is good shit! There were no words exchanged, though, because we could no longer use them. We communicated telepathically.

We went to take a walk outside and get some air. The carpeted hallways of the condominium building were full of tiny dragons slithering along beside, below, and above my feet. Getting into the elevator was particularly frightening, so we abandoned it and just took the stairs. When we made it to the outside world, I don't know where we thought we were going, maybe to the beach? But we didn't get more than a block away from the building. My spirit kept leaving my body and entering a dimension full of bubbles. The bubbles were other spirits, souls, some of which were people dreaming, others were ancient spirits completely disconnected from their flesh. I somehow got it across to Alex that it was too difficult to be out in the open space. Too many bubbles were distracting me, trying to lead me away. Back at the condo it was safe, but at some point we learned that Alex's grandmother was due to return. Day was turning into night. We had to get out of there. He talked me into driving, and I don't know how he was able to do that considering my condition.

While I was driving, I kept telling him that I couldn't do it. I made an official declaration that I was unable to drive. He responded with reason: "But you are driving, aren't you?"

"Yes, but what I'm saying is that I can't do this. You're going to have to take over."

"But I can't drive, I'm waaay too high!" he'd reason.

This went on like an Abbot and Costello routine.

Meanwhile I felt like I was made of rubber. As the vehicle turned a corner, it stretched out in a semi-circular shape. My legs stretched out with it. My sweaty hand glued to the steering wheel. My body was at one with the car. My foot felt like it was way, way, way far off in the unreachable distance. My body was contorted into different shapes as I rounded different corners. There was blinding traffic all around and somehow I was driving through it all. I pulled over at one point into the campus of Florida Atlantic University and tried again to convince Alex to drive. He kept winning the argument by stating that I was already doing it. I already had the experience on my side. There was no way he was going to chance it.

I continued to drive taking all the side roads. At one point, just a few blocks from our destination, a cop car pulled up behind me at a red light. We were in the left turning lane. I was panicking, heart thumping out of chest. The light turned green and I stomped on the gas, but the car wouldn't move. The engine kept revving... I was tripping hard, scared out of my mind, trying to make a left turn. It seemed like forever. "Shit! It's not moving! I've got my foot on the gas, what the hell? Alex, help me!"

"Dude, your other foot is on the brake!"

"Oh, right, of course."

We made the left turn and the cop car followed. My heart was racing. I drove slowly. Was I driving toooooo slooooow? Any second now, those reds and blues were going to start flashing and we were going to have to ride the rest of the trip out in jail. At the end of the next street, I made a right turn and the cop went left. Wheee! Close fucking call!

Back at the private housing development where Alex lived, we managed to get through the gated security without looking the guard in the eyes. But I knew he was on to us. Alex's parents were home and awake. It wasn't safe to go inside yet. We ran around the palm trees and palmetto bushes and imagined we were at war against the security golf carts that patrolled the neighborhood. Occasionally being bombarded by the sprinkler systems. The enemy was everywhere, but we managed to survive unscathed. Well sort of... I still have these random twitches, white blotches that appear on my skin, and the occasional night terrors where I wake up screaming. As for the bubbles and the dragons, I've experienced them at other times in my life tripping, dreaming, and sober too. I don't question them anymore.

CHAPTER 11

Our Kind Of Zoo

After my "bank robbery," Jesus Greg dropped Heather, me, and the new kids off at the Cal Expo Amphitheater. He said he wanted nothing more to do with these crazy Grateful Dead people, and we all went our separate ways.

My new connections inside of the Dead camp kept me informed on who the undercover DEA agents were and how to spot them in the parking lots. This kept my friends and I from getting busted. Their shiny black shoes especially were a dead giveaway, and the brand new blue minivan they were driving was easy to spot. From a distance, I would watch them make deals and take down kids who weren't in the know. It was sickening to see.

The boys opened up a great three-night run with an enthusiastic "Bertha" with Jerry's licks soaring effortlessly over Phil's occasional bass bombs. This run had the perfect set of openers for me. The second night's "Hell In A Bucket" could have healed the crippled—"You must really consider the circus..." Bob Weir suggested. The closing night kicked off with an angelic "Help On The Way." They segued into the "Slipknot" jam superbly and majestically landing into the perfect "Franklin's Tower"—one of my personal anthems. It was so healing to get lost in the music, the shows, the scene, and put all my worries behind me and just roll away the dew.

It was still business as usual in the lot. Several of the Middle Earth crew were on the scene, including Celeste and Bama Boys, JB and Kilgore. I managed to run into Gayle–the girl from that mall in St. Louis. I think she was originally from Philly; alas my memory isn't so certain anymore. Cal Expo is where I was supposed to meet up with Summer–there was no sign of her. That worried me some, but I shrugged it off and put my faith in the bliss of the Universe. As long as the music never stopped, I could continue to hide in it and seek my shelter there as if it were an invisible force protecting me.

I remember having such a great time inside the shows, dancing with Gayle and just letting all my worries go. Getting high with friends, lost in Jerry's guitar licks, the rhythm devils, the laughter, the dancing, and nothing else in the world seemed to matter anymore. It was my spiritual exodus from the world. I always felt a little better when I came out of a show, even when assaulted by the twisted faces of the carnies leaning over a fence from the amusement park next to Cal Expo. I told Kilgore that someone should put up a sign: DO NOT FEED THE CARNIES! We rolled on out in deranged laughter. Now *that* was our kind of zoo.

The next set of shows was set for Shoreline, south of the San Francisco Bay. The Bama Boys were heading that way as was Celeste and most of the people I knew. Gayle was heading back east, and I lost her just before I got to say goodbye or get her contact info which I figured was probably for the best anyhow.

Another travel option came up from a dude I knew from the Rainbow Gatherings, Forest. He was heading back to the Rocky Mountains for another Gathering. It seemed like a great option. I could get back there, go to the Gathering, then find a ride back for the '91 East Coast Summer Tour. The Dead were planning to play Buckeye Lake, Ohio, back near my native homeland that summer and I knew that would be the perfect time and place to get back to Springwater.

CHAPTER 12

Chasing Rainbows Down
A Dead End Street

F orest gave me a ride all the way back to Colorado's snow-capped Rocky Mountain peaks, but not to the Gathering. We ended up at Carter Lake to meet up with some of his family; his plans had changed. He delivered me back to Summit County (my former winter retreat) where I stayed with Sticker Dave for a few days.

My friend from the Sunshine Cafe, Dan and his girlfriend Tonya, were interested in heading down to the gathering. But at the last minute Dan couldn't make it happen, so Tonya and I hitched our way toward the San Juan Mountains. We witnessed several breathtaking rainbows along the way. The majestic splendor of the San Juans absolutely blew me away. We got very lucky with a few great rides. It didn't hurt that Tonya seemed to have a lucky thumb and very nice legs.

The Gathering was held in a place that could best be described as heaven. It was a two-mile pack-and-hike in, along the First Fork of the Lower Piedra River, nestled in remote black bear country. There were hot springs nearby, surrounded by breathtaking peaks. It was one of the most beautiful places I had ever been to. The vibes were nothing but positive, completely the opposite of the previous Cumberland mess. Happy and creative people shared their smiles and loving energy with everyone. A sweat lodge was built along the creek, and I experienced spiritual bliss inside its muddy walls. A masked, mad doser ran around randomly puddling the masses with some fine quality liquid LSD, as gods and goddesses danced in naked worship to a magnificent full moon. It was hedonistic paganism at its best. Dancing bears could be imagined in the distance as a thousand or so freaks boogied, sang, played music and had the time of their lives.

Once we arrived, Tonya went her own way. One night by the fire there was a beautiful girl, Sadie, who wanted someone to keep her warm. I was one of many dudes sitting around that fire. One by one, each guy was trying to convince her why she should go back to his particular tent. She looked over at me expecting a plea, but I politely told her that I was doing fine and didn't really need any company. So of course, she chose to spend the night with me.

During the days, I mostly hung out with the Doctor, whose true identity I have vowed to keep secret. He was an old school family chemist who had let me into his inner circle. He was known to produce some very good quality crystal LSD.

Tonya got a ride back to Summit County after the gathering to meet up with Dan, and I secured a ride with Doc to Boulder, which gave me a chance to ask him a lot of detailed questions about the LSD manufacturing process. He was very open to telling me about it; I had gained his trust. I'm pretty sure I told him my life story. I think he was impressed with my affinity to his chemical expertise and my quest for the sacraments of psychedelic production. He explained the subtle differences in producing the much-sought after White Fluff in comparison to what he shared with me at the gathering as the final stages of the crystallized Silver. He bragged to me about having a great formula for Needlepoint crystal, which is just about as good as acid can get. When we got to town, he dropped me off at a house that he owned near the university where I crashed out for a few days.

Dan and Tonya arrived in his orange VW microbus that he had nicknamed Love Street. The plan was to head off toward Deer Creek, Indiana where the first summer show would be. I had secured plenty of LSD to sell. First though, we had to make a stop in the small town of Freedom, Indiana. A "family" friend of Tonya's had a honey farm there. A massive pre-Tour party was under way with several hundred crazy hippies camping out. A herd of candy-colored modified school buses were parked in the field. It was like an unofficial mini–Rainbow Gathering.

A man named Honeybee was in charge of the farm and with his help I unloaded several vials of Doc's sacred silver concoction.

I sold this old hippie named Tree a couple of vials, and he invited me aboard his bus where I partook in the process of laying the liquid onto sheets of perforated blotter. There were several different designs; most were oriental patterns, but he also had sheets that featured Homer Simpson. Before we distilled the crystal, we shared in a sacred thumb print ritual, which consisted of a very large unknown amount of pure LSD soaking into my skin.

By nighttime of I-can't-recall-what day, acid was dropped by pretty much all in attendance, either by choice or by just being dosed somehow. The party raged into the wee hours of the morning while naked hippie girls ran around all covered in honey. That's right, young naked hippie girls running and frolicking about with sticky honey dripping off their majestic perky breasts. What a scene! Then we all witnessed one of the more outrageous things any of us had seen in our lives.

At first I thought it was just me from the intensity of the acid thumbprint I had done in the school bus. The dark night sky, with its millions of beautiful stars, started to change color and shape. Wild cosmic dragon clouds started floating in from above with their dark ultra-dimensional spectrums. The heavens opened up the sky and folded back layers of stars to reveal a celestial dance of waving rainbow-patterned nebulas. The rowdy folks all seemed to calm down for a few hours and stood still, gazing upward as if the Mothership were arriving. There was great silence at first, but then wild accusations and varying degrees of panic. When the mysterious sky formations were suddenly joined by a creeping illumination along the horizon, we all BELIEVED that the world was actually coming to an end. Which no one was afraid of, but thought was a rather glorious and groovy thing. We were more freaked out when we realized that the brightness along the horizon turned out to be the morning sun and not the rapture after all.

The heavens could not have delivered these beautiful, naked, honey-covered freaks a more spectacular cosmic show. We found out the next day that we had actually witnessed a rare display of the northern lights! It was amazingly unpredicted and we greeted it with pure awe and astonishment. A northern lights show is a must-see experience, and for it to just happen upon a crazy Indiana summer night, descending on several hundred acid-filled heads, was a completely mind-blowing experience. What a fantastic way to kick off a long, strange Grateful Dead Summer Tour!

The next day, Dan, Tonya, and I headed off toward Noblesville's Deer Creek Music Center for the show. I had complimentary tickets and passes already set up, waiting at the box office. The band opened with a very welcomed and powerful "Jack Straw" and continued to deliver a stellar performance throughout.

We skipped the second night at Deer Creek and headed straight to Athens, Ohio, where Springwater and her sister Bo were hosting a party. I was extremely excited to see her again. It was all I had been thinking about for months. We arrived at their place kind of late, and she was noticeably distant. I couldn't understand it. I was extremely nervous and most definitely had some sort of expectation that everything was just going to be magically great when we saw each other. Alas, the Universe was going to make me work for her affection again. The party itself was a much mellower scene than the Honeybee Farm: just a couple dozen people around a bonfire. I ended up sleeping alone in Love Street, wondering why Springwater wasn't more excited to see me. Something was amiss.

CHAPTER 13

Heaven, Or The Night
I Cross The Line

T he day of the Buckeye Lake show had finally arrived. The venue is less than an hour's drive from my hometown, Coshocton, and just a stone's throw from my actual place of birth. In the 1970s and '80s, the place had been named Legend Valley and was the scene of many giant Central Ohio rock festivals. My older siblings and cousins had all gone to see great concerts there. I was envious as a kid and had always hoped to see a concert there someday.

Just about everyone I knew from Tour and the Gatherings had shown up to Buckeye Lake, including my Middle Earth friends from Alabama. This was a huge venue that boasted a capacity of 80,000. The setting was primitive, with the stage built in a large field surrounded by rolling hills. It was absolutely the perfect scene for a summer Dead show. The parking lots themselves were the hills across the highway. It was good to have a big show away from the concrete lots and plastic-seated amphitheaters for a change.

We all caravanned up from Athens. Springwater rode up with her sister and a few of their college friends. I rode along with Dan and Tonya in Love Street. After we parked I discovered the Bama Boys had parked Calvin, the little red Ford Escort, just a few aisles away.

Springwater and I were hanging out, walking the lots, having a good time together. It was our first actual Dead show together. All was beautiful and blissful as I introduced her around to many of my tour friends. We sat down in the grass and I played a song on my guitar that

I had been writing for her. But then she seemed uncomfortable, a little overwhelmed perhaps. We talked about our ideas of the future, and I told her how I'd like to her to travel with me on the rest of the tour, and then we could relocate to Colorado, and maybe even get married for real, legally. She kind of froze when I mentioned that last part; it was obvious that it scared her. Maybe I was just too excited to see her again? I eased the tension by telling her to not worry about it and that we should just focus on having a good time together. I'm not sure what I was really thinking by getting so heavy on her like that so soon. Maybe the road stress was getting to me. Or the stress of not knowing anymore about Summer's situation with the baby and all, which I was still keeping to myself at the time. Maybe I was doing too much acid. I just know that I missed her terribly, and I really wanted things to work out.

But I wasn't the only one withholding information. What I didn't know but sensed, was that something else was going on with her. On our way into the show, her sister pulled me aside and had a little talk with me. She said that I should know that on the way up from Athens, Springwater's friend, who was a young professor at the University, had just confessed his love for her. He was there with us going into the show. I then realized that he had been acting odd all day. It seemed to add up. Springwater was in a very confused place and I had just put some more weight and stress on her. I wished she had told me herself. It would have made a big difference to what I said to her. Then her sister laid it on me that I had some kind of magical hold on Springwater that she had never seen with anyone else before. It weighed heavy on me as we went into the show.

We made our way toward the front and caught the end of the Violent Femmes opening set. This was one of those occasions where the Grateful Dead had an opening act. I tried my best to ease Springwater's worries during the intermission. We found a spot with Bama Boys Kilgore and Freeman in the Phil Zone. Springwater's sister and the young professor had disappeared when we first got in. So it was just Springwater, me, and the Bama Boys when the show started. The first set opened with a newer, spooky number, "Picasso Moon," and then ripped into the classic "Sugaree." Toward the end of "Sugaree,"

Springwater turned to me and put her hand on my face and said, "I'll be right back".

I had that sinking insecurity that I would never see her again. The chorus of the song would later haunt me as Jerry begged for his name to be forgotten, by his darling, Sugaree.

I made an emergency decision to drop some more acid and just enjoy the show the best I could. Confused? Bewildered? Insecure? Go ahead, take more drugs! That should help. I stayed in that spot with Kilgore and Freeman the whole show. I doubled, and even tripled, my dosage by the time the second set started. "Crazy Fingers" was unreal, the best I ever heard. By the end of the show, I was tripping really, really, really hard. Springwater never returned.

The encore of the night was Dylan's "Knockin' On Heaven's Door," which emotionally overwhelmed my acid-drenched body. Kilgore and I walked along the top of the hill overlooking the valley of melted cars below. I stopped in my tracks when I saw her standing next to Love Street. She was just standing there, looking around, waiting for someone. I stood at a distance and watched. She could not see me, but I knew that she was looking for me. I could feel it. The anxiety and the drugs were too much, and I couldn't move my feet or decide what to do. I wasn't sure how to face her and be subjected to a rejection. I was officially out of my mind and so fucking overwhelmed. It was then, in an LSD-fueled state with heavily distorted emotions, that I made a controversial decision... I just walked away.

I retreated to Kilgore's car, Calvin, and nestled in the back, succumbing to my own cowardice and sorrow, and cried. The Boys sat out in lawn chairs and drank beer as the carnival atmosphere rolled on. Every thirty minutes or so throughout the night, a golf cart would stroll by with a security person shouting into a megaphone for everyone to get in their cars and head out. No one listened.

We laughed at them and reasoned, why get in a line of cars just to sit there? The parking lot party raged on all night. The sun broke over the horizon and there seemed to be just one line of cars now waiting to get out. We decided that it was time to start the car and get in line. Just as we pulled up to the back of the line, someone in the car noticed something interesting off in the distant corner of the field.

There was an open gate to the highway that no cars had yet discovered. We pulled Calvin out of line and veered toward the exit. The rear view mirror captured scores of other cars racing behind us. A flawless and beautiful getaway, which provided some much needed comic relief.

I wasn't too concerned with the belongings I had left behind in Love Street; I knew Dan and Tonya would be at the next shows in North Carolina, and I would catch up with them there. The Bama Boys drove on, with their pathetic love-stricken acid casualty in the back seat. I may have self-indflicted the pain that I was going through, but for some mysterious reason, it seemed necessary for me to let my heart go. I didn't want to be a source of conflict for Springwater. We were both very young and stubborn people then, which only added to our difficulties, and clearly I had some issues to sort out.

After a couple of days, the drugs finally wore off and I tried to phone Springwater multiple times. I realized that I had made a mistake. I wanted to jump off Tour and head right back to Ohio and fix things, but each time I called, Bo answered and told me that she was unavailable. On my final attempt, her sister just bitched me out and told me that Springwater never wanted to speak to me ever again. I was admonished to stop calling her. I apologized and replied that I couldn't blame her. I had to accept my actions and my choice to continue on. Although at the time I still felt really confused having failed to properly read the situation. When I saw Dan in Charlotte, he told me "that girl" was waiting at the van for me and that she had something important to tell me. It nagged me that I didn't exactly know what she was going to say. Maybe she was going to say "yes" to my haphazard proposal.

Jude, a beautiful Middle Earth bohemian sister, and I traveled to several shows together on the '89 and '90 Dead Tours, and she was there, again, in Charlotte, to help me sort through the drama. I nicknamed her "Hey Jude" and would often sing it out to her. Jude and I had a great friendship. We often confided our relationship woes to each other. I'm pretty certain we made one of those "If we're both not married by 40, then we'll marry each other" deals. I'm not sure I could've gotten through the days following Buckeye Lake without her. We had a great time at the shows and I shifted my focus to more positive thoughts. I had to quickly roll away my troubles and accept that my relationship with Springwater was now history. I managed to screw it all up somehow, but I had to also accept the error of my ways and move on.

Inside the Charlotte Coliseum, Bob Weir belted out that he could not stand the rain. Inside my heart, I was coping with my decision to move on. My self-inflicted pain seemed to know no boundaries. Garcia drove it home with an over the top "Morning Dew," and reminded us all that it just didn't matter anyway.

CHAPTER 14

With No Direction Home

Little Feat opened the show at New Jersey's Giants Stadium. I dropped some LSD and got my groove on to that "Spanish Moon". And then the boys took me home by teasing their space-driven anthem, "Dark Star." They had been hinting at it all summer. The Giants Stadium show was no exception. They teased the jam in and out of every other song that night. It was unlike anything they had done in recent years. It was beautifully spooky, much like that summer itself. And at some time, while twirling around to one of the jams, I hooked up with Zoey. We made out quite passionately during the second set and acknowledged that we really wanted to be together. She was getting ready to relocate to Arizona for college in a few months and we promised to keep in touch.

She was a friend of Middle Earth Jersey Jay, from the same city near Morristown. In fact, I think their families were neighbors. So they grew up together. We hung out for the Giants and D.C. shows. I found her to be extremely stunning and a bit of a bad girl. Jay told me that she was nothing but trouble and to stay away from her. I think that caused me to be attracted to her more. She had a petite figure, curly long sandy hair, a wild look about her, and she looked downright incredible in a sundress, just my weakness.

I continued to receive hundreds of letters for publication in *Inspiration* containing poems, artwork, and writings from fellow Deadheads, according to my old buddy Rob Pena, who was collecting my mail for me back in Boca. A certain portion of these letter writers were from incarcerated 'heads like this one who wrote to me in the spring of '91:

> *Now on a more serious note, I would like to spread a little light on the War on Drugs. Kids, they mean business. The number of brothers and sisters doing time for selling drugs in and around Grateful Dead host cities has tripled in the past six months. No kidding Sherlock. So please get a clue and think about your choices. The War on Drugs is real, please don't become another casualty.*

His advice I took very seriously, especially considering my insider information about the DEA's operation. I had a personal code that I never sold acid to any strangers who approached me. I would become friendly and hang out with my potential customers before I ever let them know what I had available. It was a simple method. I also instructed people to never ask me for any more. It would be me who would let them know if I had anything available. If they continued this practice for themselves, then things could remain less risky as long as no one got too desperate. At one of the Jersey shows, I had to run through the lot crowd to escape some undercover cops who tried to bust me. The thing is, I wasn't even selling to them. They witnessed me make an exchange with a friend and then they approached me for doses. I told them I didn't have any.

"C'mon, man, I know you got doses bro... just sell us a couple hits." I refused to. They followed me for a little while and confronted me again. This time one of them pulled his jacket back to reveal a badge. As he was about to grab my arm, that's when I didn't even hesitate, I just took off before he could get a grip. I lost them pretty quickly in the Shakedown Street crowd. It was a pretty close call that scared the the shit out of me.

There was still no sign at any of the shows of Summer or even her boyfriend, but the situation still weighed on my mind. I was hoping to have some sort of resolution at some point. Here I was, still in limbo, traveling aimlessly around looking for some deeper meaning to my existence. I was also really hoping that Springwater would appear around the next corner.

The tour trucked its way up to Buffalo, a typical Summer Tour stop. Then it was off to Michigan for another run of bizarre shows. I was still traveling with Dan in the Love Street van, and things were again about to take a serious turn.

We were on our way from the Michigan shows to Chicago. There were six or seven of us in the vehicle. I was sleeping in the far back next to the engine. Someone nudged me for a light. Apparently their spliff had gone out, and I was being summoned to provide an igniter. Abruptly I opened my eyes to see flames at my head and felt an amazing rush of heat. By pure coincidence, the engine had caught on fire right then. "FIRE!" I yelled, but the stoners up front responded with laughter. "YES, WE NEED FIRE!"

"NO … really … FIRE!"

Dan screeched Love Street over to the shoulder of the road. We all barreled out. Someone grabbed the beer cooler and dumped water on the engine, which was just enough and in time to stop it from spreading. But significant damage had already been done. Love Street was dead. Much like my own desires that summer, she had gone down in flames.

The police and fire crews showed up. We sat around for hours and were advised that we would have to figure something out because there was no hitchhiking allowed in the area. We were right next to a state prison. After the cops split, we all began walking down the road hitchhiking anyway, right next to the NO HITCHHIKING signs.

Two Volkswagen buses pulled over. Not that unusual, considering we were on the road connecting two Dead shows, but then an amazing thing happened. I recognized the second van as looking extremely similar to that of Summer's white Volkswagen. And, sure enough, she was behind the wheel. We enthusiastically embraced each other and she apologized for not meeting up with me before but she had just finally made it back to tour. She informed me that the whole pregnancy was a false alarm and that she and her boyfriend had subsequently broken up. Then she introduced me to her new "girlfriend."

I was pretty blown away and excited that it was she who ended up rescuing us after the Love Street fire. What a great coincidence, but just another typical alignment that I had become all too accustomed to.

CHAPTER 15

Roll Away The Dew

T he Dead performed a heavenly show at Chicago's Soldier Field that kicked off with an opening set by Roger McGuinn of The Byrds. A fantastic fireworks display finished off the night.

Summer and her girlfriend went their own way and I ended up back with the Bama Boys again for the ride to Bonner Springs, Kansas. Dan and Tonya stayed behind in Chicago and planned to return to Michigan to deal with the van situation.

The Dead ripped it up with two killer nights at the Sandstone Amphitheater, giving some of their finest performances on the whole tour. The weather was extremely hot, and I recall the venue staff hosing down the crowds. Damn, that was absolutely the best "Help > Slip > Franklin's" I had ever heard.

Back to Denver for the last stop on the Grateful Dead's Summer Tour of '91, an outdoor show at Mile High Stadium. Santana was back on the bill and opened the show. There was a lot of strange negative energy at the show, with scores of cops beating up on fans and such. I took my spot somewhere behind the soundboard and met a cool hippie chick there from Arizona, named Scarlett. She reminded me a lot of Zoey, actually—same kind of look, but a little younger and more innocent. She had a precious and fragile quality about her. In no way did she possess a hint of the troublesome.

Scarlett and I hit it off right away and danced together during the show. Our energies teased one another throughout the night and eventually we embraced for a make out kiss at the end of the second set. Like the Giants Stadium show, the Dead again weaved in and out of the ominous "Dark Star" throughout the show, as they had been doing all tour long. I was beginning to think there was some magical love spell aura embedded in the tune. But the band's overall performance in Denver, left a lot to be desired. Fans left the stadium a little strange and disappointed. Let's face it: no one has ever disputed that on certain nights, the Dead just plain sucked. Scarlett was the best thing about that show and, for us, it seemed like a pretty good night after all.

In the lot, she introduced me to her mom, who was partying her ass off. She seemed pretty wild and crazy, and was either tripping, or drunk, or both when I met her. This was definitely a first for me—meeting a girl at a Dead show and being introduced to her mother in the lot. Mom told me to take good care of her daughter and that she was heading up to a party near Boulder. Scarlett wanted to keep hanging out with me, and I actually had no plans at all as to my next destination. I was truly wingin' it by that point. I knew that, eventually, there would be more shows in California, but that was a good month and a half away.

In Boulder, Scarlett and I became inseparable. We took advantage of many intimate opportunities. Our passions surrendered in a beautiful mountainside setting under the stars near the town of Nederland. We were attending some party hosted by the soon-to-be popular jam band, Leftover Salmon.

The shenanigans went on for about a week before her mom finally sobered up and decided it was time to head back to Arizona. This was another difficult goodbye for me. I had really fallen for that girl in the short time we were together. I did not want her to go, just when I was feeling that I had finally connected with something that might last. So much for not wearing my heart on my sleeve. Sitting under a tree, strumming my guitar on the Pearl Street Mall, I penned another love song.

CHAPTER 16

End Of The Line?

I had run out of my liquid vials early on the tour, and by the time I was in Boulder, some of my east coast distributers were asking me for more. I tried to find Doc, but was told that he was out of the country. The only source I could find in town was sketchy. In fact, it was the one and only Fast Eddie, sleazy leader of the infamous Wrecking Crew. My instinct told me to never do a deal with him, but I reasoned, just this once.

I asked Eddie to give me a sample dose for testing, which he did. I had a friend test it out and he reported it to be good. A ten lot (1,000 doses) was exchanged for cash that I had received via the standard Western Union method. The blotter had pictures of flying pigs on each dose with the slogan WHEN PIGS FLY written on them. Hmmm... that should've been my sign right there! The ten sheets were then slipped inside a *Bible* and shipped off to the south.

My guinea pig for the acid was this kid from Nebraska, Lippy. We hitchhiked to Telluride. We arrived in the small village on the fourth of July, when a great music festival was about to take place. The town of Telluride is a well-known haven for the bohemian elite—artists like Jackson Browne, James Taylor, and the Dead's own concert promoter, Bill Graham, had vacation homes there.

It was nightfall when we arrived and the holiday fireworks display had just begun lighting up the canyon walls. I had heard nothing but great things about this magical village, and this was my first time there. We picked our campsite behind Towne Park alongside Bear Creek. We built a fire, and I played a few songs on my guitar before we retired to our respective tents.

The splendor of the town's box canyon peaks was not fully realized until the morning of July fifth. It was then that I first saw the terrain by daylight. It was breathtaking and awe-inspiring. Every afternoon, the clouds would stroll into the valley and sweet misty rains would fall onto the village while the sun merged its way into a ritual heavenly dance. Rainbows would often marquee the crested rocky skyline, usually around 3 o'clock. In that environment, it was easy to understand why the place was revered as magical.

There was no lack of magic in the air on the afternoon when a beautiful, blue-eyed hippie girl named Phoebe smiled in my direction. Oh yes, here we go again! She was slender with long flowing blonde hair and a smile that was out of this world. She and her boyfriend Gus were fellow nomads who were also camping out near town for the upcoming festival. Gus seemed like a nice guy but I couldn't help but wonder if he noticed the immediate spark between Phoebe and I. Despite Gus being a potential obstacle between us, Phoebe and I quickly became close and, as fate would have it, she would become the key to a whole new life awaiting me.

One afternoon, she found me alone in town and was overwhelmed with joy. She was excited about a new opportunity. A man had approached her at the town market. He informed her that he worked as a production manager for Bill Graham Presents. He then offered her a job as an assistant for the upcoming festival. She happily accepted. She asked me if I'd like to tag along with her, and I didn't hesitate to accept. It sounded like fun. Interestingly, she didn't want Gus to be around and confided in me that their relationship was in trouble. They had been fighting quite often, and she wasn't sure how much longer they would stay together.

I was feeling guilty pleasure over her confession, but it made sense to me. It fueled my developing desire for her, but I still kept my anxieties hidden as best I could. Our new-found friendship and symbiosis seemed natural to others who simply saw us as a couple of young lovers, giggling with positive energy, smiles, and laughter. We seemed to be filling a void with one another.

Phoebe's new opportunity was a sign of great things to come. After she shared her good news with me, I headed off alone through town and back toward Bear Creek. There was a nice afternoon drizzle of rain that complemented the cool alpine breeze. What a wonderful sensation of being so close to the heavens to soak up nature that way. As I got closer to Towne Park, I noticed the usual afternoon rainbow shining gloriously over the mountain pines. It turned out to be no ordinary rainbow.

I stopped in my tracks when I noticed that just ahead of me, in the center of the park was the end of the rainbow, about 100 feet in front of the wooden framed concert stage. I walked up to the spot where it transcended into the earth and experienced what could only be described as a paranormal event. I literally stood in amazement at rainbow's end with my arms extended outward as the spectrum of colors flowed through my body and into the solid ground beneath me. No, I was not on any mind-altering substances, and it was certainly no flashback. Well, I cannot completely out rule the latter. I know that it was a real, tangible occurrence that most would argue impossible, but it, indeed, happened.

I looked around for witnesses, but there was no one in sight. As corny as it might sound, I stood there peacefully and embraced the anomaly with goose bumps of excitement. There must be gold in these hills, I thought. If I only possessed a shovel! It was a spiritual sign from the heavens that a great alignment in my life was about to take place, in this park and with the stage that stood before me. After a few moments, the rainbow faded and I made my way back to the campsite buzzing with energy.

The next day I tagged along with Phoebe as she helped out running errands for the Bill Graham people. Nigel, who had been a former tour manager for Little Feat, was a Production Manager for Bill Graham Presents and the one that offered Phoebe the job. He took a liking to me and immediately offered me a job as a stagehand, which of course I accepted.

As the days grew closer to the event, more and more of Bill Graham's California crew arrived on site. They were the same cast of characters that put on most Grateful Dead shows, and I immediately recognized a familiar face among them. It was good ol' Henry Sullivan. He was there to head up security for the festival.

Henry's approval of me played an important role in my making new friends inside the inner circle of the Bill Graham and Grateful Dead families. The crew had welcomed me in right away, but there was one problem. I was working in Birkenstock sandals, which was not very safe for my feet. One of the guys actually went out and bought me the proper shoes and socks to work in.

The first job I was asked to do was to sweep off the stage. They handed me a broom, which in my memory now symbolizes a Holy Grail moment of being officially initiated into the rock-and-roll business. A short time later, I was hanging from a lighting truss, adjusting fixtures, setting up P.A. speakers, unloading road case after road case of equipment. I loved every minute of it. Remember that KISS concert I snuck off to when I was 14 (five and half years earlier)? Well, finally, my real breaking moment into the business had arrived.

The morning of the first day of the festival, we loaded in a grand piano. Just as we finished setting it up, Jackson Browne sat down and began tinkering with it. He looked at me and asked if I could help him with something. I was speechless. I had been such a big fan of his for years and there he was asking me for help. I held up the piano lid and as he played a few notes.

"Does this sound in tune?" Browne asked.

"Sounds a little flat," I said. He agreed and called over a piano tuner to fix it. We then moved over to the side of the stage and chatted about the environment and Native American rights while piano tuner Ed Howe worked his magic.

After Jackson's sound check and just before the festival gates were scheduled to open, I was standing alone on the side of the stage while the rest of the crew was on break. Bill Graham walked past me with a broom in his hand and began sweeping the front of the stage. I immediately went over to him and asked if I could take over. He pointed to the side of the stage where another broom was and said that I was welcome to join him if I wished to. I swept along side him as the crowd began flowing onto the festival grounds. It was an unbelievable moment. I could hardly believe that I was sweeping with the legendary Bill Graham. When we finished, he smiled and thanked me for helping him. He gave me that "you look awful familiar to me" look, and I reminded him that we met in Arizona the previous year. He acknowledged the memory and then seemed generally pleased that I was now somehow working for him.

The weekend proceeded like a dream, and Phoebe and I were both having the time of our lives. She continued to help out the production staff as I was loading band equipment belonging to Joe Cocker, Hot Tuna, Widespread Panic, Blues Traveler, Taj Mahal, The Allman Brothers Band, Los Lobos, and others. We began to meet a lot of new friends.

During Saturday night's show, while on stage with Joe Cocker, the young guitarist for the Allman Brothers Band, Warren Haynes, 31 at the time, struck up a conversation with me. I had briefly been introduced to a few members of the band back in Miami, but this was the first time I had spent any quality, sober time with any of them. We talked at great length about music and, as it turned out, he was a big fan of the Dead. We shared the same dream that possibly one day the Dead and the Allmans would play a show together. Mind you, they had in the early Seventies, but it had been nearly twenty years. I also turned him on to a bag of killer weed, as I would regularly do over the next few years.

Sunday night, during the Allman Brothers set, Gregg Allman left the stage during the drum section of "In Memory of Elizabeth Reed." Warren Haynes, Dickey Betts, and Alan Woody exited stage left and were introduced to a very potent elixir that Henry dubbed "Telluride Tea." The mixture, of course, contained copious amounts of mushrooms, peyote, and MDMA. Warren did not participate, as great pot was pretty much his only recreation. Dickey and Alan however took very big gulps of the concoction. A friend helped Greg walk behind a Port-A-Potty backstage. I had a clear line of site on the needle that went into Greg's arm. He fell slightly backwards with the biggest grin I had ever seen. The two walked back toward the stage with his helper disposing of the towel that was wrapped around Greg's arm. As Greg got to the top of the stage stairs, he looked right into my eyes, smiling away, and flashed me the peace sign. I was shocked. Our friend knew that I had seen what went down and he just shook his head back and forth acknowledging the ugliness of the situation.

After the end of the Allman Brothers set, Warren invited Phoebe and I back to chill with the band at the hotel. We sat in a big hot tub with members of the Allman Brothers Band, along with a few of their girlfriends, and got really stoned. I know Gregg, Warren, and Woody were there, and possibly Jaimoe too. Phoebe was all cuddled with me and we were both just having a great time, our energies aligned. That's when it happened.

She looked up at me and after a silent pause we knew that we couldn't hold back anymore. Our lips touched passionately and we gave into our instincts with a long, deep kiss. She whispered in my ear that she would be with me that night, and that she and Gus were over. We exited the hot tub, thanked our rock star friends for the hospitality, and retreated to my campsite where we made love under the stars.

Warren had invited us to go to the Sheridan Opera House for a late night jam session, but we declined, as our interest had become focused purely on our physical needs. Haynes went on to jam with Widespread Panic until the wee hours of the morning in what many people remember as an epic night of magical music in Telluride.

The day after the festival, Nigel paid Phoebe and I a few hundred dollars each for our work. Although I had to shake Nigel down for my money, because I wasn't officially on the BGP payroll, he kindly paid me out of his own pocket. Danny, who was head of the backstage Ambience crew, encouraged me to follow-up for further employment should I end up at the next festival, which was to take place in northern California in a couple of weeks. It was a promising development. Phoebe and I made plans to depart for California sometime later in the week.

A couple of days went by, and I decided to get a souvenir to remember the whole experience. Phoebe was off making a bad deal that I didn't know about yet, but it would soon be a problem.

I took a few swigs of Irish whiskey as the Allman Brothers Band's "Live at The Fillmore East" played in the background. One needle carved into old vinyl while the other needle carved a heart into the flesh of my sleeve surrounding a yin-yang circle. Rainbow colored wings spread out atop the heart as eagle talons etched from below gripped into my arm. A skin-illustrated ode to my Joseph Campbell "Follow your bliss"–inspired method of travel, accompanied by my heart-on-sleeve approach to romance, my spirit soaring through rainbows, while gripping firmly into flesh under the Eagle, Bill Graham's, influence and power. Well, okay, so I was a little drunk at the time, and, well, that's the tattoo I ended up with.

I staggered back to our usual hangout, Baked In Telluride, hoping to show off my new ink to Phoebe. She wasn't around, so I joined in a street hackie-sack game to kill time and sober up a little.

A Jeep pulled up and James Taylor got out. He unwittingly walked through the center of our hackie circle as I had just hit the sack with my heel. It flew up and nailed him right in the forehead. (Nearly seven months later, I would accidentally nail the Grateful Dead's Bob Weir in the forehead with a flying rubber eyeball while he was performing on stage, but more on that later.)

"Sorry about that, J.T.," I said. We invited him to play with us, but he politely declined, as he was in a bit of a hurry to pick up an order from the bakery.

Just then, the afternoon rain started coming down and we all headed for shelter on the bakery's porch. I decided it was a good time to check in with my friends back east and see if they got the acid okay.

They had been waiting for my call for a couple of weeks, because, apparently, there was a big problem. The little blotter pigs with wings were not doing much flying and a lot of people were very upset with me.

"Is this some kind of joke?" My friend sarcastically shouted at me through the phone. "WHEN PIGS FLY?!? Is that when this shit is supposed to work?! "

"I promise I'll fix it," I told him.

The entire lot was bunk. We had been ripped off. My tester must've been given a decoy dose. Maybe Fast Eddie forgot to get the blotter dipped... yeah, right.

Phoebe arrived at the bakery soon after I got off the pay phone. She gave me a big hug and briefly admired my new tattoo. But she was visibly upset and said she had to talk to me about something. I, too, had an upsetting situation to discuss with her. She confessed that she had spent all of her money trying to make a quick deal that sounded too good be to true. She had been looking all over for the guy, only to find out that he was last seen leaving town in a hurry.

I became furious. Now we had both been ripped off by a couple of scumbags. I knew Fast Eddie had to be on his way to California, and that he would more than likely be at the next festival. I had to get to California as soon as possible to resolve the "pigs fly" situation. Matters only got worse when Phoebe and I began to argue about how to handle it. I got really confused. We had previously lined up a ride, but it wasn't leaving for a few more days. I didn't want to wait. We couldn't agree on what to do. I decided it was best for me to head out right away, and hopefully, take care of the situation before we met up again.

It was one of those bittersweet goodbyes that I had become all-too accustomed with. My backpack was firmly attached, guitar case in my left hand and my right thumb waving anxiously in the air. The peaks of Telluride were still surrounding me, but not for long, as the oncoming Jeep slowed down to a stop.

Then, as if my summer hadn't been full of adventure already, the next week proved to be some of the most downright dangerous days of my entire life.

PART II
Initiation

CHAPTER 17

Ramble Onward Rose

I hopped into the black Jeep Wrangler. The driver was wearing a United States Postal Service uniform and told me that he was on his way home to Grand Junction.

"That's a good start for me," I said.

He was the Post Master General of Telluride, a very kind and talkative man. He told me all about his job, and how much he loved serving the people of Telluride. I didn't do that much talking, but enjoyed listening to his tales of life in western Colorado and about his daily commutes between Grand Junction and Telluride. My heart was a little on the heavy side as my thoughts kept drifting back to Phoebe, Scarlett, Summer, Zoey, Springwater, and Elle. I might as well have named it my Trail of Tears Tour '91. I still had not found what I was running toward yet, but I could feel I was getting closer. I had the overwhelming feeling that something bigger than I could comprehend, some kind of magnetism, was pulling me back to California.

The postmaster kept trying to get me to open up and talk more. I told him that there was a new life for me waiting for me in California. He asked about my family. I told him that I belonged to a family of traveling gypsies. "What about your biological family?" he insisted. I just blankly stared at him and avoided getting into all that.

When we arrived in Grand Junction, I asked him to drop me off by the intestate exit. He invited me to stick around for dinner, saying his wife was a great cook and, if I preferred, I could even stay over and get an early start the next morning. It was a kind offer, but my sailing shoes were anxious to get into gear. I was hoping to at least make it to Utah by sundown.

Fifteen minutes or so later, I hopped in the back of a blue Toyota pickup with two dudes up front. They were only driving west a few short miles, but were happy to help me out. AC/DC's album Back In Black was blaring out of the speakers. The sounds were a comforting reminder of growing up in Coshocton. A thinly rolled joint was passed back to me through the sliding back window. The radio was cranked up a little more and we all started singing along to "Shoot To Thrill."

The ride finished as quickly as the smoke. I hopped out of the back with my guitar and pack. The kind strangers handed me a small bag of weed for the journey, wished me luck, and drove north with the fading sounds of AC/DC.

I began walking westward toward Utah and the setting sun, humming the rest of the song to myself. I didn't get more than a quarter-mile or so down the road when a red sports car pulled over, about a hundred yards ahead of me. I hadn't even stuck my thumb out yet. My heart skipped a beat. Yes, ride number three already!

The car backed up and I was impressed to find it to be a smokin' hot late model Ferrari. What was even more impressive was the young brown-eyed blonde woman behind the wheel, smiling at me when the window lowered. I looked up at the sky, took a deep breath and thanked the good lord for the fortunate situation. We put my back pack in the trunk, barely squeezed the guitar into the backseat and away we went. I sensed a little anxiety in the air.

Rose was heading home to Moab. She had been visiting with friends in Aspen. She said that she had never picked up a hitchhiker before. Apparently her instincts to pick me up had something to do with the guitar case I was carrying and her sudden curiosity to find out what my story could be.

I told her that I wasn't really hitching and that we had actually passed my house back where she picked me up. She had that "Oh, shit!" look on her face for a few seconds. Then I laughed and confessed that I was joking. The tension broke as we laughed and felt a little more at ease with one another. She seemed to be pretty cool, and it turned out that she liked to get high.

The comfort of our stoned conversation turned to sexy flirtations as the fading sun disappeared ahead of us. There was a chemistry flowing. But, like the oncoming night, anxiety crept back in, and I began to resist Rose's seduction. My thoughts drifted again to the many women already on my mind and the thought of getting to California. This only seemed to fuel the more immediate ambitions on her mind.

I played along with the dance, but became increasingly paranoid the closer we got to the Moab turnoff—or, more appropriately, what became the Moab "turn-on."

She pulled off the exit and directly onto the gravel parking lot of an abandoned gas station. She parked in an unlit corner of the lot and turned the car off. Moab was about thirty miles south of the exit. I felt her eyes weighing intensely on me as I tried not to get trapped in them, instead looking down at my feet.

There was an uncomfortable silence as I searched for words, any words I could think of; if there was just something I could just think of to say. But I knew. I just knew we were already in that zone. As I looked up at her I noticed quite possibly the largest full moon I'd ever seen peering over the desert horizon. It was blood red. "Stay here. I've got to make a phone call," she said as she suddenly got out of the car and headed to an old rusty looking pay phone.

My mind was racing. I thought that, normally, this is where I would just get out and bid farewell to my driver and move on. But I just sat there quietly, as instructed, and watched her fiddle with the old pay phone, trying to get it to work.

She returned to the car quickly and seemed a little frustrated that she couldn't make her call. We sat there silently. I tried not to look directly at her, and stared at the giant blood red full moon instead. She, too, was caught up in its magnificent beauty.

Again, Rose turned her eyes on me. As if she had just magically stolen the hypnotic powers of the moon and transferred them into her own eyes, I was pulled in. Her hand slid to the inside of my thigh. My heart was pounding. She moved in and kissed me intensely. I pulled away with my heart beating a hundred miles an hour. My thoughts discombobulated. She sensed a betrayal in my confusion.

"I can't do this," I told her. There was a long silence.

She didn't ask what the problem was. Instead she passionately insisted that I come home with her.

"I've got to get to California," I responded.

She offered to drive me back to the highway in the morning. She also offered up another scenario: a ride with her mother who was leaving for California in three days. Until then, we would have the time of our lives, she promised.

Her hand still caressing me, my lips surrendered again in the battle. My thoughts were all over the place. Phoebe... Moab... Scarlett... Moab... California... Moab... the blood red moon... Moab... fingers in my hair... Moab... baseball! baseball! Rose... Moab... California... Moab... west... Moab is south... Moab... the west is the best baby... Moab is not west... California is west... Moab is south... California... Moab... Phoebe... Moab... nipples... Scarlett... Moab... Zoey... Moab ... fingers-in-hair... Moab... hands, legs, flesh... Moab... Phoebe... Moab... Eddie-Fast Eddie? Who the fuck is Fast Eddie?!?... Fuck him and those flying pigs he rode in on!... Moab, Moab, Moab... MOAB! Hmmm, I had never been to Moab! I had heard so many great things about Moab. This chick is hot! Holy crap we're in a freakin' candy apple red Ferrari! She's probably rich! This chick is hot! Moab! That's it; I'm going to fucking Moab man, WAIT! What am I thinking?... Moab? This chick could be crazy! Her mother? I don't want to meet her mother! Moab? Stuck inside of Moab? I wonder if her mother is hot? The blood red moon... wet fingers, flesh... Moab? What am I thinking? Blood red moon... temptress... WARNING! WARNING! WARNING! THE MOON IS WARNING ME! desert rattlesnake... lips-tongues-nipples-flesh-fingers-hair-cock... blood red moon...

I pulled her hands off of me and simultaneously our lips disengaged.

Blood red moon, the highway, the west IS the best. The Pacific Ocean, California! Like an angel standing in a shaft of light, rising up to paradise... alas clarity!

Again I repeated to her, "I can't do this. I have to get down the road."

She gave me the look of a lifetime, an "ARE-YOU-A-FUCKING-

IDIOT?" look.

She sat back and suddenly out of thin air she materialized and lit up a Virginia Slim cigarette. Up to this point I figured her for a non-cigarette-smoker. Where did that cigarette come from? Jenny used to smoke that brand.

She took a loooooooong drag, paused, and exhaled.

"Get the fuck out," she said quite calmly.

I hesitated to react as if I needed clarification.

Instead of repeating herself verbally, she merely shot me a dose of those newly formed rattlesnake eyes. I quietly opened the car door, pulled out my guitar.

She got out and opened the trunk for me.

I retrieved my backpack.

No words.

She got back in the car.

I stood there outside of the car. Clarity? Was this clarity or insanity?

She slowly revved the engine a little, then shifted. She shot me that "are-you-a-fucking-idiot" look again, flipped me the bird, spun her tires in the gravel, and, southbound toward Moab, she disappeared into the night.

I stood there for a while, just thinking, "Yep, I am probably a fucking idiot. Oh, well." That's all I could conclude. I walked westward up the highway on-ramp.

CHAPTER 18

And You Know It
Has To Get Stranger

My thumb was in the air for probably twenty minutes or so, and then I gave up. I was too tired and distraught. I walked down the highway embankment and made my bed in the dirt with a rock as my pillow. I could've been in the arms of a beautiful woman, but, instead, I slept on the side of the highway. I dreamt of being back in Telluride.

The sun brutally woke me up in the morning, and I was quickly reminded that I was in the desert. The heat was unbearable. It wasn't long before I got a ride from some old hippies in a brown Dodge van. I showed off my new tattoo to their kids who kept asking me a million questions. They drove me as far as the Green River exit where they dropped me off at basically high noon in the middle of the sweltering desert, leaving me with a bag of sunflower seeds.

Lucky for me, I didn't have to wait that long. An hour or so later another sports car pulled over. It was a guy on his way to Las Vegas who had just returned from serving in the Gulf War. I had a great conversation with him and thanked him dearly for his service to our country. He was intrigued by my tales and said he wished I could go all the way to Vegas with him. But that was far beyond my route; instead, I hopped out at the turn-off to Salt Lake City.

The next ride was just in time to miss a torrential thunderstorm, an elderly couple on their way to Ogden, north of Salt Lake City. They dropped me off on the side of the I-80 interchange. Traffic was bustling, and I assumed it would be a tough spot to get a ride, but a rusty old Ford pick-up pulled over, and I hopped in the back. The couple in front said they would take me to a great spot for hitchhikers, but I would have to come along with them while they made a couple of pit stops.

What came next was basically a kidnapping. I had no idea where I was, except that I was somewhere in the suburbs of Salt Lake City. The scene played out like a very long episode of the Jerry Springer show. The woman was the sister of the wife of the man who was driving. An attempt to stop by the man's house found the wife throwing her husband's clothes out the window and onto their lawn while death threats were shouted back and forth by all three. Apparently, the wife had just learned that her husband was fucking her sister. It was nasty. After that, two quick stops for drug deals followed. Every attempt I made to exit the back of the truck was met with stiff resistance. I was being held captive by white trash Mormons. I ended up in a shouting match with the couple as they fought with each other. It was night and we had been driving through rough neighborhoods for hours. I felt unsafe, but also knew it was a greater risk to make a run for it. Finally after hours of intense negotiations, I convinced my captors to get me to a highway, any highway would do. So where do you think these dumb ass motherfuckers dropped me off? Yep, that's right. They deposited me back at the very spot where they first picked me up.

I walked down off the highway and found a patch of sand next to the Great Salt Lake where I put down my weary body and slept off a crazy day.

In the morning, seagulls attacked me. They were angry seagulls. Mean, disrespectful seagulls. They were some punk-ass bitch seagulls from hell that had some sort of score to settle with the likes of a dirty hippie sleeping on their beach. They woke me up by pecking at my head and trying to eat my dreaded-up blonde hair, which must have resembled French fries to them. The attack didn't end on the beach. The gulls followed me out to the highway and began dive-bombing me. It was like a Hitchcock movie. The drivers that whizzed by seemed to be amused at this sight. My only path of escape was treacherous. I balanced along a narrow strip of pavement. On one side were concrete construction barriers, on the other, morning traffic barreling by at high speed. The seagulls continued their bombardment until someone felt sorry enough to pull over to give me a lift.

The driver said he had never seen such a vicious bird attack on a live human. He dropped me off a few miles down the road at a truck stop where I washed up and ate some breakfast. The news on TV told of a psycho serial killer named Jeffrey Dahmer who picked up hitch-hikers only to take them home and eat them. It was a lovely time to be on the road.

Undeterred, I headed back out to the highway to continue my journey. A trucker pulled over and, just as I was climbing up into the cab, leaned over and shouted, "Hold on jus' a sec... MY MISTAKE, I DON'T HAVE ANY ROOM FOR YA!" Confused, I asked what the problem was.

"WELL, I THOUGHT YOU'S A LADY THERE, yer long hair, ya' know."

I backed off the perv's truck immediately and responded, "No problem! I'll take the next ride. Thank you very much."

A white mini-van pulled over and a chubby Native American gentleman was behind the wheel. He had a friendly smile and seemed like a good, safe ride. I hopped in his van and we headed west toward Nevada. The back of his van was loaded with merchandise, cartons of cigarettes, boxes of candy, chips, cases of soda—all of which were offered to me free, for whatever I needed to stock up on. He explained that he was picking up goods for his general store that he and his lover ran at a nearby reservation. He then informed me that he was a homosexual and asked if that made me uncomfortable. At that point nothing seemed to surprise me anymore so I couldn't help but just laugh. The guy had a mellow vibe about him and made it clear that he wasn't hitting on me. I did not feel threatened by him at all, and I couldn't have cared less about his lifestyle. I thought it weird that he found it necessary to make that pronouncement, actually, but the rest of the time he was funny and a joy to talk to. As we neared the exit for Goshote, he invited me to the reservation to have dinner with he and his partner. I politely declined, but did stock up on cigarettes, drinks, and snacks before I bailed out.

Almost immediately, my next ride came along—a semi-truck being driven by a man resembling Paul Newman. He said he was going as far as Reno, which was a straight shot across Nevada, and that worked out perfectly for me. He taught me CB radio lingo and let me chat with a few truck stop hookers over the airwaves. He also confided that he was living a double life—he had a family in Reno and a family in Utah, and they knew nothing of each other. Eventually, he offered me a job driving trucks if I wanted, but it was just another opportunity I would have to pass on. I was amazed at how many of these doors of opportunity opened around me while on my quest.

CHAPTER 19

The Lord Works
In Mysterious Ways

The morning sun shot up very quickly over the eastern horizon of Reno. I stood on the entrance ramp, which sloped downward toward the freeway. My pack and guitar case sat idle behind me. The sun was quickly becoming unbearable, and it was impossible to escape from. I needed a ride to arrive soon.

A small pickup truck passed by and then pulled over suddenly. The driver got out and walked to the back of the vehicle. He opened the hatch and grabbed my pack to toss it in. He was mumbling something about the heat. He was an older gentleman with a scruffy presence about him. My instinct was to not accept a ride from this guy, but he had grabbed my pack so quickly. I asked him where he was headed, so that I could perhaps manipulate my way out of accepting the ride. He was too cunning and simply replied, "Why I'm going wherever I can take you to my son. Now get in. It's going to be a hot one today."

Even given everything that I had gone through so far, this time I actually had a real bad feeling; the guy gave me the creeps. I stupidly convinced myself that it would be okay, so I went ahead and tossed my guitar case in. In the cab, there was a beautiful, friendly German Sheppard he called Smokey.

I learned that Bill was from North Carolina. He handed me a scrapbook, which contained newspaper clippings of his "walks for the homeless." He had walked across a few towns and the state of North Carolina to bring attention to the homelessness plight. He explained that he was planning to drive to Seattle, where he would then walk across America to promote his cause. A religious retreat back in Carolina was sponsoring him. They gave him the truck that we were now riding in, a little cash, a box of food, and some gas vouchers to get there. He was hoping to find someone along the way that could drive his truck beside the route while he did the walks. Oh, great: another interesting job offer. Well at the very least, perhaps Bill could get me all the way to Humboldt County.

We pulled into Truckee, California and parked on Main Street. Bill said he had to pick up something. When he returned, he put down a small brown paper bag, which contained a bottle of Bullit Bourbon. He asked that I not judge him. He was a recovering alcoholic and up to that point had been bragging about his sobriety. He hadn't had a drink in months, he told me. He only needed a little taste. I had a sinking feeling.

He offered me a swig, but I declined since whiskey wasn't my thing. I had my mind on getting to northern California. There was another problem, though, we needed gas, and he explained that he was out of vouchers and had just spent the last of his money on the booze. I had no money and could only think to abandon the guy at that point. Before I could get away, though, he put the truck into gear and said he had a plan.

We drove south toward Tahoe City. We pulled up in front of a church and Bill went in and spoke to the pastor. Twenty minutes later, we met the pastor behind the church, where he was instructing us the area of a hill he wanted us do some landscaping. We were given two shovels and then he disappeared. Bill had told him that I was his son, and that we would do some work for gas money. I was becoming frustrated, but silently went along with it. I wanted to tell the pastor what was really going on, but Bill had control of the situation.

I began digging an area of rocks out of the side of the hill that the pastor had indicated, but Bill returned to the truck for a drink. He just sat there drinking his whiskey while I worked. I was getting angry. He returned and just sat on the hill instead of helping with the dig. He never touched the shovel. When the pastor returned, he was displeased at the amount of unfinished work. Bill was sweating from the afternoon heat and his drinking. He told the pastor that we were doing our best. I tried to speak up about how Bill had not done any of the work, but Bill quickly distracted the pastor with a group prayer.

The pastor stared at me, and I could tell through his eyes that he knew things weren't adding up. He decided that we, meaning I, had done enough work and he handed over some cash to Bill. It was a relief but inside I was feeling angry, anxious and tired. I was offered none of the money, but at least it did go into the gas tank.

As we continued south, I felt like a helpless prisoner again. How did I let this guy control me? Was I not free to go? He was a smooth talker. He knew that I took a liking to Smokey, so he even said that I could have her if I wanted. But, the alcohol was taking its toll, and a noticeably less pleasant side of Bill was emerging. Also, he wouldn't allow me to drive.

Danger bells were going off. We pulled over to a remote parking area somewhere in the Sierra Nevada Mountains near the place where the Donner party had descended into cannibalism 150 years earlier. Bill was drunk and mumbled about going on a hike. I sensed fear coursing through my veins.

I told myself that this guy was a psychopath and there was no way I was walking off into the woods with him. In my mind, I was going through scenarios of escape. I felt tense, stressed, and frightened. In slurred words, he kept insisting on going for a hike. Finally I just broke and just shouted at him, "LOOK MOTHERFUCKER... I AIN'T GONG NOWHERE WITH YOU! YOU ARE DRUNK AND YOU'RE REALLY STARTING TO FREAK ME OUT, MAN!"

I figured if he had something sinister in mind, then I was going to call him out right then and there. It was his move.

He reassured me that he was fine, not drunk. The whiskey bottle was nearly empty. My stance worked, but I was still fearful. I didn't want to push my luck by making a run for it into mountainous, unfamiliar backcountry. It was a chess game, and I had to think very carefully about every move. I convinced myself that the guy was probably concealing a weapon somewhere, and that if I did the wrong thing it would incite him.

The standoff was agonizing. I made it very clear that I didn't trust him. I insisted that he let me drive, but that only made him angry, so I backed off. As another car pulled into the parking area, he quickly decided to put the truck in motion again. Had I jumped out, I would certainly have lost my backpack and guitar, and who knows what might have ensued; I could have been putting more people into danger.

We headed west down Highway 50. At least we were going in the right direction. My heart was thumping rapidly as I worked out scenarios in my head. A few miles down the road, there was a broken-down Oldsmobile on the side of the freeway. We pulled over in front of it.

"Let's help these niggers out," he said.

Oh, that's nice, I thought. He's a racist, too.

"Stay here," he instructed. A minute later, he returned to the vehicle with a guy who introduced himself as James. I moved to the small back seat of the cab with Smokey. James' wife and baby were left behind at the car and Bill had agreed to take him to the next service exit to get a hose clamp that he needed to repair his car.

Almost immediately after swerving back onto the highway, James inquired about the dog, and he was met with, "She don't like niggers!"

"Excuse me?"

"She don't like niggers, and I don't like niggers!" barked Bill.

James demanded that Bill pull over and let him out. "I'll find someone else to help us, Sir."

He looked back at me and I quietly gestured that I was a hitchhiker and did not know this man. I silently pleaded for his help. Smokey sat there oblivious, her tongue dangling out. I gestured that my captor had been drinking, which it didn't take long for James to realize. Bill refused to pull over. His driving became erratic, and his racial slurs multiplied.

"Please, Sir, just get us to a service station. That's all I ask." You could tell that James was clearly thinking of the safety of the wife and baby he left behind at the car. James was a big dude, and could have easily knocked Bill out if he wanted to, But we were barreling down Highway 50 at a high rate of speed swerving from lane to lane.

Bill claimed to know where there was a service garage ahead. He mumbled something about a sister of his who lived near Placerville.

Sure enough, we pulled off the exit where he claimed one would be and there was a BP service garage there. The truck swerved into the station and screeched to a diagonal stop in front of the garage. James and I got out. Bill was slurring half-hearted apologies, "Juss tryin' to help out... my sister lives here... gonna collect some aluminum cans... take care of Smokey... she's a good dog." His head was bobbing around, eyes rolling back, drool on his mouth. His head came to a rest on the steering wheel.

I got my things out of the back while James found the part he needed from the garage. He let them know that they had to do something about the drunk driver who now appeared passed out in their lot. He talked to some people who were getting gas, and asked if they could give us a ride back to his car. He offered to get me where I needed to go. "I just need to get to Sacramento," I told him. Friends of mine from Boca, Misty and Linda lived there.

The ordeal was finally over. Before we left with our new ride, I let Smokey out to pee, and then put her back in his truck. I decided that he needed that dog more than I did, but I couldn't help but feel sorry for her. I like to think that she ended up at Bill's sister's house.

We got back to the car and fixed the hose. We were back on the road, and I was so thankful and relieved. We laughed about the ordeal and I thanked James for saving my life. They eventually dropped me off in Sacramento but in a very questionable and suspiciously bad neighborhood.

CHAPTER 20

Highway To Hell
(Yet Another Abduction)

I called Misty and Linda and hoped they would rescue me from the seediest section of Sacramento. Cars drove by in slow motion and creepy, perverted old men stared out the window at me. Frustrated, I learned from one of the many wildly dressed street walkin' ladies that people thought I was "'working'."

Finally the sisters arrived, but with bad news. Linda's jealous, controlling boyfriend wouldn't let me stay at their house, so the girls got me a motel room. I told them all about my crazy ordeal while we ate take-out. They wished I could hang around for a few days, but I still wanted to get to Humboldt County and the sooner the better. It was so great to get a shower, clean up, and relax a little.

In the morning, I headed out to I-5 North and got my first ride. As soon as I sat in the passenger seat, I noticed that the guy was wearing a gun. Alarm bells go off again. What the fuck?

"It's okay; I'm a cop," he told me. "You know, you're not allowed to hitchhike here, right?"

I just shook my head in disbelief. Was this really happening to me? Considering that the officer picked me up in his unmarked car directly at a NO HITCHHIKING sign, of course I knew that.

The gun wasn't the only thing weird; he also had an open can of beer in the cup holder.

"Relax, you're not in any trouble. You want a beer?" He nodded toward the cooler in the backseat.

"Um, no thanks."

"Where you headed?"

Gee, Officer, I'm a hippie heading to Humboldt County. I have a job waiting for me in the redwoods. No, no, better not tell him that.

"To work a music festival up near Garberville."

"Well, I'm heading way up north and I know a great spot where you can get a ride over to the coast. It's a not far from here."

"That sounds great." I said.

"First though, we're going to go fishing."

"Thanks for the offer really, but I don't have a lot of time to go fishing."

"No, I insist now. We're going to go fishing." He dictated.

"No really, I'm on a time schedule and I'm running behind as it—"

"Listen son, YOU ARE GOING FISHING WITH ME!"

His tone got dark, very dark. He motioned to his gun.

My heart started racing again. I sat silent and took a deep breath.

"Don't make this difficult."

"With all due respect, Sir, you have no idea what I've already been through."

His voice responded louder and darker.

"WE ARE GOING FISHING!" he declared, stern and forceful.

My leg started to shake uncontrollably; fear was overcoming me. There was a long silence, which gave me a chance to work things out. Okay, what the fuck is going on? I've already survived two abductions, and here I am being tested yet again. Or, perhaps it's just my destiny to be murdered by a serial killer.

"Okay, it's cool man. I'll go fishing with you. In fact, I'll take one of those beers now."

"That's better. Don't worry, we'll have some fun." There was an evil grin as he reached over and patted my leg. That really enraged me. I had to start thinking of a way out of this.

I played it as cool as I could, but he would occasionally have an angry outburst about random things. I knew I was dealing with a serious psychotic. This situation made those previous experiences with Bill and the white trash Mormons look tame.

The conversation swung in and out of tension. I reasoned that my previous run-ins were just preparing me for the real deal. This time, I could see my captor's gun. I just prayed that he didn't pull off at a remote exit somewhere, but realized it would be inevitable. It was best to just go along with whatever he said until I could find an opportunity to fight back or escape.

The car exited in a small California town and pulled into a corner store gas station. My heartbeat was faster than it had ever been. I knew this would probably be my only chance. I was now convinced that my life was in serious danger. Without hesitation, as soon as the car came to a stop, I opened up the door and ran for it. I ran around the building and jumped over some bushes. Everything happened so fast, I had no idea if I was being chased or not. Everything was blurry.

I ran past a couple more buildings and into a Denny's. I quickly composed myself to not draw attention. I asked for the bathroom. I regained myself for a few minutes, but was still frightened. I assumed the asshole was waiting out there for me. Perhaps he would flash his badge around. I figured that if anything went down, it would be best to go ahead and make a scene so people would remember me. I was surprised to not see him when I came out of the bathroom. I sat down in a booth and ordered a glass of water. I told the waitress I just needed a few minutes to relax. I accepted that I had left my guitar and backpack with my camping gear behind. This time I reasoned the items were a necessary sacrifice.

There were drugs in my pack, too. If he searched my stuff, he could've easily called for backup and made up some story about apprehending me earlier and how I escaped. This was a bad situation.

I waited inside the Denny's while fear and paranoia consumed me, waiting for the inevitable. I kept looking out the windows for a sign of him or his car. Every car that drove by looked like his. Every person within my eye's view looked like him. Eventually the paranoid hallucinations wore off and I gained enough nerve to step outside for a smoke. There was no sign of him or any other cops for that matter.

I was little more than a couple of hours north of Sacramento. I wished that I could call Linda and Misty for help, but I knew that would only complicate things on their end. My only real option was to start hitchhiking again. I was still shaken up, but in the middle of who-knows-where and now with nothing except the clothes on my back. As I walked across the street toward the corner store where I had made my escape, I noticed that my backpack and guitar were resting against the building. The car was nowhere to be seen. I couldn't believe it. Naturally I thought it was a trap, but quickly realized that I had just gotten another lucky break.

CHAPTER 21

Help On The Way

H our after agonizing hour, I stood along the highway's edge hoping and praying for a ride. I was distraught, hungry, weak, and on edge. The sun faded as did my strength, and I took refuge in an island of trees about fifty yards from the road. I set up camp and rested for the night.

In the morning, I set out again to find a ride. I was still too weak to do much walking. Hours again went by at what could best be described as the worst place in the world to hitchhike.

The afternoon sun beat down on me hard. Surely, I was entering into the initial phases of dehydration and starvation. The hours lingered on as the occasional vehicle roared past without even a thought to pull over. The realization hit me that I had now been in the same spot for twenty-four hours without a ride. My attempts to walk north toward my destination had only yielded a mile or two of progress.

The sun again thought of fading from the harsh day, and I honestly didn't know if I would survive another night. Just then, I spotted an oncoming Volkswagen van. As they came closer, I started jumping up and down and waving my arms. I wasn't going to let this one get away. They passed me with looks of confusion but quickly pulled over ahead of me. I grabbed my things and ran toward my rescuers. Dead stickers covered the back window. I got to the van, opened the side door, and threw my belongings and myself in the back. The couple in the front was taken somewhat by surprise at my assumptions.

"You okay, man?"

"No. I've been in that fucking spot for twenty-four hours and I feel like I'm on the verge of death! Oh, and I'm heading to Humboldt County, but wherever you can get me will be fine."

Josh and Tari were from Nevada, and as fate would have it, they were also heading to the Electric On The Eel music festival in Humboldt County. There couldn't have been a better alignment. They kindly offered me their fruit, granola, and liquids, which replenished my weary body. They explained that they didn't normally pick up hitchhikers, but because I was frantically jumping up and down, they had pulled over.

A few hours later, we drove into the grounds of French's Camp, which was nestled alongside Humboldt County's Eel River. One of the first people I ran into when I got out of the van was Phoebe. It was a happy reunion. She had found a ride with one vehicle straight through from Telluride, and she had beaten me to the site by an entire day. Now if that ain't a bitch. If I hadn't been so anxious to head out in the first place, I could've had the same ride and avoided all the insane situations I ended up in.

Phoebe and I retired with our sleeping bags in the middle of a field, and we stared wildly above at heaven's stars, and I proceeded to tell her about my crazy adventure.

In the morning I was awakened by an off-road motorcycle that pulled up alongside my sleeping bag. Considering where we were, I thought to myself that it must be Bill Graham's dirt bike that I was hearing.

"You can't camp here on the festival grounds." It was a familiar voice. I lifted up my head and smiled.

"Henry Sullivan!"

He smiled back. "Hey, I thought that was you two. Let's get you over to my camp."

CHAPTER 22

Join The Party

There were two music festivals scheduled to converge on French's Camp. The first weekend was the Jerry Garcia Band playing a festival called Electric On The Eel; the following weekend was Reggae On The River. I helped out Henry with some security duties and also joined in Danny's backstage ambiance crew, setting up the dressing rooms for the bands. The latter mostly included moving couches, tables, lamps, and rugs—something that would soon become my full-time job. The vibe backstage was beautiful. It was mostly old school Hog Farmers and Merry Pranksters around. Jerry Garcia and Ken Kesey's old flame, the infamous Mountain Girl, was organizing things in the catering tent while Kesey and Garcia reminisced in the hospitality tent. I felt honored to be in the presence of such psychedelic royalty.

The Bama Boys made it to the festival, and I would hang out with them when not with Phoebe or doing some backstage work. The scene was incredibly peaceful except for some federal agents that were camped out on the hill, spying on everyone through their binoculars.

There was no lack of getting high and it seemed that my behind-the-scenes initiation was well under way. The production office was located in an old hippie school bus, which belonged to the Hog Farm Commune.

One night, I was sitting on this bus with Henry, getting high, when things started to really take off. Ken Kesey, Wavy Gravy, and Bob Weir appeared. Bill Graham made a brief appearance along with several of his top people, including Bob and Peter Barsotti.

Shortly after Graham left, a full-fledged carnival began. There was nitrous flowing, drinks passed, joint after joint after joint after joint of
some serious space ganja being toked, mushrooms eaten, pills popped,
and powder snorted. The bus was buzzing and pulsing with energy.

At some point, I was finally so high I just couldn't toke anymore. I
couldn't keep track of everything going into my system and the crowd
of voices and laughter surrounding me. Bob Weir was sitting to my
right and Bob Barsotti was directly across from me. The three of us
were locked into some hysterical laughter of unknown origin. I stood
up but couldn't maintain my balance.

"Where are we going?" I shouted to Weir. He continued his laughter and replied with something typically cryptic. I returned the laughter holding onto my gut. "No, really, where is this fucking BUS going
man? We're moving tooooo fast maaan." I stood and staggered in the
cloud of smoke that filled the aisle. Wavy Gravy danced past me and
muttered something funny about the bus rolling on forever and ever.
I had no idea exactly where I was and how I ended up in such strange
company. I didn't recall being informed as to where we were headed.
It was like the spirit of Neal Cassady himself had been summoned to
drive us madly through the giant redwoods. Weir and Kesey were having quite the laugh at my expense. I, too, was laughing, but with utter
confusion as the bus bounced from left to right while I pulled my way
to the front. Henry was standing at the front and offered to help.

"You need some air?"

"When are we going to stop maaan?"

"Just step outside for a few minutes and get some air. You need
a drink. Here, drink this." He tried to hand me bottled water with a
brownish liquid inside.

"No more Mushroom Peyote tea, or whatever that is. Must get off
this bus." Some Spanish lady who sat in the front seat passed a joint to
me. The energy was still buzzing from the back of the bus to the front.
The party was raging. "Can you ask the driver when we are going to get
to wherever? I don't want the bus to stop on my account." They were
all laughing at me. It was night, and I could not see very well into the
dark and blurry landscape.

"Here kid, try some of these," someone else suggested. Playing along, and always the good tripping shepherd, Henry leaned over to the driver's seat and asked the invisible driver something. Oh, that was just more confusing. Nothing made any sense anymore. Who was driving this bus? Was it the invisible psychedelic cowboy, the very ghost of Cassady? Why were we rolling down a hill out of control with no one behind the wheel? Mammoth redwoods whizzing by us in the dark! For God's sake, someone at least turn the headlights on!

Henry helped me to the steps. "Go ahead, you can do it." He nudged me towards the outside. I staggered on the bottom step as the trees and ground went flurrying by at high rates of speed.

"You want me to jump?" I laughed. "Can you slow the bus down at all?"

Henry convinced me that the bus was moving slower and slower. It was safe now to jump. So I just did it. I jumped off the carnival bus and rolled three times in the grass and came to a stop with my eyes staring into the night sky above. The sounds of the bus were now a cloud at my feet. I leaned my head up and noticed the bus parked with an enormous giant redwood towering firmly in front of it. So we were never moving in the first place? I'm really that high? I continued to lie on the ground becoming one with the earth, squirming and wiggling. Some time passed and a familiar face appeared over me smiling. It was Phoebe. Her words seemed to warp in and out of focus, but I managed to hear her say, "... something-something I've been looking all over for you beautiful something-something..."

She eventually got me back on my feet and we went for a walk down by the river. It was there where she wanted to discuss "us". We had never talked about any kind of exclusive commitment nor was it really assumed. She described our relationship as "just a thing" as she put it. It became pretty clear that she had some other plans on her mind that didn't include me. Which was really okay since I hadn't thought things out too far in advance anyway. My mission to California had started to make sense once I fell into the inner circles of the Bill Graham folks. I now had a job with them and it seemed to fulfill some sort of obscured destiny that I was seeking. Phoebe and I said our fare thee wells and I felt somewhat sad in the moment, but also reassured with the great opportunities I knew were ahead of me.

CHAPTER 23

The Burning Ground

I traveled with Henry in his old, rusty, green Dodge van, a.k.a. The Green Machine, to the next Grateful Dead run at Cal Expo back in Sacramento. The shows were very lovely, especially the second set of the third night when the band segued "Cold Rain and Snow > Box of Rain > Looks Like Rain > Crazy Fingers." Usually they would go right into the "Drums" segment of the set after three or four tunes, but we were treated to some extra pre-drums jams with "Estimated Prophet > Supplication > Uncle John's Band." Six songs before Drums made for a very rare show indeed.

On the previous night of the Cal Expo show, I ended up leaving early and found myself back at The Green Machine having a sexual escapade with a BGP (Bill Graham Presents) security girl, Kelly, who I would end up having a casual relationship with over the next few years.

Following the run of shows at Cal Expo there were three more shows at Shoreline Amphitheater, during which the great San Francisco psychedelic poster artist Rick Griffin died from a motorcycle accident. On the first night, the Dead broke into a rare first set "Dark Star" in his honor. A costumed Grim Reaper solemnly walked across the stage as the band played. The freshly inked tattoo on my arm that I got in Telluride was my interpretation of Griffin's unique style of art and a sort of ode to him. From the first night at Cal Expo to the third night at Shoreline, the band never repeated one song during this six night run. To my knowledge this was the longest set of consecutive shows they ever did without any repeats. Their performances at the Cal Expo shows seemed slightly average to me, but the Shoreline shows were absolutely exceptional, the band was on fire.

Squaw Valley Music Festival took place on top of the ski mountain above Lake Tahoe. Jerry Garcia Band and the Neville Brothers headlined. Reggae great Jimmy Cliff also performed as did mandolinist David "Dawg" Grisman. I worked on Danny's ambiance crew setting up the backstage hospitality tents and dressing rooms, which became my main job for BGP over the next few years.

On the day before the festival was to start, I was finishing up some backstage work with Jeff "Bundy" Perin. We were zip-tying some tent walls and chatting when I heard the sound of a helicopter approaching. Bundy joked that we had better finish up quickly since Bill was coming home.

I stopped working for a minute and watched Bill's helicopter descend on the landing area adjacent to backstage. An eerie premonition entered my head as I was locked into a trance with the flying machine. It was a flash of the helicopter crashing in some other dark and twisted environment. It was a disturbing thought, and I had no idea where it had come from. Bundy was calling out my name. "Dewey, Dewey! Hey man! What are you thinking about?" I couldn't repeat the awful images that had gone through my head. Was it natural to think such an awful thing? I felt uneasy about it.

"Nothing. I don't want to say it, man. It was a crazy thought, and I'm not going to repeat it out loud."

Bundy gave me an understanding look and shook his head. "Okay we're finished here. Let's go welcome Bill."

Graham walked into the backstage area where his employees had formed a loose receiving line to say hello, give him hugs, or just shake the legendary promoter's hand. Bundy and I were the last in line, waiting as Bill took his time to acknowledge each person individually. Bundy shook Bill's hand and welcomed him home. Bill smiled and then turned his eyes to me. I shook his hand and thanked him for the opportunity to work for him.

"It's an honor to be working for you. Thank you so much for still doing what you do so well. And that I can be a part of this, well it means a lot to me. Thanks!"

Bill just smiled and replied, "You are a part of this family now. I can't do what I do without you guys. I should be thanking you. It's good to see you here and thank YOU!"

Bundy looked over at me with a "Wow, that was cool" expression. Then Bill called out to all his stagehands to gather around. He announced that he would a host a party at his quarters that evening, and that he especially wanted his stagehands to attend, in appreciation for all the great work.

BGP put us up in ski lodge dorm rooms, and because of my friendship with Henry I was hanging out with the bluecoats (BGP security). We had a party of our own that was kicking off when a few of the guys mentioned heading over to Bill's crew party. I was still the new guy and felt awkward about imposing around the veteran stagehands. In a most regrettable move that I still kick myself for today, I did not attend Bill's party.

The next day, it was all the crew could talk about: how Bill sat around and told stories of his days with Jimi Hendrix and Janis Joplin. They said that it was rare for Bill to hang out like that with the stagehands. Most of the crew had never hung out with Bill socially. It was a once in a lifetime event, a hell of a party, et cetera, and et cetera. The guys were rejuvenated with a refreshed respect for their boss and mentor. I was mad at myself for missing the party and told myself that I wouldn't pass up the next one.

CHAPTER 24

Weird Scenes Inside
The Paradigm

B urrowed between 98th Avenue and Hegenberger Boulevard, just across from the train tracks, were the grounds of a rundown warehouse complex. It resembled an ongoing parking lot scene at an eighties heavy metal concert, like those scenes at the old Hollywood Sportatorium in Florida, but much more condensed. This was Paradigm Studios, rumored to have been constructed on an ancient Indian burial ground, an unlikely Shangri-La for crystal-meth-peddling bikers who mingled among struggling homeless rockers and the occasional stray hippies. The East Oakland air was laced with industrial pollutants. There was a sweet, yet bitter quality to it that you could feel burn in your lungs if you took too deep a breath. The dark passageways inside the Paradigm were also drenched in pollution, of the deafening variety. Loud and mostly toxic heavy metal vibrations seeped from nearly every chamber. Navigating the unpainted halls often gave one's eardrums the sensation of being sonically violated. This would be my home for the next two and a half years.

When we first arrived in San Leandro, Henry let me stay at his place for a few days. On my twentieth birthday, he dumped me off at the Paradigm. Kelly said I didn't belong there. She didn't want to see the place corrupt me. But I quickly settled into a couch in one of the back warehouses and started supplying the tenants with acid.

I called into the BGP offices to check for more work, and Danny informed me that there was a problem. He had plenty of work for me, but one of the production managers said there was an issue over something that happened at Squaw Valley. I went into the Bill Graham offices right away. Apparently someone of importance claimed to have seen me granting access to "one of my girlfriends" who had a laminate around her neck. The girl in question was Phoebe.

Smokey, a BGP production manager, knew of my relationship with Phoebe in Telluride. He told me how serious an offense it would be if I were sneaking people into the shows. Wow, I couldn't believe the drama churned up over little ol' me! I recalled riding in the gondola with Phoebe—that was the main entrance into the Squaw Valley Festival—and, yes, she was wearing a laminate, but I didn't give it to her. When I asked her how she got it, she wouldn't tell me because she didn't want to get that person in trouble. I admitted to knowing about her getting in that way, but I honestly had nothing to do with it. I was just at the wrong place with her at the wrong time and was seen by the wrong person. Phoebe knew other people on the inside, too, not just me. After all, it was she who got me that job back in Telluride. Smokey appreciated my honesty and took a liking to me. He understood the situation and gave Danny the green light to continue to book me more work. He then took me on a tour of the offices and Bill Graham's incredible vintage poster vault. I even got to say hello to Bill again.

Back at Paradigm, things couldn't have been stranger. It was such a raw and nasty, drug-fueled wasteland—a dark contrast to a Grateful Dead parking lot scene. Loud music, the smell of burning meth, and wild parties bounced off the warehouse walls twenty-four hours a day. People that resided there barely ever slept. The popular thrash metal bands Dirty Rotten Imbeciles, Testament, and Exodus all had studios there. I supplied them with LSD. I also kept up on my mail order operations, receiving contact via one of those old vibrating pagers. I picked up money at the local Western Union and made my phone calls on a pay phone in the Paradigm lobby.

The studios were a mile walk from the Oakland Coliseum and Stadium complex, where I did most of my work for BGP events. The area I lived in was affectionately known of as the "kill zone" for its rampant gang activity and high number of drive-by shootings. I often heard gunshots in the distance as I made the walk from the BART

(Bay Area Rapid Transit) station to the warehouses. I was also often propositioned by creepy old truckers at a truck stop a couple of blocks to the south. It was a dangerous place, but the locals must've assumed we were all insane to live there, so we were mostly left alone. I grew to absolutely hate that walk. There were two sets of railroad tracks, one just on the east side of San Leandro Boulevard which bordered the seriously bad neighborhoods and one just to the west behind a string of industrial junkyard complexes next to the Oakland Airport. There were occasional upsides to the walk, like once a week when the enormous Sunshine Cookie Factory would emit the most wonderful sweet baked fragrances. And then there were the temptations of the Taco Truck (roach coach) that was set up on the corner of 85th Avenue just across from a police impound lot. I still long for the taste of those fried, greasy quesadillas! Yum!

At Oakland Stadium, we set up for one of Bill Graham's infamous Day On The Green concerts. This one was an early October show with Metallica, Faith No More and Queensryche. Our crew was always the first on site and the last to leave. We would take more than a week setting up the backstage area with mobile trailers and tents filled with all sorts of wild amenities for the artists to enjoy. We would still be there, tearing down and loading out, for up to a week after the one-night show.

It was really fun to tweak out in the stadium at four in the morning, setting up Christmas lights and odd décor in strange places. There were often just four or five us there with the whole venue to ourselves. A few overnight BGP security staff would be on scene keeping us safe, but we pretty much had the run of the place. We would sleep in the dressing rooms and shower in the locker rooms before anyone else showed up on site. My special access meant band members and their crew looking for recreational substances often approached me. And on this occasion, I supplied members of Metallica and Faith No More with some good quality acid.

Sometime shortly after the Day On The Green event, there was a massive firestorm in the Oakland hills that destroyed more than 3,000 homes and killed a couple dozen people. We could see the flames from the Paradigm. My friend Jeff Andrews, who I often jammed with, and I sat on the roof drinking beers and watching the hills burn. We saw houses explode, one at a time. It was a horrific thing to see, and such an intense place to be while that was happening.

I eventually got my own studio room in that back warehouse at the Paradigm. Inside was parked an RV, where a grumpy old man named Jan lived. He recorded cheesy soundtrack music to bad pornographic films on his Casio keyboard. His impromptu recording sessions would occur at the oddest hours, usually keeping me awake. At quiet times, I was often disturbed by the scurrying sounds of large rats in the walls and ceiling of my industrial hideaway.

CHAPTER 25

Bill Graham's Dead

"Bill Grahayam's dead! Bill Grahayam's dead!" were the words I awoke to on a Saturday morning, the 26th of October, 1991. It was the voice of Wallace, a drugged-out auto mechanic who lived in a shanty little camper in the junkyard adjacent to my studio. Interestingly enough, Wallace's own life would also be cut short just a few months later when he would be found dead in the camper from a heroin overdose.

"Wallace? Is that you?" I yelled through the walls. "What did you say?"

"Bill Grahayam's dead Dewey! He died in a hellacoppah crash last night!" Wallace's urban slang shouted back. This was how I awoke that morning: the junkie next door told me that Bill Graham had died. I didn't believe him, because I had to go to work that day. We were scheduled to load in for the Halloween Grateful Dead run at the Coliseum. Bill couldn't be dead. I thought it was a bad dream or perhaps a flashback to some previous cobwebs in my mind.

I walked into the main lobby of the studio complex. There was Top Hat Ray with a solemn look on his face. He also worked BGP security, Henry was there too, and a couple other BGP people.

"So I guess it's true."

"Yep," Ray confirmed it.

Henry just sat there teary-eyed and in a sad shock.

There was a message in the office to call Danny. I called him and he officially confirmed that Bill had died in a helicopter crash shortly after midnight. It was important that I get to the Coliseum a little early for a meeting.

It was somber at the Coliseum, very somber. People hugged each other and stared aimlessly in disbelief. It was like the president of the United States had died or something. This was big. Bill Graham was a monolithic figure in the rock-and-roll world, and now things were about to change, but no one seemed to know how or what to do about it yet. Our leader's chariot had literally been struck down in a lightning storm, crashing into one of those giant electric utility towers. It was a very sad day to work, but it was a good place to be. The employees all comforted each other. After all, this was Bill's family and his motto was always, "The show must go on!"

That day, plans were made for a huge memorial concert to take place in Golden Gate Park on November 3rd, just following the Grateful Dead Oakland run. We would load out the Dead shows and take everything straight to Golden Gate Park for the mammoth event. The funeral itself was set for Monday, and I was invited to attend.

The Dead opened the first show on Sunday night with "Sugar Magnolia," said to be Bill's favorite song. It was a healing and appropriate environment to be in considering the loss. Carlos Santana and Gary Duncan sat in with the band. There were all sorts of celebrities and rock stars backstage from Sammy Hagar to Bob Dylan all consoling each other. I was introduced by my friend Lou to Huey Lewis, who actually made the observation, "Hey, we're Huey, Dewey, and Louie."

It was a Huey Lewis concert at the Concord Pavilion in the North Bay that Bill actually attended the night of his death. Bill had gone there to personally ask Lewis to perform at a benefit concert for the recent fires in Oakland. It was a stormy night and Steve "Killer" Khan had been advised *not* to fly. Why is that always the case? Like with Stevie Ray Vaughan and so many others. I mean, who gets in a helicopter on a stormy night after a rock and roll show? It was a fatal decision that took Bill's life along with his companion Melissa Gold, as well as Khan's. I was haunted by that eerie premonition I had had back at Squaw Valley.

Bill's funeral was held on Monday and everybody who was

anybody in the Bay Area music scene was there. It was a beautiful and fitting farewell. The Dead continued the shows at the Coliseum, finishing up on Halloween night with an encore of Warren Zevon's "Werewolves of London." I took my friend Janine as a date to one of the shows; she was, at the time, the separated wife of a famous glam rock star. Janine didn't quite get the whole Dead thing, even though her head was filled with loads of acid. Though she was quite fun to party with, she was not on the bus.

We began loading in at Golden Gate Park in the middle of the night. This happened only a few hours after the Dead closed out the Halloween show. I remember having to drive a big ass RV into the park with remnants of acid still dripping through me. God that was so much fun! We set up tents and moved in all the couches, tables, lamps, and rugs. Staging began to arrive with the daylight, as did the people of San Francisco, who started camping out in the field in front of the stage. They say over 300,000 were in attendance. An airplane flew over the crowd and dropped thousands of roses.

The show was called "Laughter, Love, and Music: A Memorial for Bill Graham." The backstage energy was just incredible. I sat and listened to comedian Robin Williams in the production office tell jokes to Bob Barsotti and production manager Tom Howard. He had everyone practically rolling on the floor in hysterics. I was called into the Dead's tent to fix a lamp and witnessed Jerry Garcia and David Crosby negotiate over the last jelly roll donut, while Blues Traveler's John Popper lingered over them for a taste (they split it in three equal parts).

I also had a couple of interesting personal conversations with Garcia. I shared a joint with Carlos Santana, as we sat on the grass next to the stage looking out at a sea of bodies. What an incredible day and amazing tribute honoring Bill. The Dirty Dozen Brass Band opened up the show. Bobby McFerrin sang the national anthem. Jackson Browne did a couple songs on the piano including one of my all-time favorites, "For A Dancer." Joe Satriani played a set. Aaron Neville sang "Ave Maria." Santana played a set. Robin Williams did about ten minutes of stand up. Journey reunited for three songs. Tracey Chapman performed acoustic. Crosby, Stills, Nash and Young did a big set. Then the Grateful Dead played. John Popper and Carlos Santana sat in.

John Fogerty sat in while the Dead backed him on four Creedence Clearwater Revival songs. And the band closed with the "Sunshine Daydream" coda that they left out of the "Sugar Magnolia" from the opening night of the Halloween run. Then Neil Young came up to the stage to sit in with the Dead. "I got a letter from Bob," he said, "and it goes like this..." And they broke into Dylan's "Forever Young." A "Touch Of Grey" encore was thrown in. Finally the celebration ended with Joan Baez singing "Amazing Grace." Wow, what a day of incredible music and memories that I will never forget!

CHAPTER 26

Main Line Florida

In late November or early December, I went back to South Florida again for a brief visit, since I had an incredibly awesome job and was making good money. My memory is real fuzzy on how this next part happened, but I think I was with my friend Rob Pena who introduced me to the very attractive Tiffany Piper. She happened to have the same birth day and year as me. We really hit it off with a nice connection, and had agreed to meet up at a Crazy Fingers show in Delray Beach the following night.

So I was at Boston's On The Beach in Delray catching up with my friends Mike Green, Al Zilinsky, Bubba Newton, and Pete Lavezzoli from Crazy Fingers. I impressed them with stories about my experiences working with Bill Graham Presents and backstage at the Dead shows, and so on. I'm almost certain that my friends Corey Dwyer and Rich Friedman may have been sitting in with the band. I think Corey might have been playing keys with them.

But more to the point was meeting up with Sunshine again. She had returned from Ohio not too long after the Buckeye Lake show. Her friendship with Springwater had deteriorated and so there wasn't much she could update me on. Sunshine did however jump right back into work with the Palm Beach County Coalition for World Peace, the group that she, Springwater, and I had started together. She also formed a southern chapter of *New World Rising,* which had originated with Grateful Fred's Rhode Island hippie movement. One of her new friends in the group was a shy girl who went by the nickname Blossom. I was expecting to meet up with Tiffany but she was a no show and so I ended up hanging out on the beach with Blossom. She had heard a thing or two about me from Sunshine and she was well aware of stories about Springwater too. In fact, I remember her being quite inquisitive about Springwater. Or maybe it was me that couldn't get Springwater out of my head; I really don't know anymore how I was thinking about it then. Considering the way things panned out, I'm sure that Springwater was heavy on my mind.

A sucker for a hot dame in a sundress, I hooked up with Blossom, but not on that night. We met up on another night at another Crazy Fingers show. I'm pretty certain that it was in Boynton Beach at the Phoenix Bar. Actually I think the band we saw might have been a side project with Al, Corey, and Rich, who eventually merged into Crazy Fingers after Mike Green left the band. Blossom showed up looking extremely sexy and all interested in getting together. So, we went to the beach, and one thing led to another; it turned out to be her birthday, and we had a lot of intense fun. And, once again, I tangled up my heart with another.

On one of my last night's in town, Rob Pena, Sunshine, Blossom, and I and a few other friends all went to the Art Bar in West Palm Beach for yet another Crazy Fingers show. I remember the band ripping into an excellent "Morning Dew" in my honor. And that's when Tiffany showed up, wanting to hang out with me, but noticed I was with Blossom. It was a little awkward at first, with both girls being all "Who's that girl?" and drama shit. We narrowly averted a catfight in the parking lot after the show, and Rob almost ended up in a scuffle with some drunken dude. It was a strange evening.

My last night with Blossom was really intense; it seemed like a serious relationship might actually evolve. She seemed like a pretty serious girl, who was quite interested in what was going on inside of me.

Rob picked me up from her place early in the morning and drove me to the Miami airport for my flight back to San Francisco. We were having a philosophical discussion like we always did when suddenly out of nowhere we witnessed a giant, flaming orb rapidly descend from the sky, suddenly stop, then shoot off at a forty-five degree angle at an unbelievable rate of speed back up through the clouds into oblivion. We were driving south down Interstate 95 and Rob almost wrecked the car. It was so cool to actually see this phenomenon, whatever it was, with someone I had considered my best friend for many years. And, *no*, we were not high!

CHAPTER 27

For Auld Acquaintance

I t was an unbelievable year for me, 1991. I witnessed many strange things in the sky and took part in several bizarre rituals, initiations, and lucid spiritual encounters. I shared wonderful moments with many fine companions and ended up landing a dream job close to my favorite band. I was only twenty years old.

I returned from Florida just in time for the Bill Graham Presents staff Christmas party, held at San Francisco's Warfield Theater. What a wild time that turned out to be. Of course, it was a little somber since it was the first one held without our leader, Bill Graham. I still didn't quite know all the office people yet, but I had a great time and listened to everyone tell wonderful stories of Bill. There were so many joints smoked and lots of liquor passed around. There was also this legendary and dangerous batch of psychedelic cookies present. No one could eat a whole one, and just a tiny piece put me out of my misery. Whenever anyone spoke of the party in the weeks following, all they could remember was "the cookie."

Back in Oakland it was time for another run of Grateful Dead shows, this time for New Year's Eve. Since the mid-seventies, Bill Graham took major pride in presenting the Dead on New Year's Eve. Each year, an elaborate stunt of some sort would happen for the midnight countdown and Bill would be the centerpiece, like dressing up as father time and hovering over the stage in a spaceship, or a giant model of the Golden Gate Bridge, or riding over the crowd on a massive joint. It was always a huge spectacle. This would be the first New Year's show without Bill, and the band announced that this would be their final New Year's Eve run, ever.

In the backstage catering area, my co-worker John Bajor pulled me to the side with a serious look on his face. "Dewey, man, do you realize what we're doing here?"

"Yeah, I think so." I was trying to keep it together because we had both dropped acid. "Phil's room needs a light bulb, and Hornsby wants the basketball net setup. Right?"

"No, man, not that. I mean, we're working for the Grateful Dead, man."

"Well, actually, we're working for Bill, you know? It's just—"

"Seriously, who is standing behind me right now?"

I peered over his shoulder and noticed Jerry standing about ten feet away, eating a hot dog. "Well, that would be Mr. Garcia over there, Captain Trips, yeah, he's eating a fucking hot dog, dude." We laughed.

"We're going to look back on this one day, man, and realize how lucky we were to be doing this. There are people who would kill to have our jobs, man," he said.

In that moment my mind focused and locked into the trip he was laying out there. It was heavy indeed. My concentration was broken as I noticed Bruce Hornsby walking toward me. At the same moment, my radio squawked. "Dewey, did you get that basketball net set up yet?"

"I'm on that right now," I replied and gave Bruce a reassuring nod. I turned back to John: "You got Phil's light bulb, bro?"

"Yeah, man. Phil's light bulb. Got it." He walked off in that direction, smiling.

The ambiance gig was, indeed, a cool and unique job—especially setting up all those dressing rooms. In addition to moving lots of furniture around, we also did a lot of backstage decorating. At this point, Jerry's room was the one I mostly took care of. I even kept the Oriental rug for his dressing room in my personal possession at Paradigm. And there were other perks: nitrous oxide tanks, confiscated from the parking lots, often ended up in the dressing rooms—and on occasion found their way back to Paradigm. My friend Kelly's security position was Jerry's dressing room door. I would often stop by and talk to her and

Jerry. Once, Jerry told me that he would leave a gift for me in the room after the show. I was almost always the first one in after the band left. That night, I discovered a massive joint of serious kind bud had been left in the ashtray for me. There was one toke missing. After that, Jerry almost always left a joint behind for me.

On New Year's Eve, the final night of the run, a couple of visitors from Arizona showed up for me. It was Jersey girls Zoey and her sister Ashley, who both had recently relocated to Scottsdale. The show was fantastic as usual, and the load-out a little twisted, because a few of us on the crew had dosed pretty heavily. I gave the girls the keys to my studio, and they were waiting for me there when I finished. Zoey and I didn't waste any time, and got right down to kinky business on my studio couch, while her sister got herself off a few feet away, on the floor.

I believe I turned to so many girls that year to mask my pain over the incident at Buckeye Lake, scared to death of what Springwater's answer might have actually been. I just couldn't take her possible rejection, and I obviously wasn't ready to be as serious as I thought I wanted to be. Admittedly, I had some growing to do. I took her disappearance at the show as a rejection, and, as a result, my life was altered drastically. It was like running away from the carnival that I originally ran away to, only to keep running and join the bigger circus. Part of me was running from my own fear, but I was also running to something, something more tangible. I initially thought it had to do with Springwater, but all the confusion, mixed signals, and missed connections pushed me to keep moving down the road. No matter how much I missed her, life made much more sense for me in Oakland, with all the new opportunities that had opened up.

CHAPTER 28

The Lion's Den

One night, inside the Coliseum for one of the usual Grateful Dead runs, yet another profound experience came to me, while tripping hard on acid, of course. I was walking along the concourse and began to hear random words from people talking as I walked by them. No one was speaking directly to me; they were speaking to their friends. Their fragmented words began to form sentences that seemed to be speaking directly to me. They were arriving to my ears in bubbles as I passed through the crowd. From one person...

"The magic is—"

...and another...

"—no longer—"

...and then:

"a mystery"

"be careful"

"he"

"is"

"close to you"

"he's a"

"cop"

"i wouldn't trust"

"him"

"get out"

This really freaked me out; I struggled to realize these were not my own thoughts, but actual random words from strangers.

Suddenly, I bumped right into a new friend, Minglewood, and the bubbles stopped. I just stared right at him, quickly losing my mind.

"Hey Dew, you alright man?"

"No, I ... I ... I gotta go, man," I responded with the best tripping-my-face-off composure I could muster, then headed over to the exit and out the Coliseum doors. I didn't look back. I floated my way down the railroad tracks toward Paradigm. The Coliseum itself became a bubble that dissolved behind me, along with all the thoughts floating out of my head. I could hear the music quietly dissolving behind me. It was a good thing I didn't have to work a load-out that night; my headspace was a mess.

The Grateful Dead scene had transformed for me. I used to absorb the magic around me while the whole process remained a mystery. But things had changed drastically. I was now working behind the scenes and becoming a responsible part of creating that magic. The veil had been lifted, and I knew what was going on behind it. The mystery was eroding. But, I also felt more purpose to my life. The Dead had been a mechanism for me to easily follow my bliss. I had become a part of that mechanism in an amazingly short period of time. My interest in continuing to publish *Inspiration* had faded. I had become too distracted and overwhelmed.

As for Minglewood, he worked for the band, but in what capacity I did not know. I was never clear what his official title was, but he always had unrestricted access. He was introduced to me backstage by Cosmic Charlie, who had also introduced me to Bear (the great Owsley Stanley). I was told that Minglewood was an important person who could "fix" situations and protect certain people. In fact, it was he who had taken care of that bad acid deal with Fast Eddie, and I was eventually reimbursed with a larger quantity of decent product. I asked Calico about Charlie's and Minglewood's credentials. If there was anyone I could trust, it was definitely Calico—she was old school Grateful Dead/Hog Farm family and carried around with her an infinite positive vibration. She warned me that I should stay away from those characters, but refused to go into details. Eventually, an even more revealing interaction with Minglewood gave me more insight into his role with the band.

Meanwhile, back at the Paradigm, I had been jamming regularly in the studios with guitarist Gordon Frasier, who also played in the mildly popular punk band MDC, as well as vocalist and drummer Mark Crowl, and bassist John Foote. I switched between acoustic guitar and Hammond B-3 organ. We called the project Mulligan Stew. We played a few shows at the Paradigm, in Berkeley somewhere, and I'm pretty sure we did a show or two around San Francisco at some point.

At BGP, I was as busy as ever working all kinds of shows from the Pixies to the Cult, Lenny Kravitz, Dire Straits, and Souxsie and the Banshees. I helped out with Seva's Blues For Blindness benefit at the Berkeley Community Center, and got to work with John Lee Hooker and Hot Tuna. Backstage, Wavy Gravy and I watched Jorma Kaukanan, Jack Cassidy, Norton Buffalo, and John Lee Hooker do an impromptu dressing room jam that gave me chills. One day, while doing a spring-cleaning of the BGP warehouse, the set designer, Eleanore, asked us to throw out this giant old scrim. When we got our hands on it, we unfolded a giant painting of Stonehenge. Eleanore said it was the stage backdrop for the last American Led Zeppelin show from Oakland Stadium in 1977. She let me keep it, and I displayed it inside one of the Paradigm warehouses.

For the Mardi Gras 1992 run of Dead shows at the Coliseum, we set up floats for a parade that marched through the crowd while the Dead jammed on the opening rhythms of "Aiko Aiko." Jeff Bundy and I were the lead carriers of the jester float. We were also tossing out little rubber flying eyeballs into the crowd with our free hands. Just as we neared the front of the stage area, I tossed one over my head toward the stage as Bob and Jerry approached their microphones. Bundy and I observed the eyeball flying straight at Weir. They were just about to open with the first, "Hey, now!" when suddenly the flying eyeball pelted Bob smack in the forehead midway through. "Hey—" was all he got out. Jerry cracked up and Bob stepped away from his microphone and waited for the next measure to come around. Oops! Bundy and I laughed so hard we almost dropped the float. The mandolin-playing jester and sexy maiden we were carrying on the float both shot us a dirty look; yet another tragedy narrowly averted.

CHAPTER 29

Rave On

I n 1992, I began hanging out in the emerging underground San Francisco rave scene. I hit raves all over the Bay area with two dynamite, stunning French models—Coralie, who went by "Coco," and Marie, a photographer. I developed a serious crush on Marie, but you couldn't really blame me: we were high on ecstasy most of the time. Through the rave scene, I befriended DJ Noah Massey, who then moved into a studio at the Paradigm. Before long, he began planning a series of massive raves.

The Woopy Ball was his brainchild, put together with the help of everyone at the Paradigm. Henry Sullivan managed all the security details. The five or so acres of Paradigm were transformed into a miniature Disneyland of techno-beats-day-glo-lollypop-Dr. Suess madness. There were DJs spinning, multiple sound systems, and crazy lighting setups in an ever-imaginable corner, rafter and den of the labyrinth warehouse grounds of the Paradigm. We borrowed several props from the BGP warehouse and a couple of my friends from the ambiance crew even lent a hand in the production setup. There were a few hiccups, but overall the turnout was a massive success with thousands in attendance. The phenomenon of the rave scene was still in its infancy in March of 1992, having arrived in American cities only a few years earlier from England. The Woopy Ball was one of the largest raves in the Bay area up to that point. In a way, what we were a part of was comparable to many of the counter-culture events of the sixties, like the Acid Tests and the Summer of Love. There was a spiritual element, sometimes tied in with political messages, but fundamentally the scene was driven by the passion of public assembly, free expression, and the love of music (and good quality MDMA, too). Clearly the idealism of the sixties was still alive and well and not just in the Grateful Dead subculture—but also in the rave scene.

Besides hanging with Coco and Marie, I was also going to raves with this girl, Nicole, who was dating DJ Noah. One of the coolest parties we attended was at the beach near Half Moon Bay, which had been the site of many legendary raves. There was one very scary and intense experience in Oakland when Nicole and I mistakenly walked in the wrong direction from the BART station in search of a rave and ended up running for our lives from a street gang. Luckily, we flagged down a taxi and escaped just in the nick of time.

It was a very busy spring for me. Besides jamming in a band, attending raves, and continuing my backstage work at BGP, I also began volunteering my time at the International Indian Treaty Council, which I heard about from their show on KPFA, the public radio station out of Berkeley. The Treaty Council worked for the rights of indigenous people around the world, focusing a lot on Native American issues. I walked into their San Francisco office one day and met their director Tony Gonzales and just said, "I'd like to volunteer a couple afternoons a week." Even considering all the work I was doing with major stars at the time, my work at the Treaty Council office was the most rewarding and humbling of anything I have ever done. We put on sunrise ceremonies at Alcatraz Island, conferences with Nobel laureate and Treaty Council board member Rigoberta Menchú, and performed lots of volunteer services in the local community. I learned invaluable lessons about the struggles of indigenous peoples and I also learned quite a bit about humility. Mostly, though, I helped out Norma Scheurkogel, who became a dear friend and inspiration to me. When Norma was young, she had cancer and complications from surgery left her in a wheelchair for life. She had a very kind, strong, and determined spirit. She taught me so much from just being in her presence. Norma had an infectious smile and was also a poet and percussion player. The light that she emitted in this world was a lot of fun to be around.

Although Oakland in and of itself was a bit of a negative wasteland, and parts very dangerous and disturbing, I felt at home in the Bay area. It was a quick and easy jaunt over to San Francisco where I spent most of my time anyway. The weather was always unpredictable and there's nothing like a refreshing, sweet San Francisco rain, especially when the fog unexpectedly creeps over a hill in front of you and you've got Van Morrison's "Saint Dominic's Preview" stuck in your head.

Around this time, I was receiving some very intense love letters from Blossom, who was back in Florida. She mentioned wanting to move out to Oakland, get married, and have children with me. She was moving way too fast as I was no longer in the same heart space for her. I gently eased her away and advised that she get a puppy, which she did, and named her Cherise.

Zoey also sent me letters and talked about getting together at the upcoming spring Dead shows in Vegas. I bumped into Summer on Haight Street and she looked a total mess. She wanted me to get high with her, but I sensed it was the needle that she was referring to. I felt there was a dark sadness surrounding her, and our encounter bothered me so much that I continued to return to the Haight many times searching for her with the hope that I could somehow help get her off the streets; sadly, she had disappeared.

CHAPTER 30

A Gold Ring And A VCR

At the end of April, 1992, the Jerry Garcia Band was putting on a series of shows at San Francisco's Warfield Theater while Bama Boys J.B. and Kilgore happened to be paying me a visit. We parked Calvin a few blocks away from the Warfield, in front of the Civic Auditorium, and walked around the area a little. We noticed a couple of punk rockers putting up a flyer on a light pole. The flyer read:

FUCK THE POLICE:
Rally against the Rodney King verdict, 4pm today

Within minutes, the crowds marched in from different directions, and began meeting up at California and Van Ness near the steps of the City Hall. We stood near the rear of the crowd, listening to folks air their grievances when some disgruntled kid next to us began shouting that we needed to get the crowd on the move and "do something." People started turning around and listening to this kid. I remember giving him a high five just as he managed to get the crowd of thousands to start marching again. Kilgore's recollection is that I encouraged him quite a bit and gave the kid that extra bit of confidence he needed to speak out in the first place. I'm not going to admit to that because what followed became a very ugly incident that I'd rather not assume any responsibility for.

I looked over at the kid who had gotten everyone going and

watched him pick up a rock with the very hand I had just high-fived and then I witnessed that rock soar through the air and smash a window in San Francisco's Federal Building. At the very moment the glass shattered, the crowd of thousands all gasped in unison. And then it was on. A full-blown riot started as we all approached the police line. All the violent punks that were there suddenly jumped out in front and engaged the cops, throwing rocks and bottles at them. We had no choice but to move forward with the crowd. The cops backed away and let the mob have it. To our left, cars were being smashed and flipped over. To the right, a carnival was setup in the square, but no one messed with the carnies as they created a barrier between the mob and the square, standing firmly with lead pipes and wrenches in their hands. It was absolutely surreal. J.B. and Kilgore knew for certain that their little red Ford Escort, Calvin, parked nearby, was probably going to get a good beating.

Helicopters buzzed above us. The cops scrambled around in the distance but the streets belonged to the people. The crowd was made up of many colors, as people from all ages and walks of life marched, some hand in hand. You could clearly see the tears on many faces as they felt this was a necessary but difficult action to do. The mob was moving straight ahead toward Market Street and the Warfield Theater, where the hippies were all camped out looking for miracle tickets, swinging doses, and bartering kind grilled cheeses and veggie burritos.

I knew this was going to be a mess and thought immediately of how I could get over to the theater to warn Henry, who was there running security for the Jerry Garcia show. Somehow I managed to get out of the mob and head up hill two blocks into normal everyday San Francisco, where there was no sign of civil unrest. It did not seem real to me. Suddenly the whole riot was gone. But I knew the peace wouldn't last long, so I scrambled down a few back streets and over to the back door of the Warfield and met up with Henry. I told him about the riot and the chaos that was about to go down. Just then, it hit Market Street and seemed to be spreading like wildfire. The peaceful gathering of hippies in front of the theater was ambushed by looters, as window after window on Market Street met their shattered fates.

Jerry Garcia stepped out the back door and onto the sidewalk and stood next to Henry and me.

"Wow, what's going on over there?" he asked curiously, as we all stared down at the mess that was Market Street. A guy pushed a shopping cart by with pieces of a drum set and a TV on top of it.

Jerry chuckled, "Someone get me a gold ring and a VCR!"

Two street guys stumbled by, drinking forties out of brown paper bags, and one of them recognized Jerry.

"Jehhreee Gahceeeuh! Shit! How ya' doin', Jehhree? Haven't seen you in looong time."

"Hey, man, yeah," Jerry replied, like they were old friends. "I've been good. Playin' here at the Warfield tonight." They slapped hands.

"You take care now, Jehhree, and be careful. It's crazy out here tonight!" The two men walked on, although the man's friend looked confused.

"Who was that?" he said.

"That was Jehhree Gahceeuh! You don't know?"

"Never heard of the man."

"He used to play da park a looong time ago." The two drunks stumbled on toward the chaos on Market Street.

Jerry's guitar tech, Steve Parish, opened the back door of the theater to let him know that they were ready for him. They disappeared back into the venue.

A few minutes later, swarms of San Francisco's Finest, all riot-geared up, marched by like Storm Troopers in a Star Wars movie. Two blocks away, my friend Celeste was loading her wares into her van and witnessed someone being shot in the head at point blank range—apparently a random act of street justice. She didn't know why it happened; it just seemed part of the melee swirling everywhere. The helicopters continued to buzz overhead. Trails of tear gas flowed in from around corners. There were homeless people scattered about, wearing brand new shirts and shiny Reebok tennis shoes. The place was a war zone.

After the show, I met back up with J.B. and Kilgore and we compared stories as we walked back to the car. All the parked cars had been smashed in, some set on fire, a few were still smoldering.

Yet, there sat Calvin, barely touched, while the cars on either side were hardly recognizable. We drove our lucky red chariot back over the Bay Bridge into Oakland. We could see large fires all over the cities; it was an unbelievable time, like we were in a movie. There was a sobering feeling that life would never be the same again, that we had entered into an age of urban warfare. It was truly frightening.

CHAPTER 31

Nothin' Shakin'
On Shakedown Street

A lthough it didn't seem like it was going to happen, life did, somewhat, return to normal soon after the riots. I was still living in
the Paradigm, working concerts for BGP and hanging with Henry's
crew of girls: Katie Mae, Trina, Jennifer (Jendog), Michelle, and Kelly.
I worked a small run of shows for Bob Dylan and then we all went to
Vegas to work the Dead's run there at the end of May.

This time, Vegas was quite a different experience. For one thing,
I was being paid to be there and there were no hassles. We also hung
out with the members of Blues Traveler, who I had befriended back in
Telluride. They were playing a show at Bally's Casino with Col. Bruce
Hampton's Aquarium Rescue Unit. Gina Thompson, who worked for
the band, offered me a gig working on their upcoming summer tour,
which was an opportunity I promised to follow up on. I cannot say
enough great things about how kind Gina has been to me over the
years. I've always appreciated her friendship and her level of profes-
sionalism, passion and commitment. She is simply one of the most
wonderful persons I've ever met in the music business.

At the Dead shows I was hanging out with Amy Fogerty, who I
had made a nice connection with. She claimed to be closely related to
CCR's John Fogerty but I wasn't all that convinced. Then I bumped
into Zoey, who was up from Arizona, and I spent a little time with her,
too. Amy spotted me dancing with Zoey and that didn't go over well;
I tried to explain it, but Amy wasn't having it, and so she ditched me.

At the old Sand's Casino one night, Jendog and I were wallowing in our lovesick, lonely woes. We got so drunk that we joked about getting married to each other by an Elvis impersonator. We stumbled off in that direction to find a chapel, but Henry showed up and distracted us with something that seemed important enough at the time for us to forget all about it.

Henry managed to take in another stray. She was a runaway girl from New York who had been living off her parents' credit cards. Her name was Karen, but we called her "Krazy-with-a-K" because, as we found out later, she was bipolar and off her medication. She ended up back at the Paradigm in Oakland, of course. One weekend she took me to Monterey to look for a sister of hers, and we had the time of our lives; but, she was definitely not all there. We found her sister, and then they got into a huge blowout. I think it was mostly due to the fact that she was on the run from some situations back home and without her Lithium. After a few weeks, Henry finally located her parents back east and got her medication sent out; and arranged for her to go back home.

Just before the whole Vegas trip, there was an incident after a Shoreline Dead show. We had been invited by Bob Weir to attend a party in Woodside. Our friend Robbie was driving his old copper-toned Oldsmobile, Trina was in the passenger seat, and I was in the back with Jendog. We backed the car into a parking spot next door in a church parking lot, while listening to a tape of that night's show. There was an incredible "Shakedown Street" played that we were reminiscing over. Robbie went to the trunk for a bag of speed. He got back in the car and handed the baggy to Trina for a blast. She nodded her head down toward the key to get her fix, but just then I noticed someone walking out of the dark toward the rear of the car.

I quickly and abruptly announced in a hush tone, "Put the shit away!"

The flashlight shined in immediately on Trina's face through the passenger side window. We were all frozen with fear. Trina rolled down her window and a man dressed in black with a shiny badge demanded identification. We quickly handed them over and then he walked around the front of the car to the driver's side window.

Robbie whispered to us that he had a warrant out on him and he needed someone to take the rap for him. There was a knot tightening in my stomach.

The rent-a-cop, as he turned out to be, waved his hand in the air and four headlights suddenly turned on followed by reds and blues as two very real cop cars screeched across the road to block us in. We all silenced ourselves as they emptied us out of the car and lined us up for interrogations. It was strange that it went down that way, like they were waiting for us. They must've been staking out Bob Weir's party next door.

An old, fat cop and a Barney Fife type, smart-ass rookie sent the rent-a-cop on his way and began harassing us. They found the speed stashed in Trina's bag. They found some speed on Robbie. They opened the truck of the car and found meth divided up into little baggies, a couple ounces of weed in a briefcase along with a scale, a police scanner, wads of cash, and an accounting notebook containing some incriminating evidence with the names of some associates in the Hell's Angels. The look on Robbie's face was pure horror and I knew it wasn't the cops that he was afraid of.

Trina and Robbie were cuffed and put in the back of separate squad cars. The pressure was turned to Jendog and I. We had no drugs or paraphernalia on our bodies. Barney Fife pulled my fanny pack out of the car. Yes, I used to wear a fanny pack back then; had I overlooked mentioning that up to this point?

"Is this yours?" he asked.

"Yes."

"Mind if I search it?"

"You're going to anyway," I responded.

He dumped the contents on the hood of the car. There was a bag of mushrooms that fell out.

"Hmmm, what's this here?"

"I don't know. It's not mine," I told him.

He got angry and started picking up various items one by one.

"Is this your wallet?"

"Yes."

"Is this your hair brush?"

"Yes."

"Is this your baggie?"

"No."

He jumbled around all the contents and asked again in a different order, throwing the baggie in at random, trying to trip me up.

I said yes to all the items except the baggie every time he tried the futile tactic.

He was getting very frustrated and poked his finger in my chest while shining the flashlight directly in my eyes and said, "I know you're snow-blind, you little punk and I'm going to get you!"

I politely and calmly responded: "No sir, I am not snoooow-blind. That is not my baggie; I do not know how it got in there."

"What is this anyway?" he asked. He actually could not identify that they were stems and pieces of mushroom dust, about an eighth's worth, and at one point he tried to say that it was rock cocaine.

I laughed and said, "With all due respect, that does not look like rock cocaine, Sir. I think its just dirt."

The old, fat cop couldn't identify it either and so they just put the baggie back in the fanny pack and surprisingly handed it over to me. They towed Robbie's car, hauled Trina and Robbie off to jail, and let Jendog and I walk over to the party. We quickly gulped down a few mushroom stems on the way.

Bob Weir had split the scene once the cops showed up, the party had fizzled out because everyone was so freaked about the police activity. The hosts, who were longtime Grateful Dead family members, were very kind to Jendog and I, being sympathetic to the bullshit we just went through. I shared the remaining mushroom dust with everyone and we tried to make the best of the rest of the night.

This incident had actually sparked a long and involved aftermath process that went on for some time. A Hell's Angels lawyer got immediately involved, as did one of their bullies, Pete. Pete arranged for me to visit Robbie in jail to deliver a message. I was chosen for this task since I was involved in the incident and had a clean record with no traceable ties to the motorcycle club. Robbie was surprised to see me there. I motioned a secret coded message with my fingers on the glass between us as I spoke to him on the phone.

"Do you know what this means?" I asked him.

"Yes," he replied with a somber look on his face.

"They are handling it, okay? Just do your part."

He nodded in acknowledgment, but still looked very frightened. That was all that was said and he got the message. Essentially he had no choice but to take the fall. The club involved did not mess around in these situations.

Robbie ended up doing some time and Trina's case was dismissed. Jendog was in fear of her life because of some further involvement with Pete. She eventually fled the state for a while. I stayed clear from the situation but ended up getting entangled with Pete in a personal situation about six months later.

CHAPTER 32

But Anyway

I met up with psychedelic guru Tim Leary again in July, at the Lollapalooza event that I was working at Shoreline Amphitheater. We shared a joint next to the side stage while we watched a new progressive band called Tool. Stoned out of my mind with Leary (needless to say, he had incredible pot), I was approached by a girl who was traveling with the band. She asked me if I would wrap her up in cellophane so she could go out on stage and do an interpretive dance. She then undressed and stood naked before me while I stretched plastic wrap around every inch of her exposed flesh from the neck down. And I was getting paid for that. What a horrible job, this rock and roll business!

Later that month, I followed up on the opportunity from Blues Traveler and went to work on the first ever H.O.R.D.E. Tour (Horizons Of Rock Developing Everywhere). Jam bands Widespread Panic, Phish, and the Spin Doctors were on the bill. At that time, Blues Traveler and The Spin Doctors were the big bands in the scene. Widespread Panic and Phish were not yet the mega bands that they would eventually become. It was a unique experience to be in on the ground level, working closely with these groups as they were on their way up in the emerging jam scene. The first show was in Portland, Maine at the Cumberland Civic Center. I was helping with the organization of the concourse tables for the advocacy groups, which included the International Indian Treaty Council where I had been volunteering. My Middle Earth friends, Boca Alex and Jersey Jay, were there to help out, too.

On the way to the show in Syracuse, we witnessed a van swerve off the road and crash into a ditch. It was an elderly couple and the old man who was driving had apparently fallen asleep at the wheel. We were carpooling with a couple of friends from the Rainforest Action Network, Eric and Alison. We pulled over immediately and were the first ones on the scene. It was all bloody inside the van and we all did everything we could to help. Eric was especially helpful in that situation, having some sort of EMT experience. They closed down the freeway and a helicopter landed. They flew the man out, but it didn't turn out well for him at all. We found out later that he had died from his injuries.

We all arrived a little late for the load-in at the Syracuse show. The tour buses were all behind schedule, too, because the highway had been closed. It was a very sobering day. I gave the boys from Widespread Panic a golf cart tour around the vending area and spent some nice, relaxing time with them exploring the New York State Fairgrounds.

The next stop was at the Garden State Amphitheater in New Jersey where Warren Haynes showed up and sat in with Blues Traveler. In Jones Beach, I got to introduce the band Phish in front of the crowd after presenting a live raffle drawing. Backstage, Chris Barron from the Spin Doctors and I were busted by a police officer for smoking a joint in the stairwell. He let us off with a stern warning.

Of all the people I got up to shenanigans with on that first H.O.R.D.E. tour, Blues Traveler's bassist Bobby Sheehan was the one I formed a good, lasting friendship with. There were a couple of occasions that summer, when Blues Traveler were opening for the Allman Brothers Band, that we sat together in the dressing room and jammed a few tunes together. There were also great memorable nights that we hijacked a couple of dive bars and guitarist Chan Kinchella tended bar after hours—once in New York City and another time in San Francisco at a bar on Haight Street. The San Francisco incident became truly legendary and Jendog got to impress the boys with her incredible singing, too.

After the H.O.R.D.E. tour, I was back in Oakland continuing the ambiance gigs and also my volunteering for the International Indian Treaty Council. We were preparing for a big event in October celebrating 500 years of Native American resistance. In addition to assisting Norma, I also worked with my friend Kira Tashjian on public relations.

The culmination of all the IITC's work that year was a big show in October. Originally, it was an event that Bill Graham was personally invested in; it was near and dear to him before he died. It was by pure coincidence that I had stumbled into this role working for the IITC while Bill was planning his big event with them—I had no idea about it until after I had already started volunteering with the Treaty Council. The original plans were for a huge festival-style event in the Arizona desert, but the tribes were conflicted about being represented that way. After Bill's death, it was settled as a weekend of events at Shoreline Amphitheatre and in San Francisco's Civic Center Park, the very same area of the Rodney King riot in April.

I had the honor of working closely on the production team with the charity reps for Bonnie Raitt and Jackson Browne. Carlos Santana would stop in to the Treaty Council office on a regular basis to check up on progress as we planned the all-star event.

The whole shindig was really the inspiration of Native American activist and artist Oren Lyons. It was quite an education for me, at only 21 years old, to be interacting with Lyons, Chief Bill Means, John Trudell, and Floyd "Red Crow" Westerman. What an amazing group of teachers and spiritual people.

In all, the efforts and responsibilities I had taken on outside of my BGP work had made an impression on my supervisors there. Several of them told me that they were proud of me and could see that I had a bright future in concert production. It felt nice to be recognized and encouraged.

CHAPTER 33

Pistols And Daisies

W e were putting on another epic BGP production at Oakland Stadium. This time it was for a monster metal show featuring Metallica and Guns N' Roses. Again, I was working the usual ambiance gig, setting up the backstage dressing room areas and general backstage décor. Most big promoters would not go out of their way to please the artist as much as Bill Graham Presents. I'm pretty sure BGP was the only promoter of that size that had it's own department, Ambiance, just to put in a little extra artist pampering. My job included building little mini-theater sets in the backstage environment including video game rooms, pool tables, ping-pong tables, and the occasional hot tub. A few finishing touches might include miniature concert lighting and even a sound system or two. Sometimes, of course, that job became a little extracurricular, and since I had hooked up the Metallica boys with good doses of LSD the previous year, they were asking for them again, but with the doses I had this time, I had to issue a special warning. This particular batch had a powerful punch, and I strongly advised to not mix in other drugs. It could easily magnify your experience to the power of ten. Within an hour, they returned for more, claiming that Slash wanted in, too. I obliged, but again issued the caveat.

After the show, around three in the morning, the backstage party was in full rage. I had been invited into one of the trailers to party with a few of the band members. There was no lack of hedonism in this particular room. I noticed that Slash was totally smashed out of his mind and that he had not listened to my warning. At one point, he got up and stumbled out of the trailer. Slightly concerned, I followed him; as I left the trailer I noticed one of the Metallica guys began urinating in a fish tank.

Slash stumbled off behind the trailers away from the backstage crowd toward our crew trailer. Anxiously, he began pacing back and forth and scratching his arms. I approached him to ask if he had a cigarette. Instead, he asked me for one. He was mumbling somewhat incoherently, very pale, and sweating madly. I knew that a bad situation was quickly developing. I heard Danny calling out to me from the trailer. I looked over and noticed he was signaling me with a "what the hell are you doing" look. He didn't understand the situation as I did.

Slash stopped his pacing and looked up at me; his eyes were in another universe. He appeared to be on one hell of a roller coaster ride. I shouted back to Dan to get me some water, that we needed water like "STAT, emergency here!" Slash leaned his head back while his eyes frantically rolled around his head. His body was weakening, and arms shaking, sweat everywhere. He was having trouble standing up, and I helped him onto a road case when suddenly someone official-looking appeared out of nowhere, shouting that it was time to go.

"Whoa, no, wait, hold on! He needs some water right now!" I tried to explain, but before I could get my point across, Slash was being hauled off to the back gate where a limousine had been waiting. The limo driver opened the back door and in a perfect rock star moment, Slash lost his balance and collapsed to the pavement before reaching the car.

I was only a few feet away. They picked him up and shoved him into the back of the limo and sped away.

Danny appeared with bottled water.

"What just happened?"

"It's a little complicated, but I'm not really sure."

Shaking his head back and forth, he said, "You're not supposed to talk to them you know."

"Uh-huh, yea. I know."

I walked off and rejoined the party, but was still concerned for what went down with Slash.

The next morning, as we were cleaning up the mess and beginning to disassemble our world, I heard the rumor. Henry told me that he had heard that Slash had died from an overdose last night. At first I thought he had heard about the limo incident and my involvement and perhaps he was just fucking with me.

"WHAT? DEAD? He's fucking dead? Are you sure?"

"No, he's not still dead. They rushed him to the hospital and revived him," he explained.

"You're fucking with me, aren't you?"

"Nope, that's what I heard."

I have to admit, I was having a hard time believing him at first, but I checked with other sources on site and there seemed to be some truth to the rumor.

Fast forward to 2007 when Slash released his autobiography, *Slash*. I came across it in a bookstore and decided to thumb through to see if I could find anything on the incident. Sure enough, he mentions an episode of being dead for five minutes occurring around this time, but he places the incident in New York a day or two before the Oakland show. I had never heard about this New York thing until I read it in his book. It's possible the rumor going around in Oakland that day could have been referring to something that had just happened in New York; I really do not know for certain. All I know is that the man was seriously fucked up in Oakland and I know what helped put him there.

CHAPTER 34

The Master Of Puppets

She, who shall remain nameless herein, came with me to the Paradigm after the Metallica show. She wanted my backstage laminate as a souvenir. It was negotiated that a challenging game of pool would be the deciding factor. If I won, she would come back to my room and fuck me. If she won, she would get the pass. She won the game, but still came back to my room and we fucked all night.

A week later, she needed a place to stay and since I needed someone to be with, I gave her a key. I was just trying to help her out. I had no intention of hurting her. I never lied to her and I certainly didn't want to be lied to.

One night we fucked for hours and hours, and I just could not come. She came too many times to count. She called me a god.

I wasn't that naïve to think I was the only one, after all. But she just had to go there. She looked deep in my eyes pinpointing my exact moment of vulnerability, the edge of my soul. Then she slowly said it as if it were her dying words: "I love you."

"What the fuck are you talking about?"

She didn't let up and took her stare to a new level until I was hypnotized into stupidly repeating the words back to her.

She would disappear every couple of days. I began to hear rumors. I was an emotional wreck. Who the fuck was this person that suddenly had all of this control over me? I couldn't sleep. She finally showed up and we talked it out for hours. I was "paranoid," she said.

I was "trippin'," she said. I was "too intense," she said. It was all just "crazy shit in my head," she said. She was a great convincer, one hell of a liar. I fell for it again.

A few days later, the cycle repeated itself and I lost more sleep. I packed up her things and wrote her a note. I piled up everything of hers outside my door. When she returned, I simply told her that I wasn't going to talk about it anymore. It was done.

She had nowhere else to go but to the one person I warned her to stay away from, a big, grizzly biker dude. He took her in. They fucked.

She blamed me. I was the asshole, she said. She wouldn't talk to me. I wouldn't talk to her. But she still hung around. We saw each other every day, even more than before. Nasty looks were exchanged, stone cold eyes. I wondered if she had already been fucking him or if it was the other two I had heard about. Maybe it was all three. I didn't care anymore.

A few weeks went by and then she just disappeared. He was still around and one day told me that she was with her parents back in Sacramento. A month went by and then she appeared in my dream. There was a crow and there was a child. It was disturbing.

The very next day she was back. I was just sitting in the office next to the desk when she walked in staring at me with the strangest look I had ever seen. She turned to ask for change from the woman behind the desk. I looked downward and noticed her hand patting an obviously pregnant stomach.

She looked back at me and gave me an intense look. Nothing was said between us. She walked away.

I ran into the biker. He gave me a weird look and again nothing was said.

She stuck around for a few days and then was gone again. People were talking, gossiping, and I ignored them. One day he showed up at my door. I opened it and without saying a word, the big, grizzly biker just punched me in the face. He was disappointed that I didn't immediately fall, so he punched me again, and I fell to the ground.

"What the fuck?"

She lied to him too. He believed her. She was the master of puppets. I was the asshole. I was the punk. She told him that we never even fucked. I was told not to have anything to do with her or him ever again. He threw the doctor bills at me.

"Mine!" he shouted.

CHAPTER 35

Don't You Let That
Deal Go Down

I got a call from my major LSD source who warned me that someone close to our chemist, a mutual friend's girlfriend, had been
busted, and people were afraid she might snitch. Everyone in our little
family was extra paranoid. I had a big deal of my own that needed to
go down and I was feeling a little sketchy about it. This time, it was a
large transaction with Minglewood, and we had decided to meet up at
our usual spot, the Round Table Pizza, just across from the Warfield.
There was another run of Jerry Garcia Band shows going on at the
time, so I was there a lot.

The deal had been delayed for reasons I cannot remember, so we
ended up having to make the transaction on the street in front of the
theatre. The scene was typically bustling, with the usual pre-Jerry
show crowd scene. Hippies selling their wares, burritos, crystal neck-
laces, patchouli stench, small drum circles huddled on the sidewalk.

I noticed a man on the opposite street corner with a telescopic lens
taking photographs. The lens was pointed directly at Minglewood and
me. It was the same person that I noticed Minglewood talking to just
a few minutes before I handed him the money. I went on immediate
alert.

"Who the fuck is that guy you were talking to, who is NOW across
the street taking PICTURES of us?"

He pretended not to know what I was talking about at first, but
then I squeezed it out of him.

"Yeah, don't worry about him. It's complicated," he tried to reason.

"Look man, you better tell me what the fuck is going on."

The paranoia had reached a new all-time level. He already had the money in his pocket and I had yet to receive the goods. I was certain that all the hippies around me were going to suddenly pull out weapons and shout for me to get on the ground. EVERYONE looked like a cop to me. I felt like I was going to vomit.

He quickly shoved the vials in my jacket pocket as he looked over his shoulder toward the photographer.

"You should know by now."

"What the fuck does that mean?"

"They've had your number for a long time bro. They know all about you."

"They? Them? Or you? Are you them? Are you a part of them? Is this a fucking set up?"

"No man, calm down. I've been protecting you." There was a long silence. "You've got nothing to worry about."

My thoughts were a million miles an hour.

"Fuck you, dude!"

And with that I turned in absolute fear, sweating, heart thumping, and stomach knotting up, and quickly dashed away from Minglewood through the crowd in the opposite direction of the theatre. Everything was in slow motion and tunnel vision as I nervously bumped into one hippie after another. I had to get the fuck out of there as soon as possible.

I broke from the crowd, expecting that tug on my shoulder any second. Any moment, they were going to take me down; I could feel it. I was about to go down hard. Maybe their unmarked cars on Market Street would screech over and they would jump out and tackle me. I kept looking back and barely noticed the blurry vision stumbling in front of me. A drunk, fat Mexican man was staggering toward me, but I wasn't concerned with him. I was so nervous about the possible take down behind me. Suddenly and without warning... BAM! Mother Fucking Shit!

A massive and shocking physical punch to my gut; I was out of air, stumbling back, gasping for breath, dizzy. Looking up, I realized that the fat, drunk Mexican just randomly sucker punched me.

"Better wake up kid!" he slurred at me and stumbled backwards with his fists clinched. He was looking for a rumble.

I took a few steps to the side, holding my gut, but kept my progress moving away from him and the scene I just left behind. There was enough acid in my jacket to put me away for many lifetimes. I had to keep moving. I crossed right into traffic, caught my breath, and dashed across the busy Market Street and disappeared into the city.

In the days following, I mailed off my score. Minglewood paged me a few times, but I ignored his attempts to contact me. I slipped into months of paranoia over the incident. I should've followed Calico's advice when she advised that I keep away from him.

CHAPTER 36

The Brokedown Palace

S hit was really starting to hit the fan at the Paradigm. The bikers and their meth operations had really taken over. The criminal element was becoming too much.

One night around four or five in the morning, I awoke to the sounds of someone creeping into my studio room. It was a burglar—knit cap, knap sack and all, if you can believe it. I rubbed my blurry eyes, thinking it was a bad dream, but then realized I was staring right at a genuine thief.

"Hey! Who the fuck are you?" I startled him.

"Oh, good morning, my apologies, Sir. I didn't mean to wake you. I'll leave," he intoned, as politely as if he were my butler.

This took a few seconds to register in my brain as the man tiptoed back out of my room and closed the door behind him. I got up, now really pissed off, opened the door up and noticed him in the main area of the warehouse, unplugging my microwave.

"Hey! What the fuck are you doing man? That's my microwave!"

"Oh, this is yours? I'm so sorry about that. I'll leave it," he whispered.

"How the fuck did you get in here?"

"Oh, the keys were left in the door, Sir."

I then flashed back to my stumbling in drunk a few hours earlier. I must've left my keys in the door.

"I'm calling the police!"

"You don't have to do that, Sir. I'm leaving now." And with that he exited out the warehouse.

I opened the door and noticed him looking into people's cars. So I shouted as loudly as I could, "Someone call the cops. We've got a thief here!"

He stopped what he was doing and went back to a little rusted Toyota that was packed full of merchandise.

"Do you know anyone who wants to buy a car battery, Sir?"

"Are you fucking kidding me? You're about to get beaten to death, dude!"

"My bad, Sir. I'll be leaving now." He hopped into his little Toyota and sped off. Just about then, a few of the bikers and musicians had come out of their rooms and warehouses to see what the chaos was all about. I got the license plate number and we gave it to the police who later informed us that the car had been reported stolen.

"He was very polite," I told the officers.

I kept having recurring dreams about Springwater. I had the feeling she was in some sort of struggle. I made a few phone calls, trying to locate her, but, again I got nowhere. I wrote to Sunshine in Florida to see if she had heard anything, but got no reply.

My dear friend and Buddhist teacher, DeWood, helped me through this time immensely. Meanwhile, my only means of escape from the Paradigm was Boca Alex, who had now been living in San Francisco.

Alex was living with his college buddy from Pittsburgh, "Toad." Toad's girlfriend Kat was hooking up with Alex whenever Toad was passed out drunk, which was often. They were all living in this tiny one-room studio apartment on lower Haight Street. It was my only place of refuge at the time, and so the four of us proceeded to live in this one-room nightmare, getting totally smashed drunk each and every night.

They played this college drinking game called Volumetrics, which was a fraternity version of Yatzee. It never ended well. The idiocy escalated with each round of the game. Alex's attitude always quickly became "everyone just fuck off and leave me alone." Toad's attitude was depression and blame toward Alex over the situation with Kat. Regardless of how they tried to work through it, Toad was always the first one to pass out.

It was a tense situation—four somewhat miserable people living in one tiny room. Things got especially out of control and reached a boiling point one night. Alex was letting off some really bad flatulence and wouldn't let us open the window for air. In an effort to get the window open while Alex was holding it shut, my hand accidentally broke the glass, shattering the window. The pieces fell onto the ground, three stories below. There was dead silence for a moment until Alex and I burst into laughter; but Toad was pissed. Alex and I regained our composure and got all serious and apologetic. My hand was slightly cut, but not that bad.

Toad took everything to a new level. He was in a place far beyond drunken stupidity. He was ranting loudly about how Alex stole Kat from him. Shouting at everyone, he went to the kitchen for a knife. He was swaying back and forth, barely standing, but firmly gripping a large kitchen knife in his hand, stabbing it into the air in front of him. And then he held it to Kat's throat, and that's when things got really ugly.

Alex ran into the kitchen, Kat broke free and ran out. Toad quickly dropped the knife, and Alex punched him square in the face repeatedly until Toad fell back into the fridge and slid, unconscious, to the floor.

He came to and struggled desperately to get back at Alex, throwing his arms around wildly about, hitting nothing but air. The kitchen table was tossed over; pots and pans were knocked off the stove. Once decorative hanging potted plants now floated on the floor in fryer grease. All Toad could do effectively was to shout at Alex and Kat to "GET THE HELL OUT!" Alex threw in a couple more punches and then, just like that, he and Kat split the scene. Toad gathered up a few of their belongings and tossed them out the door and then he fell over in the hallway and passed out in his own blood.

Alex and Kat slept in his car for a couple of weeks until they found an apartment of their own. Toad moved out and I found myself the only one left living there, but only for a few days.

When it was time to go (before I had to pay rent or something), I put my belongings in a shopping cart, huffed them up a couple of blocks on Haight Street and made a right turn on Steiner. The hill was steeper and longer on Steiner, but once I passed Fell and Hayes, it was an easy decent along the historic painted ladies next to Alamo Square. My new destination was a classic Victorian around the corner on Fulton Street. My friend from the Treaty Council, Kira, was living there with a couple of friends, and they all agreed that I could stay there for a little while until I figured my situation out.

The vibe at Kira's was much more peaceful. Ray was the owner of the house but was hardly ever around. I think he spent most of his time in Sacramento, but he would show up on the weekends. Kira had the center room, next to the living room area. She didn't seem to spend much time there either. She spent a lot of time with her famous Hollywood friends, who would come up from Los Angeles on the weekends. She had great connections with some pretty big stars since she worked mostly in public realtions. Kira was a very spiritual person with a beautiful shining soul. We had become dear friends while working together at the Treaty Council. I let her read some of my writing and journal entries for creative feedback.

"More sex!" she said. "I want you to write more intimately about your sexual encounters."

Living in the back of the flat was an attractive brunette beauty, Shannon. I shared a room with Kira, but dreamt about Shannon, who was a seductive delight. She played a slick, cherry-stained Gibson SG guitar, which turned me on further. She had a perfectly thin sensuous body; just the perfect, perky breasts and a few well-placed skin illustrations. Her naked walkabouts in the flat continuously teased me. One afternoon, she lured me into showering with her, and almost into a threesome with her boyfriend. She was into it, he was into it, but I was not, mostly because I was aware that he had a taste for heroin.

She had a dog, a boxer, who I would walk around the neighborhood and chill out with in San Francisco's most celebrated little park, Alamo Square, which was literally right across the street. I meditated there daily. This was a perfect time and space for me to get my head together, to figure out my next move.

One particular night, Shannon came home around 3 a.m., all drunk and disoriented. Her junkie boyfriend was with her. He walked straight into their room without saying a word to me. They had been fighting. She stood there at the entrance to the hallway, swaying back and forth smiling at me and whispering my name in a sexy tone.

"Deweeeey... Deweeeey... I want you to *dew* me, Dewey..."
I was lying on the couch watching TV, trying to not get involved. She stumbled across the room and plopped herself on the couch, and leaned her head on on my chest.

"I wish he wasn't here right now," she slurred. She leaned in to my lips and whispered, "I hate him. I want you to fuck me right now. Right here on this couch."

She was so cute and sexy, but I had to resist. She was too drunk, he was in the next room; it wasn't right.

"Fuck it. I'm going to be a lesbian now. I hate men!" she proclaimed as she stumbled off to her room.

She drove one of those cute little convertible MG's that daddy had bought for her. She had no job. She was just living off her family's money. On a drive around the city one day, top down, sun shining, Wayfarers on, she confessed to me her plan to leave the boyfriend.

I was taken in again by her irresistible smile. The view from Twin Peaks was stunning. San Francisco had never looked so beautiful and promising. Her eyes were so flirtatious.

I was almost convinced to go along with the plan, but my meditations in the park had given me a clear head and confidence in my solitude. I needed to venture forward with no complications. I already had enough of my own troubles lingering behind me. Yes, I was lonely, and I could've really gotten caught up in that girl. She knew it and I knew it, but it was all too risky.

The situation was not all that dramatic; it was actually quite sweet and mellow. There was a slight tension in the house, as the weeks turned into a month and I was pressed to make a decision.

The most memorable moment of this time at Kira's happened one day when I walked down to the corner store on Fillmore and Fulton. I had just finished watching the movie

Regarding Henry. In the movie, Harrison Ford's character Henry is shot in the head when he, by unfortunate chance, walked in on a convenience store robbery. It's a very powerful and emotional film and it was still fresh in my mind when I entered the little corner store. As I stepped up inside, my senses went into overload as I noticed a large man holding a handgun and shouting at the Asian storeowner.

"Just give me the fucking money, mothah fuckah!"

"Fuck youuuuuu, niggah! You no rob my store no more! I ti-ed o' dis shit!"

Oh, it was going down, man. After having just sat through an emotional movie about this very scenario, I quickly saw my life before my eyes. It was all in slow motion. The man holding the pistol turned his head and looked right down at me. The gun didn't move. It was still pointed at the clerk. He nodded upwards at me with that "just get the fuck outta here" look. I closed my eyes, nodded my head downwards, spun my feet around, and walked right back out the door. My heart was thumping in my chest. I quickly turned the corner and headed up the hill on Fulton, never once looking back.

I could hear the shouting continue. I did not hear any gunshots, so that was good. I kept walking all the way to the other nearest corner store at Divisadero. Ironically, there was a police officer inside that store. I calmly mentioned to him that there was a robbery taking place, or had just taken place three blocks east. He ran out and hopped into his squad car, screeching off toward Fillmore. Luckily, that was the end of my involvement. But the whole thing really rattled me.

I realized I had to leave that city. I needed a break.

CHAPTER 37

Deal Reprise

T aking a break from BGP/Grateful Dead gigs for a while, I put some belongings in a storage locker and bought a one-way Greyhound bus ticket to Colorado. Waiting for the bus, I had the feeling everything was going to be all right. I boarded the bus and took a seat. Then, suddenly, all my fears became present again. A rush of paranoia hit me as I noticed Minglewood boarding the bus. He came down the aisle and sat right next to me.

"Fancy seeing you here bro," he said.

"Yeah, isn't this weird?" I was tense as ever.

"Where you heading?"

"I'm going to Colorado for a while, to see some friends. And you?"

"Tahoe. A sister."

I just nodded in agreement. All I could think about was whether or not cops were going to storm the bus. Was this it? I wanted so desperately to leave this scene behind, and here it was in my face again. My heart was racing. I mean, what were the odds? I'm trying to get the fuck out this state and one of the reasons I'm running is sitting right next to me? I thought about getting up and leaving, but that would have been too suspicious. I had no excuses to come up with. I felt trapped.

"So what happened to you? Where you been?" he prompted.

I was up front with him right away. "You gotta be straight with me man. What happened back at the Warfield was fucked up. Just so you know, I'm out now. I did my last deal."

He nodded.

After an agonizing several minutes, the bus finally pulled away and I felt a little better, but not completely convinced that I was safe.

During the trip, he opened up and confided in me some pretty nasty details about the players involved in some recent busts. We had both been involved with some of those folks. He explained how the DEA's operation had infiltrated the scene years earlier, the band's reluctant cooperation with them, and his role in all of it. The Grateful Dead had been threatened with RICO laws. He tied together all the bits and pieces that I had known about for some time. There were promises of immunity that the feds gave to certain people. There were criminal informants. Basically the whole game was rigged. The band had been backed into a corner, and the government essentially threatened to shut the whole circus down if they didn't cooperate. What choice did they have?

Minglewood had details about former deals I was involved in that he shouldn't have known anything about. It all made sense, but it also hinted that he must've been playing both sides. I couldn't make it fit together any other way. He denied it when I asked him. He insisted that another mutual friend of ours was the informant. At some level, I didn't really care what the truth was anymore. I just wanted him to know that I was definitely out.

We were both connected to more than one chemist that the feds were after, but I would never ever be a snitch, narc, or pawn in the DEA's game. I wasn't completely convinced of Minglewood's motivations anymore. Why was he on that bus with me? What a strange and uncomfortable coincidence, all the way to the state line. I'll never ever get over that unsettling fact. I'm convinced there was more to it. In fact, I know there was, but I left all that behind and refused to get myself involved ever again. No more acid deals.

Age 9, Coshocton, 1980.
(*D.W. Moffitt*)

With Timothy Leary, Florida Atlantic University, Boca Raton, 1990.
(*Jennifer Roberts*)

With the Bama Boys, left to right: Moffitt, J.B., Freeman, and Kilgore in Colorado, 1990. (*Dave Shroeder*)

Heading out to see the Allman Brothers Band with the Sunshine Café Crew, Maureen, Tyrone, Robin, Dave, and Dewey, Colorado 1991. *(unknown)*

Henry Sullivan running security at the BGP Electric On The Eel Music Festival, California, August 1991. *(Jimmy Jones)*

At Sacramento's Cal Expo Ampitheatre for a Grateful Dead series of shows, May 1992. *(Celeste Bloomfield)*

Just about to assault Bob Weir with a flying rubber eyeball during the Grateful Dead Mardi-Gras run, February 24, 1992 at Oakland Coliseum. *(© Michael Mendelson)*

Ambiance setup by Moffitt for Jerry Garcia photo shoot backstage at Oakland Coliseum, 1992. *(© Harry Benson)*

Middle Earth pranksters Bama Boy Jody and K. Fimster, circa 1995. *(Kilgore)*

Arriving in New England, fanny pack loaded and ready for the first
H.O.R.D.E. Tour, 1992, Boston-Logan International Airport.
(Alex Winske)

K. Fimster and Moffitt,
Gainesville, 1995. *(unknown)*

Kilgore in his trusty little red Ford Escort,
Calvin, circa 1995. *(unknown)*

Bags packed and ready to move out of lower Haight Street in San Francisco, 1993. *(unknown)*

Ben Harper, having just survived a near death stage roof collapse, performs in the pavilion at the Alachua County Fairgrounds, Gainesville, October 6, 1996. *(Michael C. Weimar, courtesy Gainesville Sun)*

ABOVE: StagePro setup and crew circa 1998. *(unknown)*

LEFT: Sound engineering at the Gothic Theatre, Denver, 2001. *(T. Stubby)*

BELOW: Painting the ice for the Colorado Avalanche at the Pepsi Center in Denver 2006.
(© Tim Sutherland)

With Jamaica in Denver, 2006.
(© Tim Sutherland)

With His Holiness, the 14th Dalai Lama backstage at the Pepsi Center in Denver, 2006. *(Michael Martin)*

Performing live at Cervante's Masterpiece Ballroom in Denver, 2011. (© *Tim Sutherland)*

PART III
Sacrifice

CHAPTER 38

Southbound

C olorado's fresh air and majestic mountains made me feel at
home once again. Robin Page was there in Summit County to
offer me a place of refuge. The previous few years, I had been on a wild
California roller coaster, a dream ride through heaven and at times
even hell. It was the late summer of 1993, and time for a much-needed
rest.

The locals in Summit were still throwing outrageous parties, and a
friend and local promoter, Adam Weigand, hosted just such a shindig
around the time of my twenty-second birthday. The party was held
just north of Breckenridge, at Farmer's Corner, and featured live music from my friends Bobby Sheehan and Chan Kinchla of Blues Traveler. It was good to catch up with them again, especially in a place
where I felt so at home. I can't recall if it was sometime before or after
Adam's event, but we hosted a big celebration of our own up at Robin's
cabin in Silverthorne. Local jam band Electric Mud played. We had
huge party tents in the yard and even rented a couple of port-a-johns.

Rest, relaxation and a few rumpus parties later, I was foolishly
ready to get back on the bus and head to the deep South. This time,
my destination was Birmingham, Alabama, home of the Bama Boys.

I was not sure going in how long the vacation might last, but I
ended up taking a thirty-day sabbatical there in Birmingham. The
first three weeks were spent in a total fucking haze, holed up in J.B.'s
south-side apartment. He and a fellow chemist from the University of Alabama did drug experiments on me. At first I was a willing

participant. Eventually, though, I lost track of the days. At one point, it was said that I didn't move from my spot on the couch for at least a week. I have no idea what happened in that apartment. I vaguely remember large vats of hash oil being cooked up. I remember having a time-lapse conversation with J.B.'s girlfriend on the couch. Her clothes kept changing as I slowly conversed with her in a time span that I assumed was taking place over a few minutes but was in reality over a week-long period.

Kilgore rescued me at some point, and we headed to Tuscaloosa's Coleman Coliseum for an evening concert with the Allman Brothers Band. I met up with Warren Haynes backstage and shared with him some good southern smoke. He told me that the band was heading to Florida in November, but didn't have a show lined up for November 12, a Friday. He wondered if I knew of any possibilities, and, in fact, I did, through some good friends in Gainesville (and no, not with that fraternity we had raided two years earlier—the hemorrhoids episode). He gave me the band's agent contact info and tasked me with the challenge of producing a show for the Allman Brothers Band!

My childhood friend from Boca, Rob Pena, had been living in Gainesville, attending the University of Florida. He had recently married a lovely Texan girl, Kayte VanScoy. They put me up at their place for a couple of months, where I slept in a hammock in a back pantry the size of a closet. Kayte introduced me to her friend Constance, whose boyfriend, Marshall Lowe, along with his roommate, Codi Lazar, were planning on producing a local music festival. The timing and alignment couldn't have been more perfect.

Per Warren Haynes' suggestion, I called the Allmans' agent, Jonathon Levine at the William Morris Agency, and informed him that I was working on putting together a show for November 12th near Gainesville. He said the band normally performed for $60,000 a night but could do it for $50,000, since they would already be passing though town.

Originally I tried to put together the show with Marshall and Codi at the County Fairgrounds. We considered some other out-of-town sites too. Within a few days, the enormity of the project and the time constraints became too overwhelming, however, and we realized the show was just too big for us at the time. I was determined not to give up, so I approached Student Government Productions (SGP) at the University of Florida with the idea. They were ecstatic for the opportunity, but were only willing to spend $10,000 for the band.

The numbers were pretty far apart, but the promoter spirit within me was convinced that the show must go on. I had another conversation with Jonathan Levine about price. He said they could do it for $45,000, but not a penny less. I went back and forth between him and the SGP.

We proposed that concert admission be free, to bring the band's fee down considerably. The money put up by SGP was part of their budget that had to be spent anyway, so they agreed to come up to $12,000. Levine came back with $30,000, but was not really happy about it. SGP jumped up to $20,000, and they didn't seem happy about it either. Levine didn't want to budge another inch, so I went back to SGP and squeezed another $3,500 out of them. The final offer on the table was $23,500. The Allmans' manager reluctantly accepted on behalf of the band.

I handed the production of the event to SGP and accepted a middleman fee of just $500. Originally, I had asked for ten percent, but as part of the final offer being accepted, I agreed to take a $500 payoff. It was shit, I know. I felt a little burned, but had to put my ego aside for the sake of the show itself.

The band's manager, Bert Holman, was not happy with me at all during the entire ordeal. Especially during the event, he was an asshole to me. Even their road manager, Kirk, was cold to me for the first time ever and I think that was because Bert was taking his frustrations out on him. Kirk eventually opened up and confided to me that the problem with Bert was because: 1) I had involved a band member in the process of booking the show; 2) the band ended up playing for so cheap; and 3) I was seen doing drugs with the band! I've always loved Kirk and have much respect for him but from my perspective, their managers and handlers had way bigger egos than the musicians themselves, and, believe me, that is quite typical in the music business. As for the band members themselves, they were very laid back and mellow. The music they created transcended all that monetary bullshit. I've never felt bitter when I hear them play; it's music of a higher calling in my opinion—spiritual hymns, if you will, of the southern rock variety.

On Friday night, November 12th, 1993, the Allman Brothers Band played a free concert at the University of Florida's A-frame band shell for nearly 20,000 people. When Gregg Allman stepped off the bus, he came right over to me shook my hand and said "thank you" for putting the show together. I was shocked that he even remembered me. He looked the cleanest and most sober that I had ever seen. Guitarist Dickey Betts had been on sabbatical for an incident involving punching a police officer up in New York some four months earlier. Guitarist Dan Toler, known for short stints in the band, was backstage ready to fill in, when, suddenly, Dickey showed up, apparently unannounced. It was unknown whether Dickey would even play with the band again, and if so, when that might happen. I overheard him tell someone backstage that he was doing this because it was a free show, and that's what the true spirit of the Allman Brothers Band was all about. I couldn't have felt more proud that I had something to do with bringing the band back together that day.

And, what a beautiful day it was for a free concert in the park. The sky melted into a deep purple, while white gulls soared over the horizon and not a cloud was in the sky. On stage the band broke into a full version of "Mountain Jam," which they hadn't performed in years. I had an overwhelming feeling of accomplishment and pride as I looked out into the sea of people grooving to the incredible vibe that came together on that most beautiful evening.

Derek Trucks was around 14 years old at the time and he and I were backstage playing catch football when Kirk came over and told him that he was wanted on stage. He got up and performed "Southbound" with the band—his third or forth time ever appearing on stage with them. I got to know Derek's father Chris Trucks (drummer Butch's bother) pretty well during my Gainesville years. Chris would drive over from Jacksonville occasionally to party with me and a few friends.

I hooked Warren up with some more weed and gave Allen Woody a bottle of mushroom-peyote tea that I had personally brewed up a few days earlier. Woody drank the bottle at the next show in West Palm Beach and I was told he had one hell of a night.

It is worth mentioning that Marshall, Codi and a third partner, Geoffrey May, really put their hearts into trying to pull off the show before I took it to SGP. They were all pretty bummed out about not being able to put it on, and it caused an unfortunate rift between us. Afterward, though, we called a meeting, talked it out and healed things up quickly. As proud as I was that the show went on, I was dismayed that it wasn't really "our" show anymore. People can accomplish extraordinary things when they are in a magical environment surrounded by extraordinary people. Gainesville was one of those places for me. Everything seemed to fit from day one, and it had everything to do with those friendships and bonds that we formed when working together for a common cause.

Marshall and Codi founded the Gainesville Alternative Music Alliance (GAMA) and brought me in to help out with their festival, the first ever Alachua Music Harvest. The event took place in January 1994 at the Alachua County Fairgrounds.

Part of my previous job at Bill Graham Presents was to set up and tear down the artists' dressing rooms and backstage areas, which also included the production offices. The production team at BGP would always toss away their budget sheets in the garbage cans after an event. These sheets had all the financials that it took to put on a Grateful Dead concert—from a Day On The Green stadium event, to outdoor music festivals, to arena shows of all types and sizes. Those thrown away papers were my textbooks. They were like gold to me, and I collected and studied them religiously, along with copies of industry insider magazines *Pollstar* and *Performance*. That is how I went from backstage worker in Oakland to concert promoter in Gainesville. Armed with BGP's blueprints, I was able to bring something unique to the table with Marshall, Codi and the gang.

CHAPTER 39

Southern Nights

C onveniently, Blossom, who I'd had a short fling with in South Florida a few years earlier, was now living in Gainesville, attending the university. In an attempt to flare things up between us again, I made my move too soon, as they say. Well, mostly I was too intense, which I had been guilty of before. She must've been a little scarred from my previous hesitation in California; she had wanted to move out there so suddenly, have a child with me, get married, and so on. My reluctance then must've hit her pretty hard. She had felt rejected.

I tried my best to mend things between us in Gainesville and suddenly found myself quickly falling for her all over again. The smell of the fall leaves, the chill to the air, the loneliness I felt inside—I was looking to her to fill the emptiness. I decided that it was our fate.

I had just recently learned, too, that my first love from Boca, Elle, was getting married. That was pretty devastating, but it wasn't the only blow. I also learned through a friend that Springwater was also going to be married up in Ohio. I kept screwing things up in my relationships. The reality of my knee-jerk choices was now haunting me. I wanted to settle down just for the sake of giving in. Ultimately, Blossom rejected me pretty harshly. I couldn't blame her, really, but I continued to be lovesick for a few months.

Rob's wife Kayte took a stab at playing matchmaker that New Year's Eve. She introduced me to a friend of hers, whose name was also Kate, but who went by Katie. This was a particularly unusual pairing, though, because Katie was mostly a lesbian who was only interested in a New Year's Eve fuck with a man. It was all prearranged. Kayte pretty much pimped the two of us out to each other. We both agreed to a casual, no stings sexual encounter before we had even met. Katie turned out to be pretty cool. She was a comic book artist. We became friends. She bought an aquatic frog and named him after me. We had one of those brief "friends with benefits" arrangements.

My raver friend from San Francisco, the most beautiful and lovely Marie, wrote me a letter that winter and said that she wanted to come to Florida for a visit. She opened up about previously hidden feelings for me. I was absolutely over the moon when I got that letter. I considered immediately running back to San Francisco, because I had been smitten with her, too. When I was staying with Kira on Alamo Square, Marie was living in an old Victorian flat on Haight Street. I used to hang out with her nearly every day back then, but was too shy and frightened to make any moves. From time to time, I dreamt of her. I wrote her back, but our timing was off, something went wrong. Maybe I seemed desperate. I don't know, but I never heard from her again.

Sometime during the spring of '94, I decided that I was going to make Gainesville my full-time home. I needed to return to San Francisco to retrieve my stuff from a storage unit. So I made road trip plans for that summer, which included doing some amphitheater research for GAMA and, of course, attending a concert here and there.

During the trip, I stopped at amphitheaters and investigated their construction to see what the best design for building a venue for GAMA might be. I also had the chance to catch up with my BGP friends and former coworkers at the annual Las Vegas Grateful Dead shows. I stopped at Red Rocks in Colorado for a Fourth of July Blues Traveler concert. I also jumped on a few stops of Blues Traveler's third H.O.R.D.E. Tour through the Midwest. There was also a quick side trip to visit family in Coshocton.

There was one other side adventure of note. While I was traveling over a dirt road mountain pass near Park City, Utah, the brakes gave out just as a large mountain cat jumped in front of the car. She growled at me and jumped out of the way just in the nick of time. I considered it an odd omen of sorts. I'm convinced she cursed the car.

Brian Parker, a fellow partner at GAMA, was with me for the second part of the trip and was with me in Kentucky when the car gave out. If it weren't for Brian's credit card rescuing us, I—or we, perhaps—might have been stranded there for some time. I think we ended up spending a week there, in a haunted motel in Bardstown.

By the end of the summer, I was back in Gainesville, staying at a friend's while I waited to move into a place known as the Big House, downtown. It was a cool old Victorian house that had legendary party status among the hipper Gainesville crowd. It was located next to the downtown Hippodrome Theatre. The house was occupied by: musician Scott Clayton, dready hippie Steve Cogswell, some girl I hadn't met yet because she was out all summer following the band Phish, and another person whose place I would soon be taking.

I attended a raging party on SW 1st Avenue, near campus, a few nights before I was set to move in. It was my twenty-third birthday. Blossom was there, but rudely ignored me when I tried to talk to her. Frustrated, I went back to the keg for another beer and my eyes met a stunning, young blonde girl. We exchanged a few words, then snuck off for a make-out session. She came back to my place and we fucked all night. It was very intense and emotional. In the morning, while lying naked together and giggling, I learned her name was Alyssa. I asked her where she lived and she said she lived in the Big House downtown. Uh-oh!

I moved into the Big House two days later. Alyssa and I continued fucking for a couple of months, but agreed to keep it casual since we were roomies. That was strenuous, considering we were emotionally vested in each other. It could've been that she was always running off to parties with other guys. It could've been that one of my friends (unaware of my relationship with her) confessed that he was in love with her. But, I think it was the time I walked in on her having sex with another dude and doing all of my cocaine with him—yep, that was the one that sealed it for me. She took off on Phish Tour again and did not return for a long time. Next thing I knew, she actually hooked up with

Phish drummer Jon Fishman and moved into his house for a while.

I came across an old, poetic journal entry dated about the time she and I were together. In it, I wrote about our struggle:

> *The summer was long and agonizing.*
> *The road was weary.*
> *The traveler retreats to his dreams of tomorrow.*
> *Today remains a tease.*
> *The car, Pontiac-5k, was a victim of circumstance. The universe just opened up and swallowed her into the vortex. Her tattered remains were left behind in the village of Bardstown, where the haunted ghosts of another time had better use for her.*
> *The traveler finds a side job at the Heritage Club—kitchen work again, ugh! His dreams would have to wait.*
> *Good golly, Miss Molly, Alyssa from Virginia, a mad drifter, suck the traveler into another vortex, an unexpected 23rd birthday bonus.*
> *Wild passions and foolish promises unleashed— like blood dripping on stone, they fall into the vortex.*
> *The traveler, now an employee of time, seeks refuge in his dream machine, rolling onward.*
> *Midnight calls the drifter, and she breaks away. She stumbles, hesitates, and slowly concedes a brief glimpse of reality. He reassures her and swallows the time.*
> *The storm rages—thunder, lightning, and rain echo, blind, and drench the lonely house.*
> *The traveler sits and writes, pondering his current tragedy, imagining a runaway semi-truck finding its way out of control and crashing onto the front porch of the Big House, smashing through the wall and careening to a stop at the traveler's feet. And then, just then, maybe the grill of the truck would*

animate a smile, possibly stick its tongue out, or,
better yet, spit in the traveler's face. And he would
laugh.

The road never forgets.

The rains stopped as the he gulped his time
away, surrendering to the mystery of it all.

The traveler catapults back into familiar scen-
ery. Little compassion remains for the drifter. She
cannot see the gold in his heart.

They dance.

They crawl.

Together they entwine their ecstasies of fear.

Summer dreams, but fade and retreat to the cold
reality of winter's freeze.

Together they face their emptiness.

Polarities reverse, they magnetize again.

Give the mystery a chance.

Flow — stumble, flow.

Spin, flip, and roll...

Close the door behind you.

Next.

I was running the lighting console in Richenbacher's, a local night-club, when I met Kristen. It was a typically crowded night in the bar, and she was standing next to the sound booth just staring at me. She was gorgeous—tall, slender, long dark hair, tight jeans, Chuck Taylor's on her feet. She was a bit of a tomboy, and her spirit kind of reminded me of Elle.

"Hi," she broke the ice.

"Hello."

I turned my focus back towards the band that was playing. After a few moments she spoke again.

"I don't normally do this, but would you like to hang out with me sometime?" she asked.

"Yeah, sure."

Then she just smiled and walked off. Several minutes later she reappeared.

"How about tonight?"

"Um, okay. Yeah, let's hang out after the band's done."

We went back to her dorm room on the UF campus. She put on one of my favorite records, *Bitches Brew* by Miles Davis. It was a brilliant and romantic night. Within a week I found myself in a serious relationship.

She was an audio engineer and a night DJ on the campus radio station. I used to hang out with her in the radio booth. I'd pick out cool blues and jazz records for her to play. We had some great times together—camping trips, concerts, parties.

I had a great aunt that lived in Gainesville, my mother's Aunt Oneita. She was in her eighties, and Kristen and I would visit with her a lot. In fact, Kristen would go see her on her own, too, just to check on her. She was very kind that way. Oneita loved to tell stories about her time living in California. She and my great uncle, Glen Rutiger, lived on the famous Doheny Ranch off of Mulholland Drive in the Hollywood Hills. They were neighbors and good friends with Spencer Tracy and Katharine Hepburn. Oneita often spoke of her friendship with Hepburn and would point to gifts that Hepburn had sent her, which she kept on display.

Kristen was six or seven years older; I was only twenty-three and still admittedly inexperienced with serious relationships, but her weakness was an insecurity that constantly threatened our relationship. Insecurities in relationships tend to push people away. Tipping points are made out of trivial issues and people find themselves years later looking back on foolish knee-jerk attitudes and wonder what might have been or what could have or should have been. It's often justified by saying that it just wasn't meant to be. The hard truth is that there are moments when people just don't have the strength to face their fears and let go of the struggle, the needing and the wanting, the longing to be loved. To just embrace the infinite now, the purity and loving bliss of the Universe. It's a powerful thing that at most times people just do not fully embrace.

With Kristen, those possessive and jealous qualities eventually got the best of us, along with my lack of mature communication. It all went bad when I was working late in the recording studio one weekend. She accused me of seeing someone else. The following day, it all blew up on the phone, and I was sick of trying to defend myself. I hung up on her and then ignored her for two weeks. One day when I was in the office of the recording studio, one of the engineers made a comment that sounded like something she would say. I mentioned that it sounded like he was hanging out with my girlfriend. I was kidding, of course, but I suddenly realized something was up when there was dead silence to my comment—what a way to find out.

It was ironic that her freak-out and lack of security, was what actually drove her into the arms of another. It was sobering. I was always faithful to her and really loved her, but realized the relationship was a lot of hard work. It was a struggle: too many arguments over silly things. She threw a shoe at me once (one of her Chuck Taylor's). Who throws a shoe?

Officially my relationship with Kristen ended a bit harshly. But the breakup taught me how to be a better communicator. I waited outside the radio station for her one night, not in a creepy stalker way, but in a melancholy need-to-talk way. She came out of the studio expecting to confront some troublemaker she thought was messing with her truck. But it was just me, sitting patiently on the tailgate. We went for a long drive and talked. We had been together for six months and this was probably the first time we ever really had a deep conversation. I confessed to her my previously failed attempts at love: the losses, the running away, the lack of commitments, slutting around on Grateful Dead Tour, and so on. It felt so therapeutic to get all of that off my chest. I talked to her more like a friend rather than a disturbed lover. She listened like a true friend.

Perhaps there was hope for us after all. We talked about starting over, but of course she had sparked things up with a new lover. It was something that only time could work out. I encouraged her to pursue things further with him. I didn't want to possess her. Eventually things worked out pretty well for her and the new guy. A few years later they got married and started a family.

CHAPTER 40

If I Knew The Way

I was very proud of the work we had all done on the first Alachua Music Harvest. I really felt that we had accomplished something great and it was only the beginning. Putting together a festival like that really brought us all closer together. We were like a family of brothers that had gone through a war together. And it was a rewarding victory to know that we were producing events that had profound effects on the lives of so many people that most of us would never meet.

Shortly following the first Alachua Music Harvest, Codi resigned from GAMA. His reasoning was that he wanted to focus more on his band, Loose Fragments. We all tried our best to convince him to stay on, but he was pretty determined to leave. Some time after that, Marshall appointed me as a director, Production Director I think. I don't really remember; I've never been great with titles anyway. But I was very proud to have a more important role on the GAMA team.

We took a beating on the second Alachua Music Harvest because there was no escaping the horrible weather. The rains had beaten the hell out of us financially. We were in the hole ten grand.

All the while, I was working odd jobs: landscaping, pizza deliveries, flower deliveries, kitchen work, and driving a taxicab, and, just after the second Harvest disaster, I started working with the local band Waterdog. Andy Levine, the genius behind Richenbacher's, was an ambitious member of the band who wanted to start his own company. I helped him launch Southland Music Company and showed him some invaluable music industry resources. Soon after, a couple of members of Waterdog merged with the acoustic duo Ken and Andrew, and the band Sister Hazel was born. Between GAMA and Southland, we managed to do a lot of work for that group, but it was ultimately Andy himself who took upon the role of personally managing Sister Hazel. Today, Andy heads up Sixthman in Atlanta, which hosts wild rock and roll–themed cruises for giant rock acts like KISS, Lynyrd Skynyrd, John Mayer, and Kid Rock .

Sister Hazel became mildly successful, as did another local Gainesville band we worked very closely with at GAMA, Less Than Jake. Other noteworthy Gainesville bands we worked with were Hot Water Music, Whoreculture, and Big White Undies. The music scene was so ripe back then. There were excellent musicians around every corner in that town and so many great bands. Bill Bryson promoted excellent bands at The Covered Dish. Market Street Pub, Richenbacher's, and the Florida Theatre were the other venues for catching great live music.

In April 1994, I went on a road trip with Waterdog to Boone, North Carolina, where they opened for my friends, Blues Traveler. A few days following, Traveler played the UF band shell in Gainesville, the same venue as my Allmans show. I can't ever forget the day because my cousin Billy died of complications from AIDS that day. He was such a wonderful, kind soul, and I knew him well; he had lived with my mother and I in Florida for some of my late high school years.

GAMA hosted a local fishing expedition for the Blues Traveler's road crew. Marshall and I partied pretty hard with bassist Bobby Sheehan that weekend. I brought Bobby and guitarist Chan Kinchla down to the Market Street Pub one night for an impromptu jam session and we all joined in with the band Fatty Tea Bags out of Tallahassee. After that, several of us in the GAMA crew went on to follow Blues Traveler to New Orleans for some more partying during Jazz Fest, and a great show at the State Palace Theater.

Bobby and I were walking in a bad New Orleans neighborhood one night close to the French Quarter and we noticed an arms deal going down at the open trunk of someone's car. As we passed the car, we pretended not to notice what was going on, but clearly there were some AK-47s being looked at. As we got to the end of the block, the guys back at the car decided to give the guns a test and began shooting bullets over our heads. We took off running while the assassins were back there laughing. When we got safely around the corner, Brendan Hill (Blues Traveler's drummer) and friends were riding by in a taxi and they stopped to pick us up. We crammed into the cab and headed uptown to see a late night show at a club called The Boot. Dave Mathews Band, from Charlottesville, Virginia were just then emerging onto the jam band scene and put on an amazing show. We partied that night until the sun came up. The rest of that New Orleans trip remains a total blur in my memory banks but I had fallen in love with the city's culture.

Of all the side jobs I ever worked, by far the most riveting low-profile job was for Gainesville's Yellow Cab. The situations I wound up in, and the people I met driving those cabs were so strange. I worked for a very short Irish-German man named Dan McCarthy. He loved to run scams on people, and by "people," I mean lawyers and insurance companies. This guy was a real piece of work. Dan had a sidekick named Kris, a very tall and fat transsexual person who constantly whined like a little pussy boy. Dan had these two Dachshund wiener dogs that received his only visible compassion. The only times you could witness any decent sense of humanity out of Dan was when it came to his dogs. Dan was a very loving dog owner, but an asshole to most humans.

While I was working for him, Dan got into trouble with the local community for proudly telling the newspaper, the Gainesville Sun, that his number one rule was to, "never pick up a young black male after dark, if the place they're calling from can't be clearly identified." Rule number two was the same, but applied to two black men, and rule number three to three black men, and so forth. People thought he was being racist, but really he was just being deliberately crass and obnoxious. In fact, his rules made sense if you knew how often we were getting robbed by people calling from pay phones and bad street locations with no clear destinations. They just happened to be black.

I really don't think Dan was a racist: he had a black girlfriend who lived with him from time to time and a couple of our drivers were black, and they were robbed just as much as anyone else, by the way. The city threatened to revoke Dan's license after the article, though, and called special hearings on the matter. In the end, Dan won the argument by explaining that he was just protecting his employees with the policy not to pick up where there was no clear address connected to a phone number. He even apologized to the community for his remarks and eventually the whole thing blew over.

I should also mention how cheap Dan was. He put very little maintenance into the vehicles. On my first day working for him, I got into an accident while driving my first fare (an elderly woman) because the brakes went out on me. I also found out that day that I was driving on a suspended license from an old speeding ticket I got in Utah that I had ignored. After a week or two, I cleared up the issue and was back on the road driving, but I always checked the brakes before I took a car.

I saw through Dan's prickly, odd exterior and felt sorrow for him. I guess I developed a soft spot for the old guy. He had lived a tough life. He had apparently been a horse jockey in his youth down in Miami, but eventually ran into some Mob trouble with some of Santos Trafficante's boys. He was constantly paranoid from all the scams he was running. I figured there was probably at least a contract or two out on him. Despite all the negativity around him, I learned a lot, mostly about how living that way wasn't a life that I wanted. Always peeking out from behind the curtains, over your shoulder, and moving quickly from one motel to another. He mostly lived in different motels and ran the taxi operation remotely. Everything with him was shady. But I made good money driving that cab.

Eventually it all came to a head when Dan ordered me to drive into a bad section of town one night, where experience had taught me to never go after dark. The crime and murder rate in Gainesville was pretty high during that period, and cabbies were constantly being robbed at gunpoint. I felt a setup and refused to take the run. The night it happened, Paul, another driver, had been robbed on a call to that same area of town—Sugar Hill. A gun was pulled on him and he abandoned his cab and ran for his life. He showed up at my apartment to relax and calm down. I called Dan to tell him what had happened and let him know that Paul was safe, but had decided to quit. Dan wanted me to go back and get Paul's cab. I think he was caving to all the pressure from the previous controversy. There was no way I was going to put my life in jeopardy by going back to that neighborhood, so I quit too. Besides, I had my hands full at GAMA anyway.

GAMA started to produce some other events around town including a Jazz-Pop festival and some one-off events with bands like Rusted Root and Bela Fleck. We took a stab at running a couple of venues in town, too. Our ambition to build our own amphitheater was always on the table. In 1995, we decided it was time for the Grateful Dead to play Gainesville. They had played there in the early eighties, at a gymnasium on campus, but the time seemed right for them to return. Plus, with all my connections and our skills to put on big events at the Fairgrounds, we were very confident that we were the ones who could pull it off. I think it was Marshall who started the petition; I don't remember exactly, but I know he was involved in overseeing the collection of all those signatures. I can't recall anymore how many we got, but it was enough to get the attention we needed. Marshall and I created our own separate company from GAMA with our friend Kevin Campbell and called it LCM Ventures (for Lowe, Campbell, Moffitt). I initiated contact with Cameron Sears at Grateful Dead Productions, who was the go-between with the band. The Dead worked very differently than most other bands. They no longer used an agent or a manger, like for example the way the Allmans did business, but instead made their decisions democratically as a band. At that point in their career, they managed themselves. Their business model was unlike any other top-grossing band—and, of course, the Grateful Dead had been dominating box office sales in the U.S. for years. We figured that we'd give it our best shot; we had nothing to lose.

We followed all of the band's reasonable requirements and put in an official proposal for a date on the Dead's 1995 Spring Tour. The catch was that we had to co-promote the show with east coast/New York promoter John Scher's Metropolitan Entertainment. Bill Graham Presents handled the Dead's production west of the Mississippi and John Scher handled everything in the East, with a few exceptions. If you wanted to produce a Grateful Dead show, you had to work with one of those two promoters. My relationships were obviously with the Bill Graham people and not with Scher's, but a friend at BGP vouched for me once we initiated talks.

There wasn't much of a negotiation, because the band simply wanted $300,000 flat, plus bonus incentives for a sell-out (and they always sold out). This pricing structure allowed their ticket prices to remain low, which was something they strongly believed in. Consider: at that time, artists like the Rolling Stones and Paul McCartney were requiring a minimum of $1,000,000 per show. We had no problem finding the $300K. Several local businesses and a few wealthy individuals were on board.

We were still wet behind the ears as far as Metropolitan Entertainment was concerned, and, overall, the pairing was a tall order from their vantage, though not unreasonable. I had more conversations with the Grateful Dead office than I did with Metropolitan. I think I only spoke to John Scher maybe two times, and he just said that he would do whatever the band told him to do. Cameron told me that the band took the offer seriously. Bob and Jerry apparently liked the idea a lot. I had heard that they wanted to get away from doing so many stadium-type shows.

Ultimately, the majority voted that our venue's parking wasn't big enough, and we needed a few bigger shows under our belt as promoters. Our bid was for a minimum two-night stand on Friday and Saturday, April 7th and 8th, 1995, to be held at the Alachua County Fairgrounds, with possibly a third night, and each evening's capacity set at 30,000. It would have been 90,000 tickets over three nights in a market they normally skipped over on tour. It still sounds like a good idea to me.

An actual show did take place on April 7th, but not in Gainesville. Instead, Metropolitan decided to put on one show, two hours south, at Tampa Stadium with its capacity of 80,000; we were cut out of it completely. I was told that the band would welcome another offer from us in the future, at least.

I went to Spring Tour's Atlanta and Birmingham shows with a few Middle Earth friends. The last stop was the April 7th Tampa show, which was the final Grateful Dead show I ever attended and the last stop on the Spring Tour. Kristen was with me, as was my brother Shawn, who was also the one responsible for taking me to my very first Grateful Dead show. The show itself left a lot to be desired. The Black Crowes were the opening act and there seemed to be a dark energy all around the stadium. There were cops everywhere, beating the shit out of people. It reminded me of so many times I had witnessed that darkness over the years. It seemed like police violence had only gotten worse. Tampa in general was not a great environment for a Dead Show. It should've been in Gainesville. It should've been our show. It would've been a much better vibe.

It had been a common myth, traveling by word of mouth in Grateful Dead circles, that if the band ever played the song "Unbroken Chain" it would be a sign of the end times for the band. It was a song of theirs from the early seventies that had never been performed live. Midway through the second set at Tampa, they broke into "Unbroken Chain."

Four months later...

Marshall answered the phone in the GAMA office and his tone became very somber. Jerry Garcia had died. The world instantly felt different. I wanted to fly out to San Francisco and be there for the public memorial at Golden Gate Park. I wanted to be a part of it like I was when Bill Graham died. But, reason settled in, and I realized that I needed to be right where I was, surrounded by my Gainesville family and friends.

We put together a tribute concert just a few days after the news hit, and held it at the Downtown Plaza with many musicians in the local Gainesville scene. It was our community vigil. The place filled up with a couple thousand Deadheads—mourning, celebrating, hugging, crying, dancing, and sharing the grief we all felt.

During this time, I was also busy in the recording studio working on my first solo album, *Not All Who Wander Are Lost*. The phrase is from J.R.R. Tolkien and many in the Deadhead community are familiar with it, especially my Middle Earth friends. I was dating Kristen at the time, and it was on a bumper sticker on her truck.

My main backing band for the recording was the Fatty Tea Bags. The lead guitarist, Chris Mulé, a native of New Orleans, and I would become good friends, recording and gigging together for many years. Marshall played drums on one of the songs and Josh Greenbaum played percussion on a few. Josh was (and still is) an extraordinary percussionist. He used to perform in River Phoenix's band, Aleka's Attic.

The Phoenix clan had a lot of ties to the Gainesville community. His family had a farm outside of the tiny village of Micanopy, just south of town. I first met Josh and his father Kenny within a week of arriving in Gainesville, back in October 1993. They were absolutely wonderful people and I knew it from the moment I met them. I never got to meet River, though; of course, he died in Los Angeles on Halloween only weeks after I arrived in Gainesville. I did, however, briefly know his sisters, Rain and Summer, and his brother Joaquin. Rain and Summer played in a local punk band, the Causey Way, with Gainesville's Covered Dish promoter Bill Bryson. That band was a lot of fun and in many ways they were the best underground music in Gainesville at that time.

Josh's father Kenny Greenbaum was a great asset to the GAMA family, and a spiritual mentor to most of us in the Gainesville music community. He was an old hippie from the Woodstock, New York area, with lots of festival experience. Having people around like that really elevated what we were doing to a better level. We really had a great sense of community in the beginning.

CHAPTER 41

A Little Bit Further
Than We've Gone Before

This is the story of Calvin, the little red Ford Escort with Alabama license plates. You've read about him in earlier parts of this book. According to Calvin's owner, Kilgore, Calvin has had a cracked engine, been stolen a few times, impounded every now and then, and been around the country more times than a yellow-bellied sapsucker. He'd been out to San Francisco and back on several occasions, and been to more Dead shows than Bruce Hornsby. If only that car could talk! He had escaped unscathed from the 1992 Rodney King riots in San Francisco and sheltered me after the incident at Buckeye Lake.

And, so it came to pass, that in the spring of '95, Calvin was supposed to be in K. Fimster's care. And you would think that Fimster would have learned, after getting Calvin stolen from some hippie named Rabbit the previous year up in the Carolinas. But, no, as the infamous jokester arrived on site at the Alachua County Fairgrounds for the 1995 Earth Day Celebration in Gainesville, Calvin was, allegedly, stolen again.

I was pulling up in my golf cart when I noticed the crazed drunk, stumbling around in a daze shouting, "Someone just stole Calvin! Someone just stole Calvin! Stop that car! Call the cops!"

That's when I noticed the little red car leaving out the back gate. Needless to say, I didn't believe him for him a second. I told him to shut the hell up, and that it was good to see him, then asked, "By the way, who's got the car?"

Fimster kept insisting that Calvin had been abducted by a mysterious unabomber with tattoos, some hitchhiker he had picked up. A hitchhiking tattooed monk? Likely story. I assumed Fimster was just up to one of his usual Middle Earth pranks. It was probably just one of the Bama Boys with the car, but when they showed up to the site, no Calvin. We all kept pressing Fimster the entire weekend, "No, really, who's got the fucking car?" Two days later, we finally decided to believe him and called in the police report.

By the way, that Earth Day event was a fantastic line-up of music. Warren Haynes' side project from the Allmans—Gov't Mule—was out on its first headlining tour. I believe it was their first-ever festival headlining slot. In addition, the infamous Col. Bruce Hampton totally mind-fucked me with his psychic abilities; the man is just plain out of this world.

A month or so after the event, I witnessed a shooting star and made a wish for new transportation. Soon after, Calvin's owner, Kilgore, called me up to tell me: "The cops found Calvin down in St. Petersburg! And if you go pick him up, you can take care of him for a while." Kilgore mailed me the registration and notarized authorization to pick up the car.

"Yes, I'm here for the red Escort from Alabama..." Immediately the guy in the booth starts laughing. "Um, could I see the car before I pay you please?"

"Sorry, that's against policy."

"Against policy? What kind of policy is that? I need to know if I can drive it out of here!"

"Well, it says here... the car is in... oh, yeah, EXTREMELY POOR CONDITION with uh... dents everywhere." He chuckled again, reading from the report.

"What's so funny? It was stolen!"

"That'll be $100 please."

Calvin was in nearly the same condition as when Fimster had it, maybe one new scratch. The items that were supposed to be in the trunk were all gone except a new pair of Converse All-Stars that fit me perfectly and one of Fimster's unopened homebrews. There was the usual empty beer cans, litter, and broken glass throughout. I found the keys in the backseat. (The police report read: no keys, no radio, dents everywhere!) He wouldn't start up right away but after charging the battery, Calvin turned over! I tied the door shut with a piece of rope I found on the impound lot and hit the road.

I fostered Calvin for three months, during which time we drove over 3,000 miles, transported several dozen flowers, delivered 500 pizzas, blew out three tires, got stuck in a cow pasture tripping on mushrooms, lost a power steering belt, blew a water pump, and threw a clutch. According to Fimster, "You could douse that car with gasoline, light a match, drive him over a cliff, and he would still come crawlin' back ready to ride to San Francisco."

While working at Five Star Pizza, Calvin was my delivery car. It was a temporary job that I planned to give up once I reached a personal goal of delivering 500 pizzas. Our final delivery was to a sorority house on the UF campus. As Calvin veered around the corner into the parking lot, the clutch gave out. I coasted into a spot and delivered that 500th pie. But, you can't leave precious cargo like Calvin in front of a nasty old sorority house, so I got the clutch repaired and got him out of there.

It was time to drive Calvin back to Birmingham and Kilgore. On the way, my band at the time, Beginner's Mind, had booked gigs in Valdosta, Georgia and up in North Carolina. We took two vehicles, of course, since Calvin wouldn't be making the trip back. The plan was for Kilgore to drive me to the North Carolina gig, where I could meet up with the band.

So, there I was with Calvin, at a rest area off I-75 northbound, between Macon and Atlanta. I had left the rest of the band in a Valdosta motel. It was Thursday morning around 9 o'clock, and I was just waking up in the car. I was so tired from the gig that I couldn't make it straight through to Birmingham the night before. The first thing I thought to do was check the oil, check the water, call Kilgore, and get back on the road. But nature called first, and I headed off to the pisser and relieved myself. On the way out, I stopped by the pay phone and called Kilgore to let him know my ETA. He was expecting me by 8 a.m.; I was way behind schedule. Birmingham was at least three or four hours away. After I got off the phone, I felt rushed, so I skipped the maintenance checks and just jumped in Calvin and off we went, bypassed Atlanta and onward to Birmingham.

I stopped at the last Georgia exit to fill up on gas. Calvin was HOT. He was running out of water. I added water, let him cool down, and prayed we would make it to the Magic City. We got back on the road and about two minutes later, as we were crossing the Alabama border, Calvin started feeling ill. He was giving out. The Welcome Center exit ramp was within sight. The scent of the sweet Alabama air was calling out to him, just as Calvin was exhausting his last fumes... "You're almost home, Boy!" I reminded him. "C'mon, just make it to Birmingham. It'll be alright." He started choking up. The exit ramp was just ahead, but, no choice, I had to pull off and UP the hill! The ramp turned a corner and went straight up at a 45-degree angle. We were halfway up the hill and Calvin gave out. Shiiiiiiit! I looked in the rear view and a Mack semi was ramming towards us, roughly 1,000 feet behind. "C'mon, Calvin!" The truck was fast approaching. Finally, Calvin gave his last spurt and kicked in just in time to get it up over the hill then he gave out again. The truck was right behind me. We had just reached the parking area and I veered off to the left, coasting into the first available parking space with the truck narrowly missing us.

I sat there for a few minutes taking it all in. Oh well, time to call Kilgore. We decided to wait it out and let Calvin cool down.

I waited about thirty minutes and then added water. The engine cracked. Calvin was dead.

Kilgore came and got me. It was an hour trip from Birmingham, and we still needed to get to North Carolina by nightfall. We left Calvin behind, taking Kilgore's other car, Hobbes, to the festival gig. After the weekend, we returned for Calvin. A quick scam from a friendly AAA card and he was delivered to a shop in downtown Birmingham. The diagnosis was not good. The repair was too costly. The time had come for Calvin to rest. He retired to Kilgore's yard, set up on blocks to silently sleep and dream of all his past adventures.

CHAPTER 42

Don't Panic

The third Alachua Music Harvest was a step up in production for us and turned out to be a major success. We hired Stage-Pro, a large staging company out of Lawrence, Kansas, to do the main stage sound, lights, and staging. We added some national headliners: George Clinton & The Pfunk Allstars, Widespread Panic, and Joan Osborne. Interestingly enough, I had befriended Joan back in New Orleans when we were doing all that partying with Blues Traveler and friends during Jazz Fest.

On the night of George Clinton's performance, things got especially funky. We had a driver for him, whose only job was to be on stand-by for Pfunk. If they needed any errands run or any member of their forty-person entourage driven anywhere, it was the driver's job to make that happen. The driver dropped George and the singers off at our production trailer, and we had a private smoke session with them. Marshall had rolled up an especially large spaceship-looking fatty for the occasion. George took a big ol' hit, paused, exhaled, and declared that the, "Mothership would indeed be landing tonight!"

After the band took the stage, George Clinton, Jr., requested a ride back to the hotel so he could deposit the band's pay in the hotel's safe. I asked the driver to do it, but he just stood there with wide eyes, confused.

I repeated, "I need you to drive George, Jr., back to the Marriott, please."

"But ... but ... I sort of ... can't."

"What do you mean?"

"Well, on the way here. George Senior... well, he uh... kind of gave me a bunch of mushrooms and I... I didn't realize they'd be this strong... and, well... I'm tripping my face off right now."

I couldn't find anyone sober enough to drive George, Jr., back to the hotel, so I had to do it. Shit, Pfunk's set was usually like four hours long anyway. There was plenty of time to get there and back. But, when we got to the hotel, we encountered some serious fucked up shit.

The man behind the counter wouldn't give George, Jr., a key to the room. He started spouting off racist shit, and I was there to witness it. I was shocked. I was the one actually paying for the room and this guy had lost his marbles. He called the cops on us. I had to get a regional manager for the Marriott on the phone to get the situation resolved. It was a crazy scene, but, finally, it got resolved peacefully. I was so outraged to see such blatant racism, but George, Jr. admitted that it was something he was used to experiencing in the south.

When we got back to the festival, everything had been going smooth in our absence. Our buddy Scramble Campbell, a local artist we hired to do paintings around the fairgrounds had painted a giant canvas portrait of George Clinton and was trying to negotiate a sale of the piece to Clinton. Scramble went back to the stage to retrieve the painting, but it was gone, so George said, "No sale." Unbeknown to Scramble the painting had been secretly loaded onto the Pfunk bus by a member of their entourage.

Sunday night, Widespread Panic headlined. A crew guy from the band asked me to hook him up with some "kind" and I just assumed he was talking about the legendary Gainesville Green. I sent over a friend with some killer "kind" bud and witnessed the miscommunication from a distance. My friend came back over with a look of shock on his face.

"What happened?"

"He wants heroin."

"What? But he said 'kind.'"

"He assumed you knew he was really talking about smack."

The crew guy was a friend of mine, so I went over and had a talk with him. I let him know that there was no way we could help him with that request. He explained to me who it was actually for and that kind of unsettled me a little. At a Panic show a couple of years later I would walk into a dressing room backstage at Oak Mountain Amphitheater (near Birmingham) at the wrong time and witness a band member preparing to shoot up in the bathroom, it was the same person who the "kind" was requested for back in Gainesville.

Besides the awkward vibe, Panic played a hell of a set for the Gainesville crowd. After they finished the show, their singer John Bell and I reminisced about our good times on the H.O.R.D.E. Tour and at the Telluride Festival.

A few months after the third Alachua Music Harvest, a girl named Leah walked into the GAMA office and said she wanted to volunteer as an intern. She was a big Widespread Panic fan and after attending our festival, she felt the desire to get involved in the music business. I was the only one in the office at the time, and I have to admit that her beauty immediately took me. I felt an instant infatuation with her. The office phone was ringing in the background, but I awkwardly ignored it. I was distracted and immediately thought that the love of my life had just walked through the door. I'm certain that I fumbled about nervously, and she probably thought I was weird, but she signed up to be my intern anyway. I almost didn't want to, thinking that her beauty would be too distracting or intimidating, or that I would spoil our potential by being her boss.

I kept a hidden crush on her for a few months while she volunteered a few hours a week in our office. I taught her basic web design, which was a brand new technology at the time. She also organized various files and made media calls for us. I occasionally tried to get her to hang out with us socially, but she was always too busy. I was too shy and subtle about it, so she didn't catch on to my feelings. I asked her out a few times, but was repeatedly stonewalled. She didn't seem interested.

Feeling quite alone and depressed one evening, I took a walk around campus and ended up at the band shell. There was no one around, and I sat under the A-framed roof directly in the center of the stage and meditated. I watched the sun set. At first, I felt lonely and sorry for myself. I thought about how the Allman Brothers concert there had been such an amazing turning point for me. I thought about how much joy had been spread to the people that night. I breathed slowly in and out, chanted a personal mantra that always helped me through these situations. The clear energy brought me around to being confident again. My depression lifted and I felt happy and blissful. I concluded that my infatuation with Leah was over. I would no longer pursue her. It was time to move on.

When I got back to my apartment, there was a message on my answering machine. It was from Leah. In a nervous tone, she asked me to go on a canoeing and camping trip with her. I was shocked and delighted. And I had just convinced myself to give up on her! I returned her call, and, yes, it was true, she wanted to go on an overnight canoe trip, just she and I.

That weekend, it was the forth of July, Leah and I went canoeing and camping along one of North Florida's beautiful spring-fed rivers. Sleeping next to her in the tent, I had an intense surreal dream of us. In the dream, we had been in a relationship for many years and there was some crazy drama going down in some other space and time. When I woke up next to her, it was unbelievable, like a strange time warp had taken place. After the trip, we slowly started dating more. Within weeks, we found ourselves in a serious relationship.

CHAPTER 43

Tear The Roof Off The Sucker

The fourth Alachua Music Harvest in 1996 was, up to that time, the most complex event I had been involved in producing. Our headliners were They Might Be Giants, Ben Harper, Speech (singer of the hip hop band Arrested Development), and returning, was George Clinton and the Pfunk Allstars.

Bad weather was hammering down on us all weekend. Torrential downpours, heavy winds. A serious tropical storm was blowing through northern Florida. The roof tarp on the main stage kept filling up with water. It was a dangerous situation. Despite the bad weather, we still had a large attendance and a great lineup of artists performing their asses off.

On Saturday night, there was a huge problem with Speech. He was late showing up, extremely late, so late that we had to bump him from the festival. By the time his bus pulled into the site, it was already the set time for the next band, They Might Be Giants. We had been waiting for him through an entire set time's worth of dead air on the main stage! When Speech stepped off the bus, I had to break the news to him.

"I'm sorry, man, you've completely missed the set time. We have a curfew here. The only thing I can offer is for you to headline our second stage tonight."

He looked disappointed.

"Can I talk to the crowd?"

"Sure, I'll let you say a few words to let them know, and then we gotta get They Might Be Giants on."

So, out he strolled to the middle of the stage and takes the mic.

"Hey, guys, we ran into some bus problems on the road, that's why we are late. But now these fuckers won't let us play! In fact, that motherfucker right over there!" He pointed over to the side of the stage at me.

"Goddamn it! Cut his mic, now!"

They cut his mic and put some house music on.

Speech walked over to me and got in my face.

"That was bullshit man! Now you are not playing at all, asshole! The second stage offer is rescinded," I yelled.

"Fuck you!" he barked back.

The other stress on my hands was a mutiny from my second stage crew. The crew consisted of my dear Middle Earth friends, including the infamous K. Fimster and most of the Bama Boys. They kept coming over to the main stage, requesting more and more beer tickets from me. They finally staged a walk out and demanded that I supply them with an endless amount of beer if I wanted to continue to keep getting free slave labor out of them. I finally exploded in a tirade and slammed my walkie-talkie into the ground screaming, "FUCK A BUNCH OF FUCKS!" Roaring laughter followed, because my attempt to break the radio failed when it bounced off the ground and magically flew up through the air and landed right back into my hand. I had proved my supernatural powers were almighty, but, alas, I lowered my head in defeat. I scribbled in sharpie "FREE BEER, PER DEWEY" on the back of their laminates and signed them. Middle Earth won that round.

Sunday night, I was on the main stage with a few of the crew members and Ben Harper, when, suddenly, I heard a thunderous roar of screeching metal. The roof above us was collapsing. That year, we had decided to go with a different staging company than StagePro. The idea was to save some money but it turned out to be a costly mistake. I was standing directly behind the drum kit near the back of the stage. Ben ran immediately toward the stage left loading ramp and slid down it to safety. The ramp was too far for me to get to. The upstage truss came screaming down toward me. I could feel the lighting cans breathing down my neck and scraping against my back. I jumped off the back of the stage, six or eight feet to the ground. I looked back up after I landed at the horrifying site of twisted metal all over the stage. Ben Harper was on the ground about ten feet away from me. We were both safe and miraculously unscathed.

Immediately, I called out to the crew who I knew were still up on the stage. There was confusion and yelling. After a few agonizing minutes, we realized how lucky we were. No one was injured or killed. The stagehands had jumped inward next to the tall guitar stacks. The mangled roof trusses had rested on top of Pfunk's back-line of double-stacked Marshall amplifiers. Those amps literally saved the lives of our crew! It was a miracle. The bottom of the upstage truss had landed about a foot above the stage deck in the exact spot where I had been standing. Had I not jumped, I would have been violently crushed and likely killed.

Ben Harper came over and gave me a hand up. He offered to help with anything we needed him to do. His band was scheduled to go on next, but obviously that would now be impossible, at least for the main stage.

An emergency meeting was called backstage. We huddled and tried to figure out our next move. There were thousands of people in the crowd expecting a show. Big Mike McCullough came up with a plan to move all the pieces of the P.A. that he could salvage from the wreckage over to the indoor exposition building. We would start to build an indoor stage over there. We moved what acts we could to the second stage. We asked Ben Harper to perform an acoustic set in the covered pavilion area. He did. It was one of those amazing and unforgettable, once in a lifetime, performances. Thousands of people sat on the ground with their legs folded while Ben performed, unplugged, in the middle of the crowd. Like one of those old Elvis TV performances. A photograph of his performance made the cover of the *Gainesville Sun*.

Inside the expo building, we were frantic. The crew put together a makeshift stage and sound system as fast as possible. It was Sunday night. We had never used the expo building in any of our previous events, so we didn't have official permission to be in there. Actually, we broke into the building. There was no power. I gave permission to our head electrician to break into the transformer box and light up the room. It was a large, empty concrete hall that could fit a crowd of thousands. We knew it would be tight in there, but we had no other choice. The show must go on. There were several sets of glass entrance doors that we kept locked until we knew for sure that we could pull off the show.

Pfunk's set had originally been slated for an 8pm start time, and it was 11pm. The crowd anxiously gathered outside the glass doors, banging on them and demanding to be let in. But we were not ready. We only had the hall's incandescent lights on, and no sound yet. It reminded me of the beginning sequence in *The Wall*. Any minute a riot could've broken out. There was no power for the sound system yet. As much of Pfunk's gear as we could salvage had been brought in. They parked their bus just outside the back of the building's bay doors. Band members kept walking into our work area, getting in the way of the setup. They were anxious to play. I sent someone off to get them more beer and drugs. As much beer and drugs as could be found, to keep them partying on the bus. Shit, there were like twenty people in the band and about forty or fifty people partying on that bus.

The pounding on the glass doors kept getting louder as the mob repeatedly chanted, "Shit, God-damn, get off yer' ass and Jam!"

I refused to have the doors opened until we had power to the sound system. I had a sickening feeling. I wanted to throw up. All the pressure was on me. I was responsible for this madness. The glass doors would soon shatter, the crowd would rush in, there would be no music, and I would be torn apart limb from limb. It was an agonizing fear.

The chanting and pounding continued, on and on.

Finally, at about fifteen minutes to midnight, the sound system fired up. I had never been so happy in my life. We opened the doors and let the monsters in. They all rushed to the front of the temporary stage area where we had built a makeshift barricade to safely separate them from the band.

The sound check was just beginning, so there was more time to wait. The crowd was very large and filled up the entire hall within minutes. People up front started to get crushed into the plywood barricade. I had to calm them down somehow. I went to the band bus and asked George Clinton to come out and help me.

"George, the sound isn't ready yet, but people up front are starting to get hurt. I need you to come out there and calm them down. Say something to get them to relax a little."

"Okay man, but I'm really fucked up. I don't know what to tell them. They might really freak out on me, ya' dig? If there's no music yet, they're gonna be mad. They might rush the stage and kill us all!"

"Well that's very reassuring, George, but I'll come up with something for you to say. I'll stand there with you and whisper it in your ear. They will listen to you before me. Okay?"

"Okay, man, let's do this."

George Clinton spoke into the microphone with his arm around me as I whispered into his ear. I remembered how the Grateful Dead handled these situations as I muttered the words to George.

"Okay, we need all you people in the back to take a step back!"

George repeated the words in his raspy funkadelic tone. The crowd was listening intently and probably thinking the show was about to start.

"Okay, now take another step back! And another step back! You see all these people up front are getting horribly smashed. They're all bug-eyed!"

It was working.

"Take another step back!"

George smiled at me. He was my puppet. And he looked like a puppet, too. Funky-colored kaleidoscope hair, feather boas around his neck, multi-colored, paint-splattered robe. He was quite the psychedelic fashion statement.

"We'll be back in a few minutes to start the show."

About fifteen minutes later, the mothership landed. Holy shit, did it ever!

We wanted the funk, we had to have that funk, and they gave us the funk!

The biggest smile I have ever had in my life was planted on my face. Along the backstage wall was Middle Earth, dancing. The Bama

Boys, K. Fimster, Marc and Celeste, the GAMA crew, all my dearest and best friends. Leah came over and held my hand. I had a tear in my eye.

"We did it! We fucking pulled it off! Yeeessss!"

Then another weird thing happened. I noticed large white flakes falling around us like snow. It was like a dream, like it was snowing inside. Fimster pointed up at the ceiling and smiled. There were large paint flakes coming off of the fucking roof! We turned that mother owwwt!

Pfunk rocked it until the sun came up. The zombie crowd crawled out of the building into the dawn sunlight having just been funked out of their minds.

The crew was unbelievable that night. There is no way that show would have gone on if it hadn't have been for all those pitching in wherever they could. The solidarity was unlike anything I had ever been a part of. Of all the shows I've been involved with over the years, that one will always stand out as the one I am the most proud of.

CHAPTER 44

Pitfall

One of my favorite Gainesville pastimes was psychedelic mushroom hunting. Alachua County and the surrounding areas are notorious for having great psilocybin mushroom fields. Some of the old-time hippies tipped me off to some good fields to hunt in, not far from some local swamps. Leah and I both enjoyed hiking out in the mornings in search of good 'shrooms.

One particular day, I was out exploring on my own and I came upon a creek that was blocking my access to a particular field. The creek was flooded out from a recent storm, and I couldn't find an adequate spot to cross it. The narrowest section was right next to an old mossy oak tree, and I only had one choice, which was to try a dead jump across the water. I was very nervous, because the water looked deep.

I threw my backpack across to the grass on the other side and got my nerve up to jump. I didn't make it. I landed in the water half way across and fell in over my head. I pulled myself up onto the embankment just as a very large alligator, probably eight or nine feet, surfaced in the exact spot I fell into. My heart thumped wildly out of control as I crawled backwards away from the water further up the embankment. My thoughts were to get up and run, but I knew there was no way to outrun an alligator. Besides I was frozen with fear, could barely move, and was covered in swampy green algae water. I flashed ahead to thoughts of at least losing a limb or two. The gator made a weird noise as if it were slightly annoyed, and then it just swam on down the creek. Blessed again! And I was rewarded a great bonus, because that day I walked away with an entire garbage bag full of wonderful treats.

One of the most enjoyable parts of picking mushrooms is that you start to feel the effects from them soaking into your skin. It should be noted, the alligator incident was no hallucination; that happened before I found any fungus.

Leah also had a frightening run-in when she was out picking alone in the same area. After she got a big score of 'shrooms, an alligator blocked her trail back out. There were swamps on both sides and no way out behind her. A momma gator was laying out across the trail with babies on her back. The sun was setting quickly and the creepy red eyes of the hundreds of gators in the swamps around her began to glow in the growing dark. She had no choice but to make a run for it as the sun faded into the night. Luckily they left her alone. A word to the wise: always bring a friend when you're out mushroom hunting in Florida swamps.

I would have been there with her, for sure, but I had recently relocated to New Orleans. Leah would soon join me and wanted to bring along some treats for when we reunited.

The decision to move to New Orleans came to me suddenly in the spring of 1997. It was in part a reaction to Leah telling me that she was going to move to Boone, North Carolina for more schooling. It would've resulted in us breaking up. I can't pinpoint exactly why New Orleans was calling me, but it was. I woke up from a dream one morning and stated matter-of-fact, just like that: I had to move to New Orleans. I know that I was getting frustrated with the Gainesville music scene. It seemed to be losing momentum and I wasn't evolving much anymore with my own music. The bands I had been in changed members too frequently, and it was hard to get any real commitments out of anyone. I always admired and loved the culture of New Orleans and I had some good Middle Earth friends that lived there, Marc and Celeste.

Leah was very supportive and quickly changed her mind about moving to Boone. She wanted to move to New Orleans, too.

CHAPTER 45

N'awlins

In late spring of 1997, I moved in with Middle Earthers Marc and Celeste in an old Victorian shotgun house in the famed Garden District. Leah stayed behind in Gainesville for a couple of months, finishing up a semester of college. Marc and Celeste had actually met and fallen for each other at one of the Alachua Music Harvests—the third one, I think. Well, there's a little more background actually: they first met during Spring Tour '91 at K. Fimster's in North Carolina that time when I showed up with Celeste and a bunch of rainbow hippies to camp out in his yard; but I digress.

Just around the corner and up two blocks from our New Orleans home was Anne Rice's house, nearby the old mansion where Jefferson Davis died. I fell in love with the rich history of New Orleans. I had already been in love with its music and culture. I was right where I wanted to be.

I took a job in the French Quarter, at the famous House Of Blues. In my time off, I explored the city's history and spent hours researching it at the public library. I also did a lot of partying. New Orleans, pronounced N'awlins by the locals, is a town that truly never sleeps and is full of sin and hedonism. My sleeping schedule was all out of whack. On most days, I would not retire to bed until the sun had already risen. The bars in New Orleans stayed open twenty-four hours a day, closing for just thirty minutes to clean. But the thirty minute cleaning time always varied from bar to bar, so you could always find one open, usually next door to the bar you were in.

Everyone lived there with the fear that, one day, the city's levees would give out and a great flood would drown the town. This fear was common knowledge back then, nearly a decade before Katrina. In our house, Marc and Celeste lived in a converted attic. Attached to the ceiling was an axe that could be used to break through the roof, should you need to escape due to flooding. Most of the houses there had axes like that in the attics, which did prove horribly true as people were driven into their attics to ride out Katrina, and sometimes to drown there.

On my first night in town, I was asleep in the front room of the house. Just after midnight, I noticed flashlights peering through the window. Suddenly, there was a knock at the door. It was the cops. I answered the door and the police wanted to know if I had seen or heard anything suspicious. I hadn't. They informed me that a robbery had just taken place at a store on the corner, and the clerk there had been murdered. Welcome to N'awlins!

Musically, I struggled to get things off the ground. I hosted a few jams at the house with some local musicians I met. I joined in on a few around town, too. My buddy, Chris Mulé, formerly of the Fatty Tea Bags, was living there at the time, and he and I occasionally jammed together. I also set up a few jams with a girl, Maggie Louie, who had once been in a Pensacola band called Buttermilk. Maggie was such a fine singer; I adored her voice dearly. I had promoted Buttermilk in Gainesville a few times. They played at the Alachua Music Harvest, too. After Buttermilk split, other members went on to form the band Particle, which became very popular in the jam scene years later.

Another popular New Orleans artist I was fortunate enough to spend some quality porch jamming time with was Anders Osborne. He also used to perform occasionally in Gainesville, and it was an honor to be able to befriend him and play a little music with him in the Big Easy. All things considered, N'awlins was a great source of musical inspiration. I penned several songs there.

As part of my historical research, I was fascinated by the old theaters in town. Two, in particular, stirred my interest—the old abandoned Civic Theatre on Baronne Street and a hidden theatre in the

Masonic Temple at 333 St. Charles Avenue. My partner in crime was Rachel Shafer, the box office manager at the House Of Blues. She and I explored these theaters together and came up with a plan to open our own venue. We set our on eyes on the Masonic Theatre. It was located on the secret thirteenth floor of the Masonic Temple building. I secured the rights of exclusivity from the building's owners (the Masonic lodge) while we worked on finding investors and getting a business plan together. We had meetings at the mayor's office, brought in a grant writer, and quickly assembled a dedicated team. I even paid my dues to join the local blue lodge there and studied up on becoming a Mason. I found the symbolism and culture enchanting. I always had a passion for old buildings, especially theaters and abandoned movie palaces. The sacred geometry of the Masonic Temples was of particular interest. The theater seemed just right, and we came very close to making that dream a reality.

Another project I had taken on at the time involved meetings with an up-and-coming promoter, Superfly Productions. Rick and Kerry were the guys behind Superfly, and they were interested in expanding their promotions beyond the house parties they had been throwing. They reminded me a lot of what GAMA was like in the beginning. They had never seen a Pollstar magazine, nor did they know such industry resources existed before I gave them a few copies to check out. I also gave them some proposal ideas on music events I was hoping to produce with them. There were some events that involved the Masonic Theater, some that involved concerts on a riverboat, and one that involved a large outdoor music festival in partnership with GAMA.

Hoping to move forward with Superfly, I asked for a position as a production manager and they suddenly did an about face. I'll never understand that decision on their part. I was under the impression that we had started a friendship and a potential business relationship, when suddenly these guys literally said to me, and I quote, "We don't need you anymore." I had trusted them with my inside knowledge of the business that I'm certain they were on the verge of discovering, but they simply showed no appreciation or respect to me. They told me that they had a production guy that they were going to partner with, a former talent buyer for the famous N'awlins' nightclub Tippitina's.

Now, certainly, this guy had similar insights into the business as I did, but I know they weren't as far along as I was, or they would have already known certain things that they appeared to be naïve about.

Superfly went on to produce a few riverboat shows, a couple of productions at the Masonic Theater, and, after I was fed up and left town, they created the Bonnaroo Music Festival. I had a lawyer friend in New Orleans at the time who I had talked with about protecting my ideas as intellectual property, but in the end, he ended up working with them. He got my permission for them to do their first show in the theatre, which I granted assuming it would strengthen my relationship with them. I got stabbed in the back somehow, and I had no idea why, other than cold, ruthless, cunning greed on their part. All I really wanted was to be a passionate and creative part of the process with them. I wanted to continue on with what we had created with GAMA, but these New Orleans guys were shrewd, and in my own way I was naïve. I was distraught when I realized they had taken my knowledge and ideas and cut me out; eventually the confidence I had in my projects fell apart and I released my exclusive arrangement with the theater building.

Another opportunity arose with the company StagePro out of Lawrence, Kansas. I had hired StagePro to handle all the staging, lights, and sound needs for our big festivals in Florida (except for the one that the roof collapsed). I flew up to Kansas and traveled with them on a couple of different weekends, putting on concerts with them, in Missouri and Iowa. It was a test run for me to see if I wanted to travel with the company for the next summer festival season.

Back in New Orleans, things were getting rough. The town left a few scars on me. Spiritually, the town held a lot of demons and that I felt manifested in people's everyday lives. Leah and I had a tough time in our relationship there. We fought a lot. One night we got into a huge fight while we were out with friends. All of us were drunk, and I elected myself to drive for some stupid reason. I should have never been behind that wheel. I was swerving recklessly down Saint Charles Avenue, trying to avoid hitting the oncoming trolley cars. I realized that I missed the turn and pulled a quick U-turn. Another fast right, and I veered off to the left and into our friends' driveway. The police lights were flashing in my rear view mirror as I came to a stop.

"You're so going to jail!" Leah yelled at me from the passenger's seat. I got out of the car and stumbled toward the cops. I was asked if I had been drinking.

"Jus' a li'l bit, one or two maybe, but really, really, I'm totally fine."

Then I was asked about the broken glass and shattered window remains on the driver's side window.

"Well, officers, you can see, that our car was broken into tonight in the French Quarter. The bastards smashed the glass and stole a few items." Which was true.

"Where are you headed in such a hurry?"

"To drop off our friends here, and then we live jus' 'round the corner." I mumbled swaying back and forth, trying to point in the direction of our house.

"Okay, I'm going to give you a warning, and then follow you back to your place, to make sure you get home safely."

"Thank you, officers."

It was a serious wake-up call. I couldn't believe that I hadn't killed us all that night, and I was very fortunate to avoid being arrested. I was so hammered that I thought I was talking to two cops, but Leah pointed out that there had only been one. He must've had better things to do than deal with me. But that was typical N'awlins for ya'.

My friend Bobby Sheehan of Blues Traveler moved to town that winter, and that really didn't help slow my partying down. Any night of the week that I wasn't pulling a shift at the House Of Blues, I could be found at one of the town's legendary bars—the Maple Leaf, Checkpoint Charlie's, the Dragon's Den—or hanging out with Bobby doing loads of cocaine. Copious amounts of alcohol, opium, and coke were getting the best of me, and I had the notion that living in the Crescent City was going to kill me. I felt my wheels spinning again. I wasn't working enough on my music, my ideas were being stolen, my projects were falling apart, I wasn't making enough money, and, ultimately, I was burning myself out. Although I really fell in love with that town and had lots of big ideas there, in the end, I felt I was going to die if I had stayed.

CHAPTER 46

StagePro

I left Leah standing on the front porch of our New Orleans home. I got in the U-Haul truck and drove away through the misty Louisiana rain. I was sad and questioned the decision I had made. It was a brutal drive. I felt guilty, regretful, and tortured the entire time. I shouldn't have left. I knew that, but I convinced myself there was no turning back. So, off I went again, chasin' dreams.

I took a sound engineering job with StagePro. Leah stayed in New Orleans for a couple of months before moving back to her hometown of St. Petersburg, Florida. We had decided that our relationship was officially on hiatus.

With StagePro, all of my sound engineering skills were taken to another level. I was touring the country in semi-trucks, living out of hotels, and working on state-of-the-art audio gear. We were doing a lot of country music festivals, state fairs, county fairs, and mini-tours for some top-level country music acts: Diamond Rio, Sawyer Brown, Neal McCoy, Teri Clark, Travis Tritt, Toby Keith, the list goes on and on. And there was the occasional jam festival, too.

Another great thing about working at StagePro was getting to see all my friends from the road. I had amassed so many acquaintances in different regions of the country from all my Dead touring years, no matter where StagePro went I had friends showing up at the gigs to say hello. In Nashville, I got to work with George Clinton & The Pfunk Allstars again and to see some friends from Middle Earth. We also did a festival for Superfly in New Orleans, and I got to party again with most of my N'awlins buddies. Bobby Sheehan was an absolute coked-up mess; I really felt like his situation was getting out of hand and I expressed my concern to him.

Back in New Orleans with StagePro, without Leah there, I started to feel lonely. I actually hooked up with a good friend at one point and even had an encounter with a new girl. It all just made me long for Leah, though. I missed her horribly and kept in touch with her as much as I could. I wrote her a heartfelt letter and asked if she would consider moving to Colorado with me. I wanted us to work on our relationship and possibly settle down together. She responded enthu-siastically and agreed to move to Colorado.

Early that summer, Leah made the first move and relocated from St. Pete to Boulder. I took a short break from StagePro and met up with her there. We went to see our friends Widespread Panic play a show at Red Rocks Amphitheatre. She also attended a few StagePro gigs, when they were within short enough driving distance. It really seemed as though some possibilities of a decent future were emerging. At some point, she found us a house in Denver. Things were looking up.

My job at StagePro was scheduled to end that fall, 1998. For nearly eight months I had been fine-tuning my audio skills. The crew of guys that I worked with became my brothers in arms. There were some in-tense moments on and off the road. Our home base was the college town of Lawrence, Kansas, which had a similar but smaller scene and vibe reminiscent of both Gainesville and Boulder.

On our way into Lawrence one night, a particularly scary inci-dent occurred. There were four of us in the cab of the semi truck. Two guys were asleep in the bunks, I was in the passenger's seat and light-ing designer Bob Pinkerton was behind the wheel. Bob was also my roommate for a house we all shared in Lawrence. It was around 4am and we had been driving all night. All of us were dead tired from a show we had worked earlier that day. Sometimes, those after-show drives were the worst and it was hell trying to stay awake. My job was to keep the driver alert, so I would pick out the music, usually Iron Maiden, our favorite. We were only a few miles outside of Lawrence, our home destination, when I fell asleep. I might have been out for a minute or so when I sensed the danger. I heard a thumping sound. I opened my eyes and looked over at Bob. His head and arms were resting on the steering wheel. His eyes were closed. THUMP! THUMP! THUMP! THUMP! We were running over construction cones that were dividing the interstate highway into a two-lane construction zone. We were easily traveling over 70 miles per hour, way too fast. We had veered into the opposite lane with the headlights of oncoming traffic heading straight toward us. This was all happening within a few seconds from when I opened my eyes.

"Bob!" I shouted.

With lightning speed, he snapped out of his slumber and said "I got it!" He gripped the steering wheel tight and jerked it to the right. We barreled off the highway and onto the right shoulder just narrowly avoiding a head-on collision. The truck jerked so violently that the two other crew guys fell out of their bunks. We almost jackknifed! After we came to a complete stop, we all jumped out of the truck and kissed the ground. We lit up cigarettes and tried to calm down our jitters—everyone was wide awake and alert!

I liked Lawrence a lot, and I really enjoyed learning so much from the company's owner, Jay Waller, who was a mentor to me. But I realized that Kansas wasn't where I wanted to be, and the road was just too dangerous and lonely. I wanted to settle down with Leah in Colorado. The last big festival that I was scheduled to work was back in Gainesville, ironically—the sixth Alachua Music Harvest. It would be a fitting end and transition for me.

CHAPTER 47

James Brown!

At the sixth Harvest, in October 1998, the GAMA crew had done a great job of carrying on where I had left off. I was proud to be returning to Gainesville working for the very company, StagePro, that I had hired so many years earlier to run sound and staging at our festivals. That year's headliners were Pfunk, Maceo Parker, Herbie Hancock, Ben Harper, Gov't Mule (Warren Haynes' band) and the legendary James Brown. Brown's set would prove to be an exceptional experience for me and seriously tested my sound engineering skills. And it was great to catch up with the Pfunk boys again, Ben Harper, of course, and my old friend Warren Haynes.

One story I haven't shared here yet was how I got into sound engineering in the first place. It all started back in Oakland when I was living at the Paradigm Studios, six years earlier. One day, Bob Thomas, one of the studio owners, asked me to help him load-in a show at San Francisco's Off-Broadway Theatre. I think it was for a band that featured the Jefferson Starship guitarist Craig Chaquico, but I don't recall, specifically. After we had setup all the gear and Bob was ready to do a sound check, he got a call that his wife was going into labor. He turned to me. "You got this, right?"

"Um, what do you mean?"

"My wife's having the baby. I gotta go. You have to do sound for these guys."

"No problem, yeah. I got this."

I really didn't have a clue, but I was thrown to the wolves and figured everything out on the spot. The band didn't seem to realize I was faking it all, and I managed to pull it off. That was my first real sound engineering experience. From then on I dabbled here and there with the company Sound On Stage, which ran sound on most of the BGP gigs. Once I moved to Gainesville, I began picking up more sound gigs for the local bands through GAMA.

So back to the sixth Alachua Music Harvest, October 1998, and the headlining act of the weekend: the godfather of soul, James Brown. The act before Brown had just finished, and the crew was frantically setting the stage up for the man himself. There had been no headliner sound check that day, so we were going to do it on the fly, in the moment, festival style. In fact, Brown's crew and equipment had just arrived on scene, and they didn't have their own sound engineers traveling with them. So we had really no idea what to expect.

There were close to 20,000 people in attendance, and my front-of-house soundboard setup was located a good distance from the stage, in the center of the crowd. The plan was for a twenty-minute changeover between acts, so there was no time for me to walk through the crowd to help out on the stage. Things had to happen fast. My intercom light began flashing.

"Yeah?"

"Dewey, they've got two drum kits, a percussion setup, two bass players, three guitarists, two organs, six horns, and some background singers. How do you want me to do this?" It was my good friend and StagePro monitor engineer, Beau Connelly, who I had been touring with for the past eight months. The soundboard I was using was an ATI Paragon, one of the best consoles in the business. But I only had 42 inputs to work with. With that many instruments, we couldn't possibly put microphones on everything.

"Just strike it all and start from scratch. I'll zero my console out here."

"Okay, I'll start with the drums and call you back with an input list once we get closer."

"Sounds good, keep me posted."

The crew ran around even more frantically. Brown's band was

huge! There were way too many instruments up there. I was feeling a big wave of fear and anxiety. The large crowd was restless. I feared a riot. The intercom light went off again.

"James Brown doesn't use monitors! I'm striking all the front wedges. Only the band is going to get monitors, but I don't even think I have enough for all of them!"

"Do you want me up there?"

"No, stay where you're at, there's no time! Their guy says that James Brown only wants to hear the house sound. The pressure is going to be all on you! These guys are crazy up here; I'm getting really pissed off!"

"Yeah, there's no fucking walkway to the stage, man. This crowd's too big!"

"I understand, don't worry. We've got this!"

Beau proceeded to start rewiring the stage with all the new microphone setups as I cleared all the settings on the Paragon. Brown's musicians were gathering on stage and setting up their gear, calling out requests to Beau from all directions. It was the most hectic scene I had ever witnessed on a festival stage. After several agonizing minutes, the intercom light flashed again.

"Hey, this is Snowball, stage manager for James Brown."

"Yeah, how's it going up there?"

"Not so good, the monitor engineer just quit."

"What? Beau?"

"Yeah, he just threw down some cables and walked off."

"Get him on the intercom for me please."

"Hold on ..."

A few minutes later, Beau picked up the intercom.

"I can't do it man! Fuck these guys! I've had enough, I'm really sorry, but they won't listen to me at all. It's fucking hell up here!"

"So what are you saying?"

"I got everything I could patched in, but they're not fucking listening to me! It's mostly there, but I don't know where shit's going to show up. They're fucking repatching it all, man! This is bullshit!"

"Who's repatching?"

"One of their guys! I don't even know who is who up here! They can run it themselves. I need to get off this stage before I lose it!"

"Alright, that's fine, I'll just pull shit up as they start making noise. Don't worry about it. If they're treating you like shit, just go take a break, walk it off. We'll be fine."

And with that, Beau left the stage. I never blamed him for reacting that way. He had had enough, and I probably would've caved in, too, especially if people were being disrespectful. We had been in the trenches many times together and I'll always remain proud of every show that we worked, including that one. The intercom light flashed.

"This is Snowball, again."

"Yeah."

"Are we going to have a monitor guy up here?" he asked.

"Nope. He's done man. I don't know what's going on up there, and I can't get through this crowd."

"Well, the show is about to start, so I guess I have no choice but to run the monitors myself then."

"Can you give me an input list?"

"No. I'm not really sure where everything is yet."

"Alright then, we're going to just wing it! At least test that lead vocal for me."

"Okay, stand by."

A minute or so later Snowball started checking James Brown's lead vocal microphone. I scanned the Paragon looking for a signal. It was showing up in channel 42, the last available input on my desk.

We talked again on the intercom.

"Oh by the way, I patched the spare vocal into channel 43 on the snake."

"I don't have a 43 out here! I only go to 42."

"Well, you'll have to repatch it down the board somewhere."

"Alright, no worries, I'll figure something out."

"They're coming to the stage now, are you ready?"

"Yeah, fuck it, let's do this!"

I quickly went behind my soundboard and looked for a spot to patch in channel 43 from the audio snake line. The crowd was going nuts. The front-of-house sound tower was now jam packed with people crowding my whole area. There was no security posted, and I had no time to do crowd control. The spotlights were placed on the deck above the soundboard and several fans had climbed up the tower to watch the show from up there. The Paragon is equipped with "A" and "B" inputs on each channel, so I made the fast decision to just put the spare vocal line into the same channel as the lead vocal, number 42. I reasoned that it was a spare, so if I needed it, I could just hit the "A-B" switch on the channel and all would be fine. Besides, the whole purpose of a "spare" was in case something went wrong with the main microphone.

Just as the band was hitting the stage, an engineer friend showed up at the soundboard and offered to help me get the mix going. "You take the left half of the console, the drums, get 'em dialed in. I'll work the right half!" I shouted.

The band started... oh shit, no turning back. The tower started swaying from all the people hanging off of it. Worst-case scenario, we would all die.

The band started with a medley of James Brown hits that led into "Living In America," and it sounded funky, funky, funky. I started guessing at all the inputs as quickly as I could through my headphones. It was all there. The drums were coming together, the bass was heard, guitars, horns, vocals. I could hear everything! I zoomed all over the board, faster than I had ever done. It was all magically falling into place. The crowd of 20,000 were crazy, screaming, dancing, smiling, swaying, grooving, thumping—it was nuts! I had chills on my skin, a smile on my face, a shake to my hips, as I grooved along to the funk, mixing James Brown on the fly! About three or four songs into the set, the mix was getting tighter. I had never felt so good mixing before. The anxiety was gone; I was high off the adrenaline. James Brown called for everyone's attention.

"Ladies and Gentlemen... ladies and gentlemen! I gotta a surprise for you tonight, Gainesville!" The crowd went crazy.

"We are blessed tonight... very blessed! A very good friend of mine, a friend of this world, a friend of America, a friend of the children, a friend of your daddy, your grandfather..."

Uh-oh. What microphone was this *friend* going to use? I called Snowball on the intercom.

"Who's coming out on what? What channel?!"

"Spare vocal! Bo Diddly. Channel 43!"

"FUUUUUCK!"

There was no time for me to repatch.

"Let's give this man a big 'round of applause if you will, make him feel good because he lives jus' down the road from here and he is a MAAAN... Mistah Bo Diddly!" The crowd went insane. "Bo Diddly! Bo Diddly!"

So I look up to the stage, the band had started the blues anthem, "I'm A M-A-N," and Bo Diddly is walking out towards the center of the stage with the wireless spare vocal microphone. There are no stage monitors down front, so just like James Brown, he would be expecting to hear his voice over the house loud speakers. I've got my finger on channel 42's "A-B" switch, ready to go back and forth between him and James. It was my only choice in the moment. I prayed that they didn't sing at the same time.

"Ha! M!" shouted James. I hit the switch.

"A!" shouted Bo. I hit the switch again.

"N!" shouted James.

The entire song they traded off words but never sang at the same time. I kept my finger on the button and flawlessly pulled it off. It was the most nerve-racking, unbelievable, and insanely rewarding live mixing experience of my life!

Sometime later in the set, Beau relieved Snowball on the monitor desk. Snowball made his way to me out front. I thought he was going to take over or have me change the mix, but he just congratulated me on how great the sound was. He said it was one of the best mixes he had ever heard. I was simply over the moon. It was an amazing end for me to finish off my touring stint there in Gainesville, with all my old friends. The next day, I headed off to Colorado. I couldn't wait to see Leah.

CHAPTER 48

Suicide Solution

W hen I finally arrived in Denver, I was exhausted from the drive. Bob Pinkerton, my friend and co-worker from StagePro, had lent me his van for the move. In exchange, I left Bob with my car, an old Volkswagen Rabbit that I had purchased in Lawrence. I arrived excited to leave behind the stress of working on the road. I anticipated a new life with Leah. It was a chance for us to start over and to settle down together, perhaps to get married and maybe even start a family at some point.

I pulled up outside our house near Fifth and Pennsylvania in the Governor's Park neighborhood. It was nighttime. I had not even seen our new place yet. Leah had come outside to greet me. I had been sending her money from the road and she picked the place out a couple of months earlier. We talked on the phone nearly every day, but it was October and I had not seen her since July. I was so tired from the drive, but adrenaline kicked in when I saw her waiting on the steps. I got out of the van and rushed over to give her a big hug. Her hands went up.

"Wait, we need to talk."

She might as well have just kicked me in the balls.

"You're kidding me right? I haven't seen you in two or three months. I've been driving for twelve hours straight. I've missed you terribly and you won't give me a hug?" I was bewildered, exhausted, confused, and suddenly overwhelmingly anxious.

"Let's go inside and talk first before you start unpacking."

That's never a good sign.

First of all, I had no plans of unpacking until the next day anyway, but now I was being confronted with a troubling situation. All I could think of is that she must've been with someone else while I was on the road. I had to digest those thoughts pretty quickly as we walked into the house. I had made up my mind that I would accept whatever it was. It was probably my fault for being on the road for so long. She must've been pretty lonely.

"It's okay," I told her, "I just want us to start over. If you were with someone else, I'm willing to forgive you right now and work on us following through with our plan. You don't even have to tell me who it was."

"Who said I cheated on you? Did you cheat on me? What's all this?" We went back and forth.

She wouldn't admit to sleeping with anyone, but she did say that she had gone out on some dates. Our time apart had got her thinking more about her independence. She wanted me to drive back to Kansas with all my shit still packed in the van. She just dumped it all on me like that. She could've told me over the phone before I made the long trip, but, no, she waited to see me in person. I was absolutely floored that she was breaking up with me. I got depressed and angry but was too exhausted to fight with her about it. I just left the house and got in the van and drove off.

I had nowhere to go, but I was certainly not going to drive back to Kansas and there was no way I wanted to stay with her in the house that night. I tried a couple of motels but there were no vacancies. So then I found a run-down shit hole crack motel off of I-25, the Motel Seven. The lady said she only had one room that she's really not supposed to rent it out, but if I was willing to deal with it. I was so desperate at that point that I didn't care. I needed to get my head together, I needed to sleep, and I just needed a room, any room! I begged her.

"Whatever, as long as there is a bed, I'll take it!"

She had a burning cigarette dangling out of her mouth, looked like she herself hadn't slept in days, and had that "I really don't give a shit, honey" look on her face. "Here's the keys. You better look it over first."

I opened up the door and ducked under the yellow police tape to enter the room. I could not believe my eyes. It was like something out of a movie, a horror movie. There was a chalk outline of a body on the floor, shotgun holes in the wall, and what looked like dried blood everywhere. Blood stains on the walls, on the floor, and on the television. It was the most disgusting thing I had ever seen in my life. "But the bed was made and the T.V. works?"

I actually sat there on the bed. I tried to convince myself that I could deal with it. It was no big deal, I thought. Then the reality hit me. I got flashes of a really dark, evil energy. I started to feel sick to my stomach. I ran out of my room and back to the front desk. I shook my head back and forth and put the keys back on the desk.

"I can't do it. When did that happen in there?"

"Last night." She told me, while giggling.

"You really shouldn't let anyone see that."

"Yeah, but you seemed pretty desperate."

"I'm not that desperate."

I drove away from the motel in absolute shock. For the first time since I had been back across the Colorado border, I laughed a little. Up the road, I found vacancy at a Days Inn that appeared to be drama-free.

After a few tears, and a nice relaxing bath, I called Leah to tell her where I was. She was hysterical on the phone, saying that she was worried out of her mind, freaking out. I told her that I would come by in the morning and we would talk some more, to try to figure things out. But first, I needed some sleep.

In the morning, I had made up my mind that I was definitely not going back to Kansas, and, since I had been sending her money, the place was technically half mine. I was moving in and she would just have to deal with it—at least until I found an apartment. Besides, the whole idea of us moving to Denver in the first place was mine. She was in Denver because of me. This is where I wanted to live.

When I arrived at the house, she greeted me with the hug that I had anticipated the night before. We talked and I told her my plan. She was okay with it, and helped me move my stuff in. That night, we had make-up sex, and it seemed as though the whole breakup never happened.

The next weekend I was scheduled to work just one more Stage-Pro event in Kansas. The plan was for me to drive Bob's van back to Lawrence and we would exchange vehicles. But first we'd set off to do a two-day Amway Convention in Wichita before I could return to Denver to kick off yet another new life. As fate would have it, though, another devastating situation was about to suddenly arise.

Just before I left for Kansas, Leah and I had a terrible argument. I don't remember anymore what it was about, but it was apparent that we had not patched everything up. On the drive to Kansas, I had a nice soundboard Blues Traveler tape in the cassette deck. It was a show that I had patched into the board myself, from the first H.O.R.D.E. Tour, at Garden State Arts Center in New Jersey. I was about fifteen minutes or less from the Kansas-Colorado border when the tape started sounding funny. Smoke came out from the deck, so I immediately pulled the van over to the side of the highway. More smoke bellowed out through the tape deck. I got out of the van to have a look under the hood. The wind was gusting so heavy that I could barely open the hood up. But when I did, I was dismayed to see a small fire burning up a hose and dripping flames down onto vital engine components. I slammed down the hood and noticed that now the entire inside of the van was full of black smoke. I immediately thought about getting in there and rescuing some of my things but when I touched the door handle, it was too hot. I tried to open the door but I could see the large flames devourer the dashboard. I stepped back. My heart was racing and I was unsure of what to do next. Within a minute, the entire van was engulfed in flames.

The winds were so furious that day, fueling the burning van. I backed away more. Cars and trucks started to pull over. A trucker ran over with a fire extinguisher and tried to help, but the entire van was now consumed in fire. He emptied the canister in vain. The interstate traffic had ground to a halt. Vehicles were now afraid to pass because the smoke and fire were so large. The wind blew the flame away from the van and on to the grass next to the highway. A prairie fire was unleashed.

Fire trucks soon arrived and both directions of traffic were completely shut down. The wildfire was spreading to the south, growing huge. A helicopter was called in and dropped buckets of water on the burning prairie. My jacket, wallet, keys, laptop, and personal items were all inside the scorched van.

When it was over with, there was nothing left of the white van but a burnt black shell. Ashes were scattered everywhere. They put out the firestorm on the prairie, too, but not before losing about ten acres. I was in shock and had no idea on how to proceed next. The highway patrolman put me in a cop car and interviewed me. He kept asking me if there was anyone else in the van. I had to wait with him until the fire was completely out, so they could inspect the van for dead bodies. Finally, I was driven to the nearest town, Burlington, and dropped off at a local bar. It was now well into night. I went into the bar and sat down. I had no money, no wallet, nothing. I decided I had to call Kansas and let someone at StagePro know what happened. It looked like I wouldn't be making it into work. I made a collect call and I spoke to either Russ or Craig. They said that the trucks were all ready to leave so they'd have to find someone to fill in for me. My best bet would be to head back to Denver somehow.

Then I spoke to Bob. I had to tell him about the van. I felt horrible. It was in my possession and the thing just completely burnt down. He was very cool with it. In fact, he laughed because he had something to tell me that he was worried about. Apparently my car's engine had seized up the day before and he had to get it towed to a junkyard. He wasn't sure how he was going to break it to me. But since I destroyed his van, we just called it even and laughed about it.

My next collect call was to Leah to come and get me. Burlington was about three hours from Denver. She was not happy, but agreed to come rescue me. I sat down in the bar next to one of the firemen from earlier in the day. He bought me a beer and a shot, which turned into several more. "Hell of a fire you started out there today," he said.

"Yeah, well it wasn't my first van fire. I figured I would do it right this time," I said and we laughed.

Leah finally arrived and I had a nice buzz going. I thanked the fireman for his kindness, and Leah and I were soon on our way back to Denver.

A few days later, I found my own apartment and moved out. The following month, Leah moved out of the house, too, and into the apartment with me. I started doing sound at a couple of different venues around town—the Casino Cabaret in Five Points and the Bluebird Theatre on Colfax Avenue. Leah and I were arguing on and off, on and off. She kept her car packed ready to split at any time... and one day she did. She just woke up and said, "I'm going to Boulder." She never returned. I became really depressed. To make myself feel better, I drastically changed my appearance one night. I shaved off all the long hair that I had kept for a good ten years. When I showed up at the Bluebird for work the next day with a buzz cut, no one recognized me.

Leah had severed all contact with me. One night she showed up at the Bluebird and neither of us spoke one word to each other. She had a new boyfriend with her. It fueled my depression immensely. I was horribly lonely and distraught over her leaving. All my accomplishments in life so far seemed to add up to nothing. My depression worsened each day; I was becoming chemically unbalanced and mentally unstable.

Several months went by and I had gone to the Fox Theatre in Boulder to see my friends, Day By The River, perform. They were a fantastic jam band from the south that used to play the Alachua Music Harvest. Suddenly, I noticed that Leah was there. She didn't see me right away. I stood at one of the sidebars when her friend Lauren appeared and was about to order them drinks. Lauren was also from Gainesville, too, and I had known her quite well, but she didn't recognize me with my hair all cut off. I knew that she and Leah both preferred Jim Beam & Cokes, so, just before Lauren could ask the bartender, I chimed in, "Two Beam 'n Cokes, please, on me."

Lauren looked over at me, bewildered. Then her eyes widened with that "holy shit" look on her face. We chatted for about a minute then she said she would take the drinks over to Leah and let her know that I was there. I noticed that Leah was standing next to her new boyfriend. That was too awkward for me, and I didn't want any more weirdness, so I asked Lauren not to say anything. Then, during the intermission I unintentionally walked right into Leah in the lobby. I tried to say hello, but she stuck her hand in my face and shunned me.

It devastated me and I left the venue immediately, kicking over a trash can on my way out.

Now, I have dealt with a lot of depression in my life, but nothing had ever struck me so hard and so fast as when her hand went up in my face. Her attempt to pretend she didn't even know me was like a dagger in my heart—a direct hit. I had been lost, lonely, and depressed since the day she left. I had been teetering on the edge of a cliff. With that one small action of her hand in my face, she pushed me over, and my negative emotions spiraled out of control. All logic and reason were gone. I had succumbed to the deepest, darkest emotions that I had ever felt—an endless cavern of gloom.

I drove back to my small Denver apartment, pathetically sobbing the whole way. I was sad, angry, confused, and out of touch with reality. And I'll be damned if that fucking pathetic Hootie and The Blowfish song didn't come on the radio during the drive. I punched the dash and cursed Darius Rucker to hell.

Inside the tiny, dark studio apartment, I frantically paced back and forth, trying to gain an ounce of sanity; but I couldn't get a grip. I had completely lost it, and was ready to slit my wrists. I had a serous breakdown. Yeah, I admit that my battles with depression had been at times very hard, and I had contemplated hurting myself from time to time. But this was different. The negative cells in my brain had won the battle that night and they were going for an all-out victory in the war. I had decided to do it—I no longer desired to breathe anymore. It was settled. I stopped pacing and felt calm. I would soon be at total peace.

I figured that the bathtub would be my way out. I would slit my wrists the proper way, and then when the pain became too unbearable, toss in the radio for a little light electrocution, a double whammy! What the hell, might as well go out with a bloody bang and make Hunter S. Thompson proud!

The moment was approaching as I lay calmly in the tub, softly sobbing and reminiscing about my great life and the people and memories I wanted to think of in my final breaths. You would think that with all that I had been through and all the proof that life can change so much on us, so quickly that suicide would not be something I would have contemplated. But it just doesn't work that way. Depression is a nasty disease and it can hijack your brain in a very bad way. In my mind at that time, the disease had won. There was no way to truly appreciate the good people and positive things in my life, while at that same time drowning in my own despondency. The radio played a quiet static as it sat on the back of the toilet. I gathered up the courage and placed the blade against my skin. As I was going in for the cut—RINGGGGG! RINGGGGG! RINGGGGG! You've got to be fucking kidding me! What the hell? Who would be calling at this time of night? It was 3 o'clock in the morning! Suddenly my calm resolve with ending my life had disappeared. I was angry again. The phone kept ringing. It went on for several minutes and finally stopped—ahhh, peace again.

Then I was suddenly bothered with who it was that was calling. Maybe it was her calling. No, it couldn't be. It just could not be! Besides, I didn't care anymore. I wanted to die. I was all there in that moment, ready to go. Shit, maybe it was a sign? Fuck! Anger, confusion, I didn't want to go out like that. Okay, I reasoned: if it rings again, maybe I'll take it as a sign, I'll consider changing my mind—RINGGGGG! RINGGGGG! RINGGGGG! Fuck! C'mon Universe, can't you see I'm trying to kill myself here? I let the phone ring and ring and ring; it went on forever. I looked up toward the ceiling and spoke to an imaginary higher power. "If you are trying to send me a message, it better be good. Because if it isn't, I'm outta here! I promise you that."

The phone went on ringing—past five minutes, past ten, past fifteen and approaching twenty minutes. I could no longer ignore it. Among other things, I wouldn't have felt right, as silly as it may seem, taking my life while the phone was ringing.

I got out of the tub and went into the room where the phone was. I stared at it, naked, dripping wet, still convinced that I wanted to die. I screamed, "GOD DAMNIT, THIS CALL BETTER SAVE MY FUCKING LIFE!" I reached down and grabbed the receiver. "WHAT!?!"

"Hey. It's Beau."

I recognized his voice, the last thing I was expecting to hear. It was my friend and former co-worker from StagePro, Beau Connelly. Why was he calling me like that? With the phone ringing on and on, forever? At 3am? I was confused and angry at first. Didn't he know I was trying to kill myself?

"What do you want?" I snapped at him.

"I'm sorry to call you this late, but it's really important." There was a long pause of silence. "Bob's dead."

Just like that. "Bob's dead."

There was another long silence.

"But I just talked to him a couple of days ago. What, what are you... what are you talking about, Beau?"

He went on to inform me that there was an accident. Bob had been in the back of a semi-truck loading out the Country Jam Festival in Wisconsin. The stage decks in the truck were out of alignment. He was trying to fix them, slipped, and they fell on top of him, crushing his head. He died instantly.

Beau said he figured I was out at the bars drinking and he was letting the phone ring on and on until I got home. He felt it was important that I know right away.

After I hung up the phone, I realized that, indeed, the call had saved my life. I snapped out of it when he said those words: Bob's dead. The incident forever changed my life and the way I view depression. I've had my bouts with it, but never again has the negativity taken me to such an extreme place.

The morning after that fateful phone call, I received a call from my mother that my Great Aunt Oneita had died in Gainesville. Wow, talk about messages from the other side. Okay, Universe... message received.

CHAPTER 49

Things To Do In Denver
When You're Not Dead

My main sound and production management gigs in Denver were at the Bluebird and Ogden theaters. I mixed almost every night of the week and soon had hundreds of bands to add to my résumé. It was those nights in the Bluebird when I really became a much better sound engineer. The music there ranged from punk rock and heavy metal to jam and funk bands. I also worked around town for a few of the big sound companies—Audio Denver, Dowlen Sound, and Advanced Audio.

For Audio Denver, I worked a regular sound gig at the Heritage Christian Center, a non-denominational Christian megachurch. I met and befriended several great musicians at Heritage, including the percussionist José Rossy. He had played in some pretty famous bands—Weather Report, the Talking Heads, Patti LaBelle, and Robert Palmer. We became great friends, performed, and recorded lots of music together.

I tried unsuccessfully to reach out to Leah to let her know what happened to Bob. She never returned any of my messages. Later, in the summer of 1999, I made a road trip to Florida and attended my ten-year high school reunion in Boca Raton.

At the reunion, I sat next to my old friend Ed, who was the one dating my first love Elle way back in 1987. Ed and Elle had dated for a few years back then (she chose him over me that time when we got back together for a single day). Ed told me that he hadn't seen or heard from her in years, but knew, like I did, that she had gotten married. Ed didn't know that I had written to Elle earlier that summer when I was depressed. All my letters had been returned "Undeliverable."

My friends Rob and Andre never showed up at the reunion. Andre was living in California by that time, and Rob was in Texas. I still managed to party down with lots of old friends that weekend, once we had gotten away from the stuffy hotel atmosphere.

One of the highlights was catching up with Crazy Fingers again at a show on the Pompano Beach Pier. It felt like old times. I visited with Sunshine, who was now raising a beautiful girl she'd had with Corey from Crazy Fingers. There was no information on where Springwater might be; she had moved on from Ohio, apparently.

On my way back to Colorado, I stopped in New Orleans. I made a trip to Bobby Sheehan's place only to find out that he had died of an apparent overdose just a few days earlier. All of the cocaine abuse had eventually destroyed him. I felt a great sadness and guilt, knowing that I had been an enabler. Considering the last time I had seen him, I wasn't all that surprised. It was really a devastating summer.

Back in Denver, I moved out of my lonely apartment and into a house at Colfax Avenue and Fillmore Street with Scott Baxendale. Scott was a guitar luthier and owned the Colfax Guitar Shop. Although my suicidal tendencies had waned, I began to seek resolution in the bottle. I drank heavily and experienced many blackouts that lasted for months.

During that time, I casually began dating a few different girls. Sierra and I had a lot in common, as far as politics and activism. We might have had a chance at something real if it weren't for one big issue that caused me to distance myself. One drunken night, she confided in me that I had gotten her pregnant, but "not to worry about it," she said. "It was already taken care of." I never got over that, the fact that I was never given a choice to support her in the decision process. I was informed after the fact, and that damaged our potential shot at any real lasting relationship. I put up a wall, even though I felt that we had a good connection. Sexually, our fling lasted on and off for many years. Whenever we were both single and would run into each other, we would hook up.

At the Bluebird, I diverted my heart to a co-worker, Aria. She was actually in a serious relationship at the time, but would sneak away in the middle of the night to spend time with me. The maddening guilt drove our desire. She eventually left the guy and we moved in together. Living with Aria became very challenging because she liked to drink— a lot.

I cannot count the number of times that I carried her blacked-out ass into the house. She was a very depressed person and liked to drown her sorrows in alcohol. That's pretty much what brought us together in the first place, but once the guilt had disappeared, our relationship began to deteriorate.

She was a very talented artist, too. It was a shame that she wasted so much of her talent with pitiful self-destruction. It wasn't all dark and gloomy, though. We had some really great moments, too. But, eventually I sobered up, and she spiraled further into the bottle.

CHAPTER 50

Must've Been The Doses

T he most LSD I ever ingested at one time was twenty-seven doses. That was at a Dead show in Miami near the end of a tour that I can no longer remember. It was simply due to the fact that I had been tripping almost daily, meaning I had to double my dosage each day to continue tripping. After that Miami show, Kilgore and I had the time of our lives on a lost weekend in Key West. And when I say "lost," I literally mean that, to this day, we still cannot figure out what year it happened in—as if the acid created a space-time vortex. By the time I had reached the point of needing twenty-seven hits to get high, I realized that I needed to stop dosing so much.

Once I was employed by Bill Graham Presents, I cut down my dosing quite a bit. Well, I mean, not all that much, really, because there were many occasions that us crew guys dosed while we were working. Later, in Gainesville, I resorted to psychedelic mushrooms to get my spiritual fix. By the time I reached Denver, I had pretty much cut LSD out of my diet, except a couple of rare occasions, including one experimental night while working at the Bluebird.

Another sound engineer, Rich, our lighting designer Stubby, and I decided to dose while working a reggae show. I was running the front-of-house sound mix, and Rich was working the stage monitors. Once the acid kicked in, my soundboard began breathing, melting, coming completely alive. Looking up, I was overwhelmed with the visuals from the sound waves and musical notes rushing out from the speakers in a multitude of colors. I probably could've handled it, had it not have been for the 500 people in the room. Once the dials on the soundboard began to move by themselves, that's when I gave up. I went back to the monitor room, located next to the stage, and asked Rich if he would please switch spots with me. He didn't last that long out front either, though, and he soon switched duties with the lighting designer, Stubby, who had never run sound before that night. Needless to say, we all had a pretty good time.

As the millennium New Year's Eve approached, I needed a break from Aria's drinking binges and decided a solo trip to San Francisco and some good ol' psychedelic therapy was in order.

On December 31, 1999, I dropped a few hits of white blotter at San Francisco's Warfield Theatre. Bob Weir's band Ratdog, Mickey Hart's Planet Drum, and Hot Tuna performed. Now I had worked in the Warfield many times during my BGP days, but never had I realized that the gargoyles mounted to the balcony walls were actually living, breathing creatures. At least on that particular night, they were alive and smiling. It got to a point where they wouldn't leave me alone, so I left the show and wandered out into the streets. I half expected to see chaos erupting from all the Y2K end-of-the-world hype, but the streets were peaceful and in bliss. I stumbled across town to the old Maritime Hall where John Lee Hooker was playing a show with Steve Kimock's all-star band, KVHW.

When I got to the venue, all appeared abandoned. There were no security personnel and nobody in the lobby—just debris laying about the place. I heard the distant rumblings of some music as I made my way to a set of hidden stairs. I climbed several flights without seeing a single soul. Finally a hippie girl appeared, smiling and moving about to her own vibrations. "Hey, there. Do you know where the show is? The band? Is this the Maritime Hall?" I asked.

She just smiled back at me and pointed up. So I continued climbing, tripping, losing my mind, for what seemed like eternity. Where had all the people gone? I figured that I had missed the show, but with each step I could hear a little more clarity in the distant music. I finally reached the top of the stairs where I could go no further except through a small white door that was shrinking before my eyes—like the one Alice goes through. I made my way to the shrinking door and could sense that there was a field of energy on the other side. I pushed through, into another world.

I discovered that I was at the top of the music hall, in the very back of the upper balcony, and what lay before me was a sea of people grooving to a psychedelic rock show. I felt as though I had entered a time warp back to 1967. The walls of the Maritime were smooth and covered with groovy, flashing liquid lights. The place was completely packed and the crystal clear sound waves were now in my face and dancing on my scalp. I found the nearest seat. I leaned back and allowed the music to peel away several layers of my skull. My brain soaked in the beautiful melodies, while my feet melted into the floor.

By the end of the show, the acid started to wear off. I made my way back down the stairs to the outside world where daylight had already begun. I hailed a taxi and returned to my friend DeWood's house that I had been staying with in Daly City. The world had not ended, the carnival ride continued.

It's well known and believed that psychedelics possess a quality that helps people fight off addictions. I certainly attribute it to my mostly non-addictive personality. Before the millennial New Year's Eve acid trip, I had let myself get out of control with drinking. After New Year's I didn't feel the need to drink so much. This was when I sobered up, but Aria's drinking got worse. She moved out of the house by spring.

To decompress from the relationship, I took a spur-of-the-moment trip to Hawaii and spent ten days exploring Oahu, completely solo. I went snorkeling with majestic tropical fish, reef sharks, sea turtles, and eels. I let nature rejuvenate and replenish me.

After I returned from Hawaii, I started dating Stacy, a close friend who also had worked at the Bluebird. Sexually, we were very compatible. Up to this point in my relationships, things had always been messy and melodramatic. Stacy and I had a very relaxing and drama-free relationship. I wasn't used to that. I was used to drama around every corner, as it had always magnetically drawn itself to me. Stacy was also the first relationship where we had actually been good friends first, for a couple of years, in fact. She was a carefree hippie girl, and we shared a lot of common interests. My favorite memories were a couple of times that we hiked in New Mexico to what we thought were remote hot springs. On one occasion, we thought we were the only ones there, having hiked out in the middle of the night. So we had given into our sexual ambitions only to discover a couple camped out in a sleeping bag a few feet away when the sun rose. Another time, we stripped naked in a remote hot springs that was surrounded by lots of tents. The morning revealed a young Boy Scout troop still there.

Stacy and I had a lot of easygoing fun as a couple. When the relationship started to become work and our blissful feelings faded, we mutually agreed to call it quits. Well, we were really starting to want different things from our lives. Either way, whatever the reason, we ended it peacefully and with much respect for each other.

CHAPTER 51

Lovesick

My band, Dewey Decibel System, had been filling the remote Colorado Camp Fest with our own brand of psychedelic sounds before running the generator out of fuel. Had there been enough gas, we might have greeted the morning sun with our endless noodles and mindless jamming. Following our performance, I found myself at the community campfire, sitting quietly on the dirt listening to others stumble through drunken nonsensical conversations. I was feeling exhausted, slightly high, and not really focused on any one conversation except for the voice of the sharply witted girl on the opposite side of the fire. Her loud Jersey accent and intriguing presence seemed to sway back and forth in a dance with the flames. What little attention I had kept drifting to her fiery image and lunatic words. Our eyes shared a familiar gaze. I got up, stumbled around the fire, and made my way toward her. Leaning in, I whispered my opinion.

"I think you're crazy and full of shit."

She didn't know how to respond. Our eyes locked for a few seconds and then I silently retreated away from the scene for the comfort of my tent and sleeping bag.

The next day, I would see her walk by my campsite a few times. We exchanged silent glances while I relaxed in my hammock. Eventually, she stopped and we began to talk. In the background, the obnoxious sounds of drunken males were shouting in our direction. Those boys were trying their best to woo her, but she didn't seem interested in their desperate calls.

"Nice set last night."

"Well, thanks. So what's your name?" I asked.

"Jessica."

"Great song."

"Yeah, the Allmans are one my favorites. Them and the Dead. Let's go for a walk," she suggested.

She had recently relocated from New Jersey to Colorado. Slender, long, straight, sandy hair, bohemian sundress, sparkle in her eye, dimples to her smile.

We walked into the woods, found a large boulder to sit on, smoked some marijuana, and did a couple bumps of cocaine. We nicely kissed as the day faded into night. We slept in each other's arms that night, suppressing the desire for more, promising to take it slow, go out on a few dates, get to know each other.

I called her a few days later and we met up for drinks and a couple games of pool at my favorite Denver Grateful Dead bar, Sancho's Broken Arrow. I was instantly smitten with her. I remember calling up a friend immediately after the date and bragging on and on about how she might be "the one."

That summer I was the Festival Director for Performance International, producing several large music festivals in downtown Denver, including the LODO Music Festival, which attracted close to 100,000 people. She mentioned to me that she was looking for work, so I offered her a job working the festivals with me. At first, we kept our romance on the down low so that people wouldn't think that I was giving her special treatment, but it wasn't long though before everyone could see that we were, indeed, lovers.

She had quite a fiery personality and would often get all bent out of shape over the silliest matters. It didn't bother me much, and I would often just giggle during her rants. I was very much in love, again.

On the last night of the LODO Music Festival, a torrential downpour had scared most of the crowds away, and the event was turning into a disaster. I was standing on stage while members of Little Feat and The Radiators were joining in on an all-star midnight jam I had organized. I was looking out to the soundboard and noticed a familiar girl staring in my direction. It was Leah.

I went out to say hello and she gave me a big hug.

"Hey, there."

"We need to talk," she said.

"Okay, I haven't seen you in five years. Practically since the day you left. What's going on?"

"I'm moving back to New Orleans."

"Did you come here to tell me that, or did you just happen to see me here?"

"I came here to find you. I knew you'd be here. Can we get together sometime this week and talk?"

"Sure." We exchanged numbers and she left. I was curious.

Once the festival was over, the crew began the heavy task of dismantling the site, which took up four square city blocks. The LODO Music Festival was located on the streets in front of the Coor's Field Major League Baseball Stadium, where the Colorado Rockies play. Our final task was to get those stages and tents taken down so that we could hand the streets back over to the city in less than 48 hours. I had barely slept the previous few nights and knew I wasn't going to get any for a couple of more. I could barely stand up by the time the last truck was loaded.

Jessica, Kowalski, my right hand man, and I were having a celebratory beer over at a nearby bar when my cell phone rang. My phone was sitting on the bar and Jess grabbed it.

"Dewey's phone..." There was a long pause. "And who's this?" she asked sharply. "It's a girl. Leah!" She handed me the phone.

Leah wanted to meet up. Not thinking clearly, extremely tired, and a little buzzed, I invited her to meet us at the brewery where we were all having drinks. When I hung up the phone, Jessica responded angrily.

"You did what?!? Oh, fuck no. I don't want to meet your ex-girlfriend! I'm fucking out of here!" She restrained from slapping me, but quickly leapt for the exit.

"What the fuck was that?" I looked over at Kowalski.

"That was some good shit right there, brother! Bad idea on your part, but great drama," he said. With that he, too, left to meet up with the driver of the last truck, Donny, who was busy finishing up with the final load.

Ten minutes later, Leah showed up; I met her outside the bar. I explained that it would probably be best if we could catch up some other time. She agreed and split. Just then, my phone rang; it was Kowalski.

"Dewey, we've got a problem. You need to get over here right now!"

"I'm on my way."

Arriving on the scene, I noticed that our truck was sitting diagonal, in the middle of the road, along with the wreckage of two streetlight poles strewn about. They weren't ordinary streetlight poles, though. They were the tall fancy ones that lined the walkway in front of Coor's Field.

"What happened?" I laughed.

"Well, promise you won't be mad?"

"What do you mean? Is there something else?"

"Ah, forget it, I shouldn't tell you."

"Bullshit, man, you already started, so cough it up!"

"Well, Donny's got a warrant out or something, so we can't get the cops involved."

"You know the cops are two blocks away waiting on us to open these streets, right?"

"Yeah, exactly."

"Okay, so what fucking happened?"

"They were in the back of the truck smoking meth."

"What? Who?"

"Donny. And, promise you won't be mad... Jessica."

"What! Jess was smoking meth? Are you sure about that?"

"You said you wouldn't get mad."

"I did not say that, and, yes, I'm fucking pissed, dude! Where is she?"

"She took off just before Donny backed into the poles."

"Alright, let's get this shit out of the street. You're driving the truck out of here, and I'll deal with the cops."

After we got the mess all cleaned up, the truck went on its way. I dealt with the cops, and we got the streets opened back up for public traffic, albeit a half hour behind schedule. At that point, my brain was beyond fried.

On my way home to get some much-needed rest, I decided to call Jess. We got into a big argument. She was going on and on about Leah, and I was going on and on about her smoking meth. She claimed it was the first time she ever tried it and that she only did it because she was pissed at me for what happened at the bar. In the heat of the moment, I told her that we were finished and I wanted to break up. That didn't go over too well. She screamed at me and hung up. I tried calling back but she wouldn't pick up. Instead of going home, I went straight to her place.

She wouldn't open the door to talk with me; she just yelled from the other side. "No one's ever broken up with me, you asshole! Go fuck yourself!"

I decided that I needed to get out of the city. So I drove to the mountains, parked next to a peaceful stream, and meditated. There by the creek side, I finally got some much-needed rest.

In the morning I drove straight back to Jessica's to try and persuade her that I didn't really want to break up. She was having none of it and refused to speak to me.

What came next in my life was what I refer to as the post-Jessica break-up relationship months, which actually lasted longer than the original relationship.

I met up with Leah a few times. We had some great talks and re-established our friendship. She suddenly contemplated not moving back to New Orleans, but moving to California instead—if I would go with her. I wasn't sure how serious she was about it. I was too lovesick over Jess, and it was too confusing to think about falling for Leah again. I did finally get to tell her about Bob's death, and my near suicide attempt. Within a month or so, Leah moved back to New Orleans with the guy she had been dating since we had broken up.

My lovesick depression over Jess had spiraled into several drunken blackouts. I quit eating, too. I lost ten pounds in the first few weeks.

The owner of Performance International and I had a huge falling out, too, and I was suddenly without steady employment. I went to see a therapist. He put me on anti-depressants, but they were making me think suicidal thoughts again. On August 9, 2003, the eighth anniversary of Jerry Garcia's death, I decided to do something about it.

Having learned from my last major suicidal episode, and the call that saved my life, I thought of Bob. I knew I never wanted to be in that place again, and I wasn't about to let my brain get the better of me this time. So when I woke up that Saturday morning, I decided that I was going to go out and get a puppy.

The sign on the front door read:

THIS IS NOT A PUPPY MILL!

I went in to inquire about the Samoya-Husky mixes that had been advertised in the newspaper. When I got to the pen, three pretty white fluffy puppies were vying for my attention. I was trying to decide which one to get, when one of the puppies had accidently woke up a fourth puppy in the corner. Immediately the three little ones scurried to the opposite corner when she woke up and stretched. One look up at me with those baby blues and I was done. We shared a moment and I knew instantly she was the "one."

"What's the story with this one?" I asked.

"We just got her in this morning. Akita-Husky mix, only one."

"I'll take her."

I put her in the back of my Jeep. I was still mesmerized by her bright blue eyes and her soft, fluffy, tiger-striped brindle coat. Now I had to come up with her name. I started the Jeep while staring at her through the rear view mirror. She was looking right at me when Jackson Browne's voice came through the airwaves, "Jamaica, say you will..."

Four years earlier, my friend Beau had saved my life with a phone call. On that day, Jamaica gave me a whole new sense of purpose.

Puppies can do the darndest things. One of the first things Jamaica discovered in her new home turned out to be a girl's sexy red thong that I assumed she had discovered beneath the bed. I also assumed they were Jessica's, so I put them in a package along with a few of her other items that had been left behind and I mailed them to her. A few days went by and while I was out having dinner with a friend, I received the following text message from Jess:

"THOSE AREN'T MY PANTIES!"

Uh-oh, . . . awkward.

"WELL, THEY'RE NOT MINE!" I texted back.

"SERIOUSLY, FUCK YOU!" she replied.

After describing this hilarious situation to my roommates, John and his fiancé Robin, we quickly realized that the thong belonged to Robin. Jamaica had apparently dragged them out of the laundry room.

About a month or so later, I got a job working on the John Sayles film *Silver City*, which was filming locally. My job was to provide a bunch of musical equipment as props for several of the scenes. Coincidently, the musician character's name in the film was Dewey. The beautiful Daryl Hannah played his mother.

In between scenes, Daryl would meet up with me off-set, and we would play guitar together. She was very kind, sexy, and flirtatious with me. One of her scenes was a love scene in a bedroom, so when she came off set, she was wearing a thin negligee while we strummed guitars. She was downright giddy whenever a scene would stop filming and she would get a break. She just wanted to keep playing guitar every chance she got. She invited me to spend some more time with her back at her hotel. Now, I know what you're thinking. First: "No fucking way this happened." But, believe me, it did, and there were witnesses. Second thing you're thinking: "No one would ever turn that situation down." Right?

Nope, stupid ol' on-medication, lovesick me couldn't get over my ex-girlfriend, so I did not go meet with Daryl Hannah privately in her hotel room late at night. Jess found out through a friend and called me. "Are you hanging out with Daryl Hannah?"

I told her what happened, and she responded that I was a fucking idiot and she herself wouldn't have passed that one up.

I helped Jess open a coffee shop in Denver. It was a unique opportunity that just fell into her lap. She became driven and determined to have a business of her own and I was very proud of her new ambition.

I was trying everything I knew to win her back, and for weeks I showed up almost daily to help her and her friends paint, clean, and get the place ready. I had completely stopped drinking and was weaning myself off the meds. At some point, when my head became clearer, I gave up the chase. I couldn't deal with being that pathetic anymore. I needed to get my life back.

After removing myself from her presence for a few days, she called me one night, crying. "I love you," she cried. "I really fucking love you, okay? It's true. All this time." She apologized for being such a jerk.

"Thanks," I told her. It was really all I needed to know. After that call, we didn't speak for a few months and I finally started healing. I got a really good full-time job as a sound engineer at the Pepsi Center Arena. It was considered one of the best audio jobs in town. For a few years, I had been working there, but only off and on. The full-time gig came at just the right time for me.

After a few months of not drinking and not talking to Jessica, my old pal from the LODO festival, Kowalski, showed up at my house one night. He convinced me that it was time to go out and have a drink. We went to Pete's Monkey Bar on Colfax Avenue and were there ten minutes, one beer in, and who walks in the door? Jessica.

Honestly, she didn't look all that healthy. She was a real mess. She walked in holding hands with a punk rock girl who barely looked of drinking age. I knew that she was into girls, so I assumed she was with her new lover. I said hello. Jess took one look at me and stormed out. Her girlfriend scowled at me and took off after her. A good friend of hers, Annie, came over and told me that Jess had been spiraling out of control lately and she lost ownership of the coffee shop. She had gone to heavy drugs and was sleeping around with a few different girls.

I looked over at Kowalski and said, "What is it with you? The one night I go out to drink again. First time I've seen you since the festival... Haven't seen her in months, and it's drama all over again!" We laughed off the drama and ordered up some shots.

On a positive note, shortly after that, Jess got cleaned up. She got a good job as a teacher, met a great professional guy, and eventually they got married. I bump into her frequently these days, and every time I see her we are both happy people. Overall, though, the whole thing was toxic for me. Clearly, I went off the rails, and in my efforts to fix the unfixable, I became very vulnerable and pathetic. Even though I was aware of my own shortcomings, it did a lot of damage to my confidence and self esteem. It got to a point where I could barely hold a conversation with a female anymore. I swore off all relationships from that point on.

CHAPTER 52

Cry Wolf

M y job at the Pepsi Center for Kroenke Sports Enterprises went on for several years, and I became an important part of the engineering team there. I was responsible for many technical aspects of events for the Denver Nuggets, the Colorado Avalanche, the National Lacrosse League's Colorado Mammoth, an arena football team co-owned by John Elway, the Colorado Crush, and of course there were lots of great concerts, too.

Another opportunity came up in the spring of 2004: to tour as a sound engineer with the Chicago R&B band, Sonia Dada. Their big hit was the song "Lover, Lover (You Don't Treat Me No Good No More)." My boss and mentor at the Pepsi Center, Alan Schroeder, supported me so much that I was able to keep my job at the arena and still go on tour with the band. We hit the west coast, Midwest, east coast, and Canada.

In California, Sonia Dada had the fortune of playing an opening set on a show with the legendary bluesman JJ Cale. When I first met Cale outside the back door of the theater, he approached me and thought that I was someone he already knew. He had always been one of my idols, so I was very honored to befriend him. Later, I would run sound for him in Colorado, and, eventually, I released my own tribute album to him. His wife, Christine, is also very cool, and would even call me up to talk on occasion.

On tour in Vermont, I met Grace Potter, a young singer who left an indelible impression on me. Her band opened up for us at a music festival there. I encouraged them to come to Colorado, which they subsequently did, and stayed at my house. I recorded Grace's song "Crazy Parade" on the 2005 Dewey Decibel System album *Utica Street*.

At one point on the Sonia Dada tour, when we were actually playing in Denver, I convinced the band to hire my good friend José Rossy to join them as their full-time percussion player. First, he had to pass a live audition. Actually, it was a genius plan on my part. There was a great percussion riff in one of their songs, "Better Brains," and I had the idea to get José to learn that riff. The band rarely played that song live, but I convinced them to perform it in Denver when José was sitting in—without telling them it was a setup. When José nailed the percussion riffs, the band members all looked surprised and pleased. The next day, he was a full on member of the band.

In Nashville, a tornado was blowing through Sonia Dada's outdoor show at the same time my monitor soundboard caught on fire. The band was rushed off the stage and we all retreated to our tour buses.

Bama Boy Kilgore was there hanging out with us. I confided to Kilgore a story about the band's founder and songwriter, Dan Pritzker, of the famous Chicago Pritzker family. (Dan was an heir to the Hyatt Hotel fortune.) You see, Dan owned Jerry Garcia's most celebrated custom-made electric guitar, Wolf, which he bought for close to $800,000 from Sotheby's. But at the time, he wanted to keep it a secret. Of course, the first thing Kilgore said to Dan was, "So I hear you got Jerry's guitar."

There were a lot of good times on that tour, but there was somebody who was really not happy with my decision to tour: my dog, Jamaica. I had left her behind with my roommates to care for her. She would constantly break out of the house and roam the neighborhoods looking for me. I got a call one day, while in Seattle, from a woman who asked if I was the owner of a blue-eyed brindle Akita. Jamaica had apparently jumped out of a window in the house and run across the street, through a big park, and somehow got into a fenced-off dog park. All the other owners and dogs had left the park but this one woman and her dog. So she decided to call the number on the tag.

At the end of Sonia Dada's summer tour, I knew I needed to stay off the road and spend more time raising my wonderful dog. Plus, the sports teams at the Pepsi Center were about to start up their seasons, and I was needed there.

CHAPTER 53

Upon My Death

During the spring of 2005, the NBA hosted its annual All-Star game at the Pepsi Center, and an accident occurred that almost took my life. During the setup, the lights in the arena had been completely blacked out while the sound engineer for the Goo Goo Dolls, the half-time entertainment for the game, was blasting music at full volume throughout the arena.

Now, it's common safety practice in the industry that people should not be working overhead, on the arena catwalk, during loud sound checks, because, should anything fall, no one below would be able to hear the warning. The NBA production staff that had taken over most of the technical facets of the event had repeatedly ignored several safety procedures leading up to the incident. I was on the arena floor setting up some video display monitors for a courtside press table. I was plugging in the cables to the monitor and about to lean my head over it to see if it had video signal when I had the sudden notion to affix more gaffer's tape to the cable on the floor. In that slight movement of my head, suddenly the video monitor exploded and shattered into pieces. I fell backwards in shock. I noticed a large steel clamp in the center of the remains of the monitor. It would have split my head open instantly.

I looked up, frightened that more objects might suddenly fall. I shouted something, but no one could hear anything because the music was still loudly blaring throughout the arena. The song was "Give A Little Bit," originally by Supertramp, but covered by the Goo Goo Dolls, and very nearly the soundtrack of my death. I raced to the nearest "vomitory," which is what you call the arena floor entrance-exit passage, and got on my radio. I called for several supervisors to meet me outside of the building. I had been rattled pretty good and needed some fresh air.

The first thing I asked them to do was shut the music off, turn the arena lights on, and figure out who was up there on the catwalk dropping things. The responsible party turned out to be an NBA production employee who had not been authorized to be up there at that time. The steel clamp had accidently been flung off of a cable when it came barreling down at me from over 300 feet.

An hour or so later, a few of the NBA production staff wanted to meet with me. They offered an apology, a change in their safety procedures, and two courtside seats to the game. The courtside seats were really of no use to me, since that's where I worked during most of the games anyhow.

But something else was weighing heavy on my mind that day. I had received a call that morning that my father was in the hospital in Columbus, Ohio—he had been diagnosed with cancer, a brain tumor. Combined with my close call, I was rattled. I asked them: if I accepted the tickets, would they have any problem with me going out into the parking lot and scalping them? I only wanted to do this so I could afford an airline ticket back to see my father in the hospital. They said it would be okay. I went across the street from the arena and scalped the seats for $1,000. Mind you, I received free tickets for almost all events at the Pepsi Center, and I never ever sold any of them. I reasoned that, considering the circumstances, it was a special situation.

At the airport, I purchased the March 2005 issue of National Geographic that had a picture of a monk on the cover with all kinds of wires connected to his head. Something about that cover spoke to me. The articles inside discussed, among many other things, the connections between spirituality and the brain. Upon visiting with my father in the Columbus, Ohio hospital, I assumed he would enjoy the story about Buddhist monks healing the brain through meditations and spiritual practice. I read the article to him, as he lay there recovering from laser surgery to remove a tumor from his brain. It was a nice weekend visit with him, and he seemed hopeful, despite the doctors giving him only six months to live. My siblings and I all got together and discussed how to proceed with his care. It was decided that our young stepsister Renee would handle primary care. I returned to Denver.

Six months later, I got the call that it was time to come back to Ohio again—Dad's condition had worsened. When I first got home, he was in a room at Coshocton Memorial Hospital. This was a familiar place for him; his mother had suffered a long battle with Alzheimer's there, and eventually she passed away in the room across the hall from his. There were other ghosts too: his father had worked there in the sixties and got into an accident that developed into a cancer and eventually his death. So the place had bad vibes as far as my dad was concerned. His condition was getting pretty bad and most of his communication had become gibberish. In a private moment, though, he made it very clear to me that it was my duty to get him the hell out of that hospital. He did not want to die there.

We found him a private room at a nursing home that was more suitable and started hospice care. He really would have preferred home, but the doctors wouldn't allow it. We got him to the new place and put in some pictures, lamps and knick-knacks from the house, just things to make him feel like he was at home. He smiled when he arrived there and gave me the thumbs up approval. He also gave me a wink and a nod when a cute young nurse visited the room. My dad loved to flirt with the nurses and he didn't hesitate to start on her. She was very cute and I do admit that she caught my eye, too. Even my brother nudged me. She shared the name of my eldest sister, April. Well, every chance my dad had to flirt, he would, but this time he kept putting me in the middle of it. His sense of humor was still very sharp for a man on his deathbed.

There were also many dark moments when his pain medication wasn't strong enough, and we had to move him back and forth from the nursing home to the hospital. It was gut wrenching watching the amount of pain he was experiencing. My sister Sherry, who my dad never really treated all that well, was so kind and compassionate during the whole ordeal. She took charge in dealing with the doctors and nurses—as she worked in the medical field—and demanded that they up his medication so he wouldn't suffer. Renee decided to excuse herself from the entire scene, but with some unnecessary personal drama.

One day, while going through some boxes in the basement of my father's house, I found an envelope with my name written on the front. Underneath my name was written in my dad's handwriting:

TO BE OPENED AND READ UPON MY DEATH
OR THE AGE OF UNDERSTANDING

In the upper left corner of the envelope it read:

JULY, 1973

My heart sank when I saw that envelope. I was intrigued, to say the least. In July of 1973, I was just about to turn two years old. I found the letter in 2005, while my dad was lying in a nursing home, dying. I stared at it for a while and showed the envelope to my brother Michael. We reasoned it was best to open it.

I read the letter and found it to be a very touching message from a depressed man who was going through some tough marital issues. He seemed to be writing the letter, just in case anything happened to him. He was 38 years old at the time he wrote it. I was almost 34 when I finally read it.

Back at the nursing home, his condition declined. I thought about discussing with him the letter that I had found, but he had already slipped into a slow morphine haze. Michael and I got to have one last cigar with him before the final decline. His breathing became very automated over the next 24 hours and his eyes had become completely bloodshot and glossed over. A minister from the local Methodist church that our family had belonged to came by to offer some prayers.

About thirty minutes after the preacher left, dad's body color changed and his breathing patterns changed. The moment had arrived. We all stood around him with our hands on him. From his left were my sister Sherry, my brother Michael, my aunt Betty, my brother Shawn, the nurse April, and I. He hadn't looked at any of us in almost a day. His eyes were still glossy, distant, and gray. His breathing was noisy and machine-like. Then, suddenly, it stopped. Then the most astonishing thing I'd ever witnessed in my life occurred. He opened his eyes wide, and they were clear and beaming with life. His head leaned forward. There was a stillness about him as he had already stopped breathing. He took a quick glance around the room and then slowly stared into Sherry's eyes, then Michael's, then Betty's, then Shawn's, then nurse April's, then mine, all in clockwise order. His eyes then peered upwards as if he were not in a room with walls, a ceiling and a roof, but in a wide-open space with no physical materials between him and an endless sky above. With all his might, his chest suddenly thrust forward, his mouth open, eyes to the sky, and he took one final deep gasp of breath.

We were all speechless, emotional, and in awe of what had transpired. It took several minutes for us to return to our realities. We started to exit the room and I saw my eldest sister April running toward us from down the hall. We each embraced her. She knew that she had just missed it and you could see that she was really upset with herself. She then took some time alone in the room with him. About twenty minutes or so later, she joined the rest of us in a lounge area where we were sitting around crying and coming to terms with the experience. Nurse April, who, in a way, had been standing in for my sister April, could be seen getting back to her other work responsibilities, but with a shaken presence about her. There was a silence among us and then my sister looked right at me and nagged, "So this nurse, April... have you asked her out yet?"

"What is *wrong* with you?" I replied. We all started laughing. It was good to laugh again.

"Well... ?" April went on. "We share the same name, Dew. You better get on that!"

I shot her my "there's definitely something wrong with you" look as we all joked with each other to relieve our melancholy a little.

The next day, I was back at the nursing home loading up some of my father's possessions with nurse April's help. We were out at the car, and I asked her how often she sees death like that. "Quite a bit," she said, but indicated that that one had been unusually intense and unique.

We finished loading up the car and she mentioned that she would come by the house later to see how we were doing. As it turned out, she was one of my dad's neighbors. I had been struggling with whether or not it was appropriate to ask her out, considering the circumstances, but then realized that my dad would be disappointed in me if I didn't. The situation was pretty weird, so I figured why not, and went ahead and asked her. She said yes.

All this happened when I was in my swearing-off-relationships phase, and I did not feel confident anymore, since the Jessica days. April and I did go out on a couple of dates, but I felt too awkward about it all, and, besides, I had to return to my job and life back in Denver and did not want anything long distance or serious.

The overall experience of my father's passing effected me profoundly. Sadly, there was not much harmony in my life relationship with him. Though through his death I learned a great deal about myself, my origins and my capacity to embrace real compassion and a willingness to live my life to the fullest. Sure, I had accomplished many things, but in the grand scope, I felt as though there was a lot more work and living to do. Experiencing death close up with a family member or dear friend is always a pivotal life-changing event. And it's as if we owe it to them to seize the day, follow our dreams, and certainly become kinder to those around us. My father's death was no exception and as a result I espoused a deeper sense of spirituality, meditation, and a fresh sense of ambition.

CHAPTER 54

K. Fimster Rides Again

Around this time, I had been gigging frequently with Dewey Decibel System. In May 2006, I put together an all-star musical charity event at Denver's Oriental Theatre—a tribute to Bob Dylan, for his sixty-fifth birthday. It was a benefit for music programs in the Denver Public School system. My dear old friend K. Fimster rode a motorized bicycle from northern Alabama to come to the event. He ran an independent motorized bike business on his farm, which equipped standard bicycles with motors to help provide relief from rising gas prices. On the morning of my big Dylan event, I got a call from him.

"Hey, I made it to Colorado!"

"Great, are you in Denver?"

"Well, bad news, the bike's motor is vapor-locked and I'm stuck here at the Colorado-Kansas border. I need you to come get me."

"What? There's no way! It's already eleven and I have the sound check scheduled at four o'clock. It's got to be four hours round trip there and back—and what if I break down? The show would be fucked!"

"C'mon Dew. Do it for Middle Earth!"

That's all he needed to say.

I drove like a bat out of hell and swooped him up at the Kansas border. We were back in Denver in record time—less than three hours round trip and no speeding tickets!

That night, we put on an epic tribute to Bob Dylan, which has later grown into an annual event. We even raised a few thousand dollars for the cause. Keyboardist Melvin Seals from the Jerry Garcia Band played with us, and I'll always cherish him looking over and smiling at me while we jammed. Jerry used to get that smile from him on a nightly basis.

The next day I took Fimster into Sancho's Broken Arrow and introduced him to the owner, Phil Bianchi.

"Phil, I want you to meet my dear friend from Alabama. He rode his bicycle all the way out here and he's an old school Deadhead of the kindest variety."

"This guy here? He's an old friend of yours?" Phil said, pointing to Fimster.

"A friend of ours, Phil. He's good people."

"Nice to meet you, Phil. That's a great shirt you got on," Fimster said.

Phil was wearing one of his Sancho's bar shirts with a Grateful Dead Steal Your Face logo on the front. Then, in a kind gesture, Phil took off his shirt and put it on Fimster.

"It's yours now. If you're a friend of Dewey's, then I want you to have the shirt off of my back! I just met you but I already feel like I've known you for a long time, brother," said Phil.

"Welcome to Middle Earth!" Fimster replied. They smiled and hugged.

We were all pleasantly amazed at this exchange, but it was something quite typical in Fimster's world. He always said that he had never known a stranger.

Fimster stuck around for a few days and we went on a camping adventure out at a music festival on the Colorado River. My good friends in the Grateful Dead cover band Shakedown Street had invited me out to sit in with them at Colorado's State Bridge Lodge. Fimster and I had a great time again, soaking in the magic of the Deadhead scene, just like the old days—a big ol' Middle Earth party had taken over the campground by the end of the weekend.

CHAPTER 55

One Hundred Women

I t had been a couple of years since I had been emotionally invested in a relationship. The loneliness was getting to me, and I was having a lot of difficulty communicating with the opposite sex. I had become bitter since Jessica. My skills were gone. I felt angry every time I saw a couple holding hands or being affectionate in public. Every attempt to talk to a new girl would just leave me making up excuses for why I thought she was a terrible person. Finally, I had enough of my own negative attitude and decided to challenge my handicap. It was while on the phone with Kilgore that I came up with the plan to put a positive intention out into the universe. I reasoned that certainly there must be one good woman out of a hundred that I could be compatible with. So I decided that I would rebuild my confidence by trying to meet and speak to one hundred new women within one month. Just simple conversations was all I needed, like, "Hello, my name is... ," and, "What's your name?" It might sound a little silly, but I needed to rebuild my courage from square one.

On the night of my Bob Dylan tribute show, Fimster, our guest of honor, had befriended a gorgeous, tall blonde with a slender model's physique. She danced with him the entire show. After the show, I didn't get a chance to meet her, but we exchanged glances, and she whispered "rock star" to me before she disappeared. A week or so later, my plan to meet one hundred women was launched. I headed to my neighborhood bar, the Highland Pacific, in hopes to start up a few conversations. There were always beautiful girls in there—I knew this well because it was a place I played music quite frequently.

I noticed her sitting down at the end of the bar, the blonde. She whispered something to a musician friend of mine, who then looked over at me. A minute later my friend approached me with her. "This girl wants to meet you, Dewey," he said.

How weird, I thought: Girl Number One on my quest turned out to actually want to meet me, and she was the girl that caught my eye just a week earlier. Her name was Casey. We had a brief conversation, but it really helped lift my confidence. Sticking to my plan, I also made my own introductions to a couple more ladies that night, and so began my new odyssey.

A few nights later, I went bar hopping with my lesbian friend Missy and she introduced me to about twenty girls in the course of a few hours. A couple of them even made out with me and insisted that I feel them up a little. I've always loved hanging out with lesbian and bisexual girls. Within a couple of weeks, my number was already up to fifty, and I was definitely meeting some pretty interesting women. I kept a journal so I could keep all the new names straight. I didn't want to mistakenly refer to one of them by a number.

Meanwhile, I kept randomly running into Casey in my neighborhood; so, naturally, we started hanging out. Another girl that caught my eye, Laura Belle, was an actress from Texas. I also met her at the Highland Pacific and I really felt some genuine sparks. Laura Belle and I had a couple of great dates and spent a few nights together. Casey actually got a little jealous.

I had become more involved with the Oriental Theatre and eventually took over production and talent buying, in addition to my job at the Pepsi Center. As part of my deal with the theater, I became a part owner in the business, too. I performed in a show with John Oates, of Hall and Oates fame, and jokingly referred to our lineup as Dewey Paul and Oates—a play on my new band name, Dewey Paul Band. I put on a couple more tribute concerts, one to Van Morrison and another to Bruce Springsteen. I also performed in a couple of locally produced tributes for Tom Waits and a reenactment of The Band's *The Last Waltz*, that very famous Bill Graham–produced concert in

San Francisco at his legendary Winterland Ballroom, back in 1976. Martin Scorsese, of course, directed the eponymous classic film of the concert. The Denver Last Waltz shows, which my friends in the band Polytoxic produce, have become legendary on their own, and I continue to be a returning member of the cast each year.

At the Oriental, we started hosting many wild after hours parties that often left us crawling out of the venue in the following morning. Jamaica had become so used to being at the theater with me, that she would sometimes escape from the house and navigate the six blocks to look for me there. Sometimes I would get calls while I was at the Pepsi Center that Jamaica was in the theater lobby looking for me.

Laura Belle moved back to Texas, so we never had a chance to develop anything serious. Casey, Jamaica, and I began to hang out more frequently, and eventually Casey moved into my bedroom for a while. An interesting thing about Casey is that she worked for a brief time as a bartender at a swinger's club—where people walked around naked and openly had sex in front of others. Personally I found that scene to be a little unsavory for my tastes, but we would have fun counting the loads of cash she made there—after we washed and dried the money, of course.

Casey and I were sitting in a Denver Highlands bar late one night, the Coral Room, getting drunk with a few friends and many strangers. I made some stupid bet with a guy I didn't know who didn't believe that I worked for the Denver Nuggets, Colorado Avalanche, and so on. I can't recall the exact nature of what game we were playing—it may have been Quarters—but I agreed that, if I lost, I would take everyone in the bar over to the Pepsi Center to play basketball on the Denver Nuggets private practice court. Well, I lost. So, at about 2:30 a.m., I snuck in fifteen or twenty drunken fools into the side doors of the Pepsi Center Arena. I knew an obscure way into the back halls of the building, through the winding HVAC engineering rooms where we wouldn't be detected by the security cameras. I made everyone climb up ladders, duck under air vents and slide along walls to get into the practice court and locker room without being detected. I was completely drunk, reckless, and lacked any sense of judgment or concern for my job. There were no cameras in the practice court, locker room, and weight room, so once we made it undetected, we played drunken games of HORSE. Casey posed for a few uninhibited photos in front of Carmelo Anthony's locker. The shenanigans had gone on for a couple of hours before I escorted everyone out. I had to be back into work in just a few more hours.

Still feeling drunk, I clocked in for work that day and soon after received a call on my radio to report to the security office. My heart sank; I was afraid that I was going to be shown video evidence of my previous night's escapades. I also expected to see my bosses all in there, prepared to hand me my walking papers. Once in the security office, though, I was merely asked to fix an audio patch for them that had gone inoperative. Unbelievably, I had gotten away with it (until now).

The Pepsi Center was no stranger to wild party nights in any case. One particularly memorable one occurred after what was supposed to be a Cher concert. A blizzard had knocked out power in the arena and the show was cancelled. A vice president of the arena and I took the party back to the hotel with Cher's crew. Coincidently, the VP was an old friend who had also been on the stage crew at the infamous Telluride Mid-Summer Music Festival of 1991, where I had gotten my start in the business. Our party got so out of hand that the hotel staff moved us all into our very own ballroom where we would no longer disturb the other hotel guests.

The next morning, the VP practically crashed the car into the loading dock dropping me off for work. He had slammed into a pole and I banged my head against the car window. He told security to leave us, and they obeyed when they realized who was driving. I was a little banged up, but so drunk that I didn't feel anything. I stumbled into the arena and made my way up to the control room booth, which was a skybox that overlooked the arena floor. I passed out on the couch in there, stinking of booze, and slept through an entire morning event that I was supposed to be working. There were countless reckless all-nighters among many of the Pepsi Center production staff, especially in the summer when we had the run of our own outdoor amphitheater, City Lights Pavilion, located in the arena's parking lot.

Regarding the challenge of meeting one hundred women, the exercise was successful in terms of rebuilding my confidence and lifting my spirits. I gained several new friends and casual relationships with my fresh, positive outlook. As far as trying to force anything serious to occur, that was never my true intention, and besides, I've always believed that you're asking for trouble if you try to force it or overdo it. A casual, yet realistic approach was wise on my part.

CHAPTER 56

Goonga Galoonga, Goonga Goonga Lagoonga

F ollowing my father's death, I felt the need to create more of a sense of purpose in my life and also to have a little more fun while working less. I took up skiing because it was something that I literally used to have dreams about.

I would often wake up after having dreamt of skiing and was convinced that I knew how to do it even though I had never put on a pair of skis. One morning, after such a dream, I phoned my friend Kelly, who worked for us at the Oriental, and asked her if she would teach me to ski. On that first day, I achieved the sensation that I had felt in my dreams. I began to spend most of my days off commuting from Denver up to the mountain ski resorts.

At the Pepsi Center, another life-changing event took place. The Mind & Life Institute, out of Boulder, put together an event for the Dalai Lama to speak. In one of the prep meetings, I was told that I was chosen to be the one who would meet with His Holiness and equip him with the wireless headset microphone that he would use. I felt extremely honored.

On the day of the event, I had chosen Suite 69 on the Pepsi Center's club level as the room for the panel members to gather. It was a good number for balance, universal harmony, the ying and the yang—plus it was right across from the meeting room where the V.I.P. panel discussion was going to take place.

I followed Adam Engle, co-founder of the Mind & Life Institute, into the suite with the lapel microphone wireless transmitter packs. Wow, there were some heavy cats in that room. Many of the world's most revered spiritual and scientific minds of today: Father Thomas Keating, a well known Roman Catholic monk and priest, particularly notorious for having created the Centering Prayer, a unique method of Christian meditation; Rabbi Zalman Schachter-Shalomi, a founder of the Jewish Renewal movement, which focuses on spiritual meditation; Roshi Joan Halifax, Ph.D., a master teacher in Zen Buddhism and former colleague of, my favorite mythologist, Joseph Campbell; famed Pulitzer Prize–nominated author and psychologist, Dr. Daniel Goleman; and Dr. Richard Davidson of the University of Wisconsin, whose research into the links between brain science and meditation has met with wide renown. So, yeah, as you can tell, these were some heavy cats, indeed.

One by one, I wired each of them up with their microphones. As I finished, one of them suggested we all join hands in meditation and prayer. Naturally, I was about to excuse myself from the room, but they insisted that I stay and participate. Now, I had been in my share of some heavy harmonic convergence meditations—particularly in my Rainbow Gathering days—and I've taken part in some pretty cool mass peace chants, and even some meditation sessions at the San Francisco Zen Center, but this was something else entirely. The meditative energy level that we transcended in that room was something I never quite experienced, especially in such a small group of people. There were only seven of us in the room and we all held hands while each individual led their own meditation or prayer based on their own beliefs. What an incredible experience it was to participate in that once-in-a-lifetime exchange.

After the meditation, we all went into the meeting room where the conference was about to start. The high-profile guests were waiting in the conference area for the panel discussion to begin. Director Steven Spielberg sat in the front row, a few feet away from me. Tickets for this shindig were somewhere in the thousands of dollars. I sat on the side of the platform at the sound mixer and monitored the microphone levels.

The discussion immediately jumped into brain healing through spirituality and science. It really hit home for me. I hadn't realized that Dr. Davidson was the guy who led those brain studies with the monks on the cover of National Geographic, which I had shared with my father when he was going through his cancer treatment. The connection was very inspiring for me.

Following the discussion, I had a brief conversation with Dr. Davidson about the important work they were conducting. Spielberg was in the background anxiously waiting his turn with the doctor. I made it brief, because I was being signaled that time was a factor. A most important person was waiting for me in one of the dressing rooms, the Dalai Lama.

I had never witnessed such strict security in the several years that I had been working at the Pepsi Center. I've worked one-on-one with my share of rock stars, sports stars, celebrities, and politicians— from mayors to governors and even the U.S. Attorney General, John Ashcroft. The Dalai Lama was different, though. It held a special spiritual significance for me, and I felt a sense of real accomplishment.

It seemed natural to me that I was the one selected to perform the task at hand. I had known about it for weeks, since I had to clear the State Department background check. Hard to believe I passed that thing, considering all the situations I had been involved in over the years. They must've missed my DEA file. My long journey had been rapidly flashing through my brain all day as I was preparing to meet His Holiness.

Out of all the hundreds of employees who worked for the Pepsi Center (technically, for Kroenke Sports Enterprises) I was the only individual who was permitted to meet with the Dalai Lama. Not even the owner of the arena, or any of the executives or other supervisors were even allowed access into the general backstage area once His Holiness was in the building. Denver Mayor John Hickenlooper, who eventually became governor of Colorado, waited outside the room to meet with him.

My time with him was brief, but it was a jovial and enlightening exchange. I met with him again briefly before he went on stage so that I could turn on his microphone transmitter packs. My photographer friend, Michael Martin, was in the right place at the right time and snapped off a few funny-looking photos of the occurrence. Overall, the event left me feeling great about my future and the anxieties I had been struggling with subsided.

In the years I had been working for that building, I had, on occasion, been up for a job as Production Manager, which was in a different department, but it was a job I was most qualified to do considering all of my work experience. It was the job I wanted and when I originally went to work at the arena, it was a job that I was told by a VP that I would eventually get. I just had to put in some time. Well, I had been passed up for it twice already, and, finally, a third time, just after the Dalai Lama event. I can only assume that corporate politics were at play, but needless to say my enthusiasm for the company pretty much bottomed out after that. Plus the frenetic pace the job demanded of me was undermining my own personal ambitions. I had acquired plenty of new skills in my time there, but being a good politician was never one of them.

Upon my next annual employee review, right after the latest promotion disappointment, I was asked by one of my bosses what my new goals for the next year at work would be. I replied that since I had lost my passion for the job, I would like to set a record of taking a shit in every room with a toilet in the building—surely no one had ever done that! Within six months, I achieved that goal. So I got that going for me, which is nice.

CHAPTER 57

The Mountains Win Again

E arly in 2007, I left my arena job to commit full time to the Oriental Theatre and also work toward my goals of a trip to Europe. In the late fall of 2007, I had reached my breaking point with the majority owner of the theater. He kept giving me the same old run around regarding our financial agreement. I finally had enough. I was uncertain of what my next move would be. I needed to move forward somehow and find a new bliss in my life. Trying to stay in Denver didn't seem like what I wanted to do. All my possibilities were met with resistance or difficult obstacles. The Oriental had tied up my financial resources, and I hated being backed into that corner. I was feeling desperate and like a failure.

In the last minute, I made a rash decision to head for the hills. I put what I could in a storage unit, packed my car up with the essentials, and Jamaica and I drove up to Summit County—the very place of refuge I ended up in sixteen years earlier when Sticker Dave helped me out. I barely had enough gas money to make it. The snow was outrageous on the emotional drive. There was no turning back to Denver, though. A new unknown lease in my life awaited.

Dave was long gone from Summit by then. He had moved on to Texas many years before, but there was still one person there who I knew I could count on in this type of situation. I showed up unannounced, just hoping that Robin Page would be home, and she was. I explained briefly to her that I needed to stay for a while. I needed a fresh start and she was there for me. She opened her home up and I moved in. I ended up renting a room from her for the next four years.

We went out that night and celebrated by getting drunk. The next day, I needed a plan. She asked me if I remembered Bob Moon from the Sunshine Cafe. It had been sixteen years since my days at the Sunshine, but, yes, I vaguely recalled him. She said he was working at the Goat Soup & Whiskey Tavern and we should go there to get me a job. Right when we pulled into the Goat, Moon was in the parking lot taking off his skis. We caught up briefly and went inside. Within a couple of minutes, I met the owner, Scotty Jackson, who within less than a minute of talking, offered me a job. Scotty's from Massillon, Ohio, about thirty minutes north of Coshocton, and a place where my aunts, uncles, and cousins live. It also turned out we had a lot of close, mutual musician friends in common. My first five minutes in the Goat, I felt at home. I felt reassured in the bliss of the Universe again. New opportunities were, indeed, opening up for me there.

I also followed up on the offer of a friend of mine from Denver to work at his pizza shop in Summit Cove. This was very near to the place where I had lived with Sticker Dave back in the winter of 1990. Once again, I felt the healing powers of the mountains. This was a good place to be. And everything would work out just fine.

The following spring I filed a lawsuit against the owner of the Oriental for $14,630.06 that he owed me. He sent me some stupid, nasty, threatening emails, but I avoided playing into his drama. After all, he proved his friendship to me added up to nothing more than a con on his part. His habitual lies and drug abuse were more than I could deal with. It was time to let a judge decide. He didn't show up in court, but I still presented my case. The judge looked up his tax status with the state and found that he had been delinquent for many years. Based upon my evidence—I had a contract and kept a record of his payments to me and the hundreds of missed ones—and his poor standing with the state, I was awarded the judgment of $14,630.06. I felt vindicated. The very next morning after the judgment, however, he filed for bankruptcy, thus locking away my chances at filing any liens on his properties or collecting any substantial amount from him.

I was done with having negative people like him in my life.

Summit County was treating me good. I had a newfound passion in skiing, and was really enjoying sound engineering at the Goat. By springtime, I started tending bar there and booking the bands. I left behind the pizza job and co-managed the Goat in the off-season while most of the staff went back to Put-in-bay, Ohio, where the Goat had a summer location.

For my birthday that summer, my old friend from my Performance International (LODO Festival) days, Kowalski, invited me to hang out at the Jazz Aspen Music Festival. He was the Production Manager for the event and had been there since the Festival's inception some ten or so years earlier. Widespread Panic headlined two nights, John Fogerty a night, and Bob Dylan on the fourth night.

I had just arrived at the event and met up with Kowalski who hooked me up with all-access credentials. Once backstage, I walked around the corner by the artist tents and I noticed two friends walking toward me. It was none other then Cecil "P-nut" Daniels and Jimmy Herring. They didn't see me right away because Cecil was in the middle of telling Jimmy a story.

"... and then he picked the guitar back up, dragged it inside, and we finished playing the—" Cecil stopped in his tracks when noticed me, "—there he is!" He was pointing at me.

We started laughing, and greeted with some hugs.

"I know this guy!" Jimmy said.

"Dewey, I was just telling Jimmy the story, about that night we played the Goat and you hit that guy with your guitar! Man, I can't believe you're here!"

I first met Herring back in '92 in Vegas at the Bally's Casino Blues Traveler show. He was playing with Col. Bruce Hampton back then and they were the opening act. Over the years we've run into each other in many parts of the country but most notably were the Gainesville days when Col. Bruce would do shows for GAMA. Herring and the bass player Kofi Bainbridge even came over to the Big House back then and chilled with us.

Okay, so there's Cecil telling this story to Jimmy, that was actually about me, when I happened upon them backstage! What a great coincidence. Better yet, that story Cecil was telling involved one of the wilder moments I've had on stage.

Earlier that summer, I was at the Goat, tending bar and also running sound for Cecil's band, the Stanky Pockets. It was a slow night with about fifteen or so people in the room. The band was jamming on stage and, at the end of the night, they invited me up for a number. I served everyone who needed drinks and then I went over and plugged in my guitar into the spare amplifier and sat in on a good jam.

During my solo, I noticed some guy walk behind my bar. He must not have seen that I was up on stage jamming with the band. Perhaps he was going to just serve himself. He reached up to the top shelf and grabbed an unopened bottle of Patron tequila. Instead of pouring a shot for himself, he looked around to see if anyone was looking and then he stashed the bottle under his shirt. He then bravely walked out from behind the bar and proceeded to walk toward the side door, which was located next to the stage. He passed right in front of me. I abruptly stopped my solo, politely turned down the volume knob on the cheap Mexican made house guitar, a Fender Stratocaster "Squire" model, and unplugged the cable. I turned to the harp player.

"Just a second, Miles, I gotta take care of something."

I hopped off the stage and grabbed the guy by the shoulder. He turned around and, without hesitation, I grabbed the tequila bottle from under his shirt. He looked surprised.

"You fucked up man!" I told him.

"Fuck you! What are you gonna do about it?" he shouted.

I paused and thought about it for a second. I could call the cops, but he'd probably just take off running. I passed the bottle back to Miles. My Fender Strat was still strapped around my neck, so I pointed the neck of the guitar at the guy, pushing him with the headstock buried into his shoulder. I pushed him toward and into the side door. He resisted and threw up his hands like he wanted to fight.

"Really, dude? You're going to steal from this bar? From me? From the band? From our customers? That is so rude! And now you wanna fight?"

"Fuck you man, let's go! Let's go motherfucker! Let's go!" he shouted at me.

"Okay." With that I shoved him completely out the door with the head of my guitar.

I followed him outside the door and he put up his fists, ready to fight.

I looked down at my guitar and said, "Fuck it, it's a Squire!" And with that I raised the guitar like a baseball-bat. His eyes opened up wide as he couldn't believe what I was about to do.

Right upside his head—direct hit, bam! Take that, you asshole! The guitar slipped out of my hands after it made contact with his face, and then landed on the ground.

The prick stumbled back, dazed and bleeding, while I violently attacked his face with my fist. Right then, a friend of his had come out to join in, but Miles was right behind him, as was the bassist, Fleeb, followed by the guitarists, Gary and John and finally Cecil. The drummer kept playing.

The small crowd inside had all gathered at the windows and cheered us on as we beat the shit out of these two guys.

Barre, who lived in the building next to the Goat, was shouting out of her apartment window. "Keep it down out there!... Wait, what's going on?!..." After a few seconds of watching, she realized what was happening. "Kick his ass, Dewey!"

The thief and his friend were on the ground. Fleeb tore into the other guy pretty good. I was kicking my guy repeatedly. The guitar still lay on the ground, having been stepped on several times now. The whiskey coursing through my veins fueled my aggression. The blood-thirsty crowd at the bar windows were screaming for more violence. The drummer kept the beat on the stage... fucking drum solo, hell yeah!

Cecil was the civil one in the bunch. The culprits now begged for mercy, surrendering to defeat. Cecil pulled me away as I got one last kick in.

"Okay, okay... I'm sorry! I'm sorry! Please stop!" the thief begged.

"You're banned from this establishment for life, you prick! Don't let me ever see you in here again!" I yelled back.

"Okay, okay, we got it." They crawled away in defeat, beaten, bloody, and bruised.

I picked up the scuffed-up guitar off the ground and we went back into the bar. The intimate crowd was cheering.

"Best show ever!!! Whoo-hoo!!! Encore!"

The drummer was still keeping the beat. We all got back up on stage and in complete rock star fashion, picked up right back into the song where we had left off.

I normally don't believe violence is the right answer to situations like that. Whiskey, however, sometimes has a different opinion. And sometimes a little western justice is necessary when you feel compelled to defend your turf. After the show, we all signed the badly beaten "Squire" and retired it to hang on the wall at the Goat. As a reminder for those who think of stealing, don't even.

Meanwhile back in Snowmass Village, just outside Aspen, I spent the weekend enjoying some incredible music and good times. After one of the Widespread Panic sets, on my birthday, I was back at the hotel with a bunch of friends from Summit County, mostly hanging out with my friend Tiffany. We were sitting in a circle with people, passing around joints and balloons and stuff. Someone to my right handed me a tiny zip lock bag with white powder in it. I assumed it was cocaine and pulled out a key from my pocket and did a quick blast. Just as I was blasting it into my nose, the dude who handed me the bag said "Whoa dude! What are you doing? I wouldn't..." It was too late, I had already snorted a good amount.

"Yeah, man, you're gonna get really high off that."

"What do you mean? It was a just a little."

"Yeah, but that's Molly, bro."

"Oh, it's not coke?"

An hour later, according to witnesses, I was doing naked cartwheels in the hotel hallways. I vaguely remember laughing and carrying on with Ziggy Marley at some point, and partying our asses off until the dawn.

A few days later while recovering back in Summit County, I received an email from a long lost love—in fact, my first love, Elle. I hadn't heard from her in years. The weird part is, I had just recently had an intense dream about her. I had woken up crying and overwhelmed with feelings for her. Repressed feelings that had been long buried, but I reasoned, what a crazy dream, just a dream.

Her email appeared out of the blue and implied some distress in her life. She found my contact information online and decided to reach out. We communicated back and forth about her situation. She was living near Atlanta and was in an abusive relationship. She indicated a possible opportunity with her job to relocate to Colorado if things got worse, which they did. By some fateful twists, eight weeks later, Elle, my first love, was on her way to Colorado.

There was no certainty that she and I would be together again. That just seemed too much to ask for. I wanted to be there for her as a friend, first and foremost. I had always cared for her deeply and, yes, I knew that we had never really given ourselves a fair shot at a real relationship. I hadn't actually seen her in seventeen years. The very center of my heart had always belonged to her. When we reunited, she seemed more beautiful than I even recalled. The spark was still there.

CHAPTER 58

So Glad You Made It

Sometime over the next year, Elle and I did end up getting serious. It was as if all the years we had spent apart were teaching us the things we needed to learn in order to be together.

During that time, I also received an intriguing contact from another lost love, Springwater. She appeared on Facebook and sent me a friend request. Like Elle, it had been seventeen years since I had last seen her. In fact, not since the Buckeye Lake show in June 1991, when I had just walked away and left her standing in the parking lot. We spoke on the phone a few times, and it was clear to me that I still carried an overwhelming amount of guilt about the way things ended. I needed to clear the air and find out what she wanted to tell me that night when she was waiting at the Love Street van.

As it turned out, Springwater said she had been planning to run away and join that crazy circus with me after all. And when I made those calls to her in the days that followed, she said her sister had lied to me about Springwater not wanting to talk. In truth, her sister never even told Springwater that I had called, an attempt to protect her from the boy who had broken her heart. It was healing for both of us to solve those mysteries and exchange warm wishes.

In the spring of 2011, I finally made the dream of going to Europe a reality. I played a little mini-acoustic tour along the way. I hit Ireland, Scotland, England, France, Switzerland, Germany, and Holland. It was a four-week-long adventure that could not have happened if it weren't for the encouragement of some dear friends of mine from Ireland, the band Senekah. I managed to get lots of research into my family history done on that trip. One of my ancestors, Benjamin Silliman, a famous scientist and educator at Yale, wrote two books about his travels in Europe in the 1800s. I retraced many of his steps on my trip and was fascinated to explore and study many of the same artifacts that he had encountered more than one hundred fifty years earlier. I also met many new friends, discovered distant relatives, and unraveled some genealogical mysteries. I hope to release a published account of that journey in the near future.

Throughout all my travels and experiences, I've sought to maintain the fundamental and principal concepts of a nomadic Taoist. And through the rough times, life never hesitates to humble my fallible nature and remind me of the Zen Buddhist concept of Shoshin, or "beginner's mind." It is through these concepts and with my psychedelic education that I continue my eager journey through this wild world.

For the sake of love and bliss, Elle and I were joined in union in August 2011. The path of bliss is always there, running parallel to our lives, should we stumble, should we fall, it is always near.

Epilogue

K. Fimster, Deadhead to the core and beloved co-founder of Middle Earth, whose given name was Paul Crabtree, passed away at the age of 53 in 2010. He finished up a dinner meal at his farmhouse in northern Alabama and took a nap. He never woke up. Paul was quite an inspiration to his friends. He was our Dean Moriarity. Most of his closest friends were artists (musicians, writers, painters) in one form or another, and Paul himself was one hell of a good writer. I have many volumes of his letters, stories, and screenplays that I hope to get published someday. This is certainly something I'm working on, though it will take time.

I have often wondered, like most people do when they reflect on their past, how things would be different today if I had stayed in that one place with that one job or in that one relationship. I know that I was blessed and fortunate to pass through the Bill Graham and Grateful Dead families when I did and to have shared my heart and passions with many wonderfully beautiful beings. All of those experiences certainly had the most profound effects on who I am today.

Certainly the mind-altering substances of psychedelic experimentation lent its share of wisdom too, and although I no longer seek the assistance of the LSD variety, I have gained a new respect for the shamanic entheogens of the sacred plant kingdom and tryptamine families. I have never regretted my decisions to move forward seeking new adventures, experiences, people and places that have rewarded me with the knowledge and wisdom to make a difference in myself and toward others. In 2013, with encouragement and inspiration from my friends John Vandervart, Marty Walsen, and Leon Joseph Littlebird, we created a new music and camping festival in the mountains of Colorado called the Roots Retreat. I continue to perform music in two bands, the Dewey Paul Band and Postcards of the Hanging (a Bob Dylan cover act), as well as to travel, paint, write, and explore new mediums of creativity.

If there's one major thing I absorbed and learned from the Grateful Dead's influence, and especially Garcia's: it was to not be a sheep in their world, but to follow my own bliss and true passions in this life; and to spread my very own inspiration and message to others. Thank you for taking this journey with me, I hope at the very least, you have been inspired to create something of your very own to share with the world.

www.ingramcontent.com/pod-product-compliance
Lightning Source LLC
Chambersburg PA
CBHW072135090426
42739CB00013B/3197